ISBN 978-1-331-06712-2
PIBN 10140469

This book is a reproduction of an important historical work. Forgotten Books uses state-of-the-art technology to digitally reconstruct the work, preserving the original format whilst repairing imperfections present in the aged copy. In rare cases, an imperfection in the original, such as a blemish or missing page, may be replicated in our edition. We do, however, repair the vast majority of imperfections successfully; any imperfections that remain are intentionally left to preserve the state of such historical works.

Fr. H. Raphael Moss. O.P.
Hinckley. 1940

Dupl. ?

THE LITURGIES

OF

S. MARK, JAMES, CLEMENT, CHRYSOSTOM, AND BASIL,

AND

THE CHURCH OF MALABAR.

EXPLANATION OF FRONTISPIECE.

THE FRONTISPIECE is taken from one of the series of nine plates in a beautiful MS. of the Greek Liturgies now in the Vatican; but, in A.D. 1600, in the Monastery of S. Mary at Gethsemane. ; They have been engraved by Cardinal Mai, in the Sixth volume of the " Nova Bibliotheca." The intention of the designer is to show the fellow-ministration of angels with men in the Liturgy. This plate (the sixth) represents the GREAT ENTRANCE: (see pp. xxix. and 108). The Priest, carried by angels, brings in the chalice covered with the *aer :* in his right hand, he holds the paten, covered with its veil. The door, out of which he comes, is that of the prothesis. The Deacon, with a taper, and the stole marked with the Ter Sanctus, bows. To the right, an archimandrite stands up: by him is S. Michael : in answer to the prayer, "Grant that with our entrance may be an entrance of the holy angels." In front of the altar, the Priest is represented again : he wears the *stoicharion,* or alb; over it a plain *phælonion,* or chasuble : on his left (by the designer's mistake for his right) is seen a part of the *epigonation.* On the altar are the two tapers: the chalice, covered with the *aer ;* the *asterisk* covered with the veil; and behind, the books of the Epistles and Gospels. The Great Entrance, as we shall see, is the grandest piece of ritual in the Eastern Church, and mystically represents the Incarnation.

The Liturgies

OF

SS. MARK, JAMES, CLEMENT, CHRYSOSTOM, AND BASIL,

AND

THE CHURCH OF MALABAR.

TRANSLATED, WITH INTRODUCTION AND APPENDICES,

BY

THE REV. J. M. NEALE, D.D.,
SOMETIME WARDEN OF SACKVILLE COLLEGE, EAST GRINSTEAD,

AND

THE REV. R. F. LITTLEDALE, LL.D.,
SOMETIME SCHOLAR OF TRINITY COLLEGE, DUBLIN

SEVENTH EDITION

LONDON
GRIFFITH FARRAN & CO., LIMITED
NEWBERY HOUSE, 39 CHARING CROSS ROAD

PREFACE TO THE SECOND EDITION.

In this re-issue of the English Version of the Primitive Liturgies, the translation has been carefully revised and compared with the original texts, and a few additional notes have been appended to elucidate difficulties. The Liturgy of S. Basil, already printed in the Greek edition which ranges with this volume, is now given in English also. And the Appendix of Formulæ of Institution has not only been corrected, but also very considerably increased, as it now contains excerpts from the Anaphoræ of twenty-four Liturgies either unknown to Dr. Neale or beyond his reach at the time when the first edition of this book was published. These (distinguished by asterisks) are taken from Syriac and Ethiopic MSS. in the British Museum, and I am indebted to my brother-in-law, Dr. Wright, for the extracts and versions. I have added references to their places in the Museum Catalogue, to facilitate the studies of those who may desire to examine them for themselves. It is unnecessary to dwell on the cumulative weight of so much additional testimony to the liturgical doctrines and usages of ancient Christendom, all the more cogent and valuable because of the innumerable minor variations of phrase and structure which prove the independence of the witnesses, and it will suffice to say that only in the light of these documents is it possible to interpret truly the language of the Fathers touching the Holy Eucharist.

R. F. L.

LONDON, *July,* 1869.

PREFACE.

As I have said in the Introduction to my Edition of the Liturgies in Greek, it has for many years been my desire to render these most pure sources of Eucharistical Doctrine accessible to all my brethren. Hitherto the whole of them have not been procurable in Greek, except with difficulty, and at a heavy expense : in English, not at all.

I had not, however, intended to translate them; but the united advice of all the Ecclesiastical Reviews, and of many private friends, and many Priests with whom I was previously unacquainted, has encouraged me to undertake that task also :— and the result is now before the reader.

A brief introduction is prefixed; but to enter, in such very narrow limits, at any satisfactory length on the subject, is impossible.

The reader who desires to study it more deeply may consult :—1. Mr. *Palmer's* Essays on the Eastern Church : 2. My own Introduction to its History : 3. (which may easily be procured through Messrs. Williams and Norgate,) the translation of

M. Mouravieff's work on the Eastern Ritual, by
Theodore Ballianus. (ἐπιστολαὶ περὶ τῶν ἱερῶν
ἀκολουθίων τῆς ἀνατολικῆς ὀρθοδόξου Ἐκκλησίας.
Athens : Philadelpheus, 1857.)

The Translations in the present volume are as
follows :

S. MARK ⎫ The pro-anaphoral portion, new : the
        ⎬ anaphoral, slightly altered from my
S. JAMES ⎭ Introduction.

S. CLEMENT. The pro-anaphoral portion, new :
the anaphoral, corrected from Dr. Brett's
Translation.

S. CHRYSOSTOM ⎫ Slightly altered from my In-
THE PROTHESIS ⎭ troduction.

THE MALABAR LITURGY—entirely new.

I have endeavoured, most carefully, to abstain in
my notes from all polemical remarks; but one
observation I should not feel justified in omitting.
For nearly twenty years these, and the other early
Liturgies, have been my daily study : there are
very few passages in them which I could not repeat
by heart; and scarcely any important works on
the subject which I have not read. I may therefore claim some little right to be heard with respect
to them. And I say most unhesitatingly, that

while I can conceive that some passages in them might be tortured into a Calvinistic sense, were sufficient ingenuity employed; no ingenuity can make any single clause even *patient* of the theory of equivalence, which the "Opinion" of a Scotch Bishop seems to endorse. If that theory be true, the Eucharistic teaching of every Eastern Liturgy is absolutely false.

I would conclude by praying that the doctrine of these Liturgies may spread more and more widely amongst us; and that this poor little effort of mine may be blessed to that end.

Sackville College, Michaelmas, 1859.

INTRODUCTION.

1. *Liturgical Families.*

1. Primitive Liturgies may be divided into five principal families. (1.) That of S. James, or Jerusalem; (2.) That of S. Mark, or Alexandria; (3.) That of S. Thaddeus, or the East; (4.) That of S. Peter, or Rome; (5.) That of S. John, or Ephesus.

2. That of Jerusalem may be divided into three branches: the Clementine, Cæsarean, and Hierosolymitan.([1])

3. Of these, the Clementine has no branches.

4. The normal form of the Cæsarean Liturgy is that of *S. Basil.* This on the one hand branches out into that of *S. Chrysostom;* on the other, into the *Armenian.*

5. The norm of the Hierosolymitan family is the Liturgy of S. James: and this family has three

---

(1) In my Introduction to the History of the Holy Eastern Church I had classed the Clementine Liturgy by itself; but Dr. Daniel, in his observations on my book, seems to me to have shewn that it has a very close connection with the Hierosolymitan, or, as he prefers to call it, Antiochene.

divisions. (1.) *Sicilian S. James*, as said in that island before the Saracen conquest, and partly assimilated to the Petrine Liturgy. (2.) *S. Cyril:* where used uncertain, but assimilated to the Alexandrian form. (3.) *Syriac S. James*, the source of the largest number of extant Liturgies. They are these: [1.] *Lesser S. James.* [2.] *S. Clement.* [3.] *S. Mark.* [4.] *S. Dionysius.* [5.] *S. Xystus.* [6.] *S. Ignatius.* [7.] *S. Peter I.* [8.] *S. Peter II.* [9.] *S. Julius.* [10.] *S. John Evangelist.* [11.] *S. Basil.* [12.] (*S.*) *Dioscorus.* [13.] *S. John Chrysostom I.* [14.] *All Apostles.* [15.] *S. Maruthas.* [16.] *S. Eustathius.* [17.] *Philoxenus of Mabug I.* [18.] *Matthew the Shepherd.* [19.] *James Baradaeus.* [20.] *James of Batnæ.* [21.] *James of Edessa.* [22.] *Moses Bar-Cephas.* [23.] *Thomas of Heraclea.* [24.] *Holy Doctors.* [25.] *Philoxenus of Mabug II.* [26.] *S. John Chrysostom II.* [27.] *Abu'lfaraj I.* [28.] *John of Dara.* [29.] *S. Celestine.* [30.] *John Bar-Susan.* [31.] *Eleazar of Babylon.* [32.] *John the Scribe.* [33.] *John Maro.* [34.] *Dionysius of Cardu.* [35.] *Michael of Antioch.* [36.] *John Bar-Vahib.* [37.] *John Bar-Maadân.* [38.] *Dionysius of Diarbekr.* [39.] *Philoxenus of Bagdad.* [40.] *S. Gregory Nazianzen.* [41.] *Cyriacus of Antioch.* [42.] *Dionysius Bar-Salîbi.* [43.] *Abu'lfaraj II.* All these, from Syriac S. James inclusive, are Monophysite Liturgies.

6. The norm of the Alexandrian family is S. Mark. From this are derived these Liturgies: **(1.)** *S. Cyril.* **(2.)** *S. Gregory.* **(3.)** *S. Basil.*

From S. Basil another family springs, used in Ethiopia, and for the most part very barbarous. The norm of this is the *Liturgy of all Apostles.* From this, as from their source, spring the following Liturgies: [1.] *S. John Evangelist.* [2.] *The Three Hundred and Eighteen.* [3.] *S. Epiphanius.* [4.] *James of Serug.* [5.] *Our* Lord Jesus *I.* [6.] *(S.) Dioscorus I.* [7.] *S. Gregory of Armenia.* [8.] *S. Mary.* [9.] *S. John Chrysostom.* [10.] *S. Gregory of Alexandria.* [11.] *S. Basil.* [12.] *S. Cyril.* [13.] *S. Athanasius.* [14.] *Dioscorus II.* [15.] *Our* Lord Jesus *II.* [16.] *All Apostles II.*

There is a bastard Liturgy between Egyptian S. Basil and Syriac S. James, called *John of Bassora.*

7. The Eastern family is much less numerous. The norm of this is *All Apostles.* From this there spring (1.) *Theodore the Interpreter.* (2.) *Nestorius.* (3.) *Narses the Leper.* (4.) *The Liturgy of Malabar or S. Thomas.* But this last is rather collateral with, than derived from, *All Apostles.* The first four of these are Nestorian. The fifth, originally Nestorian, has since become Jacobite.

8. The Petrine family has only one Liturgy, the *Roman.*

There is a bastard between Eastern and *Petrine,* called *Romano-Chaldee.*

9. The Ephesine family may be divided into two orders, (1.) The Mozarabic. (2.) The Gallican.

But springing from the mixture of these with the

Roman, are [1.] *The Ambrosian Liturgy.* [2.] *The Patriarchine*, or that used in the province of Aquileia.

And these are all.

II.   *Difference between Eastern and Western Liturgies.*

By Eastern, I mean those of
> S. James,
> S. Mark,
> S. Thaddeus,
> S. John.

1. The Eastern have, the Western have not, a distinct invocation of the HOLY GHOST, without which the transmutation of the Elements is not considered perfected. It is true that this has been obliterated from the Mozarabic rite, but there it was originally: in the Gallican it is still visible.

2. The Western—and that of S. John—have varying Collects, as well as Epistles and Gospels—the others have not.

3. The three purely Eastern—S. James, S. Mark, and S. Thaddeus—have only one Preface for every day in the year.

4. The Mozarabic, Gallican, and Ambrosian, have a different one for every festival: the Roman had, and has several still.

III. *Distinctive marks of Oriental Liturgies.*

These are principally to be found in the position of the intercession for quick and dead.

(1.) In the Hierosolymitan family, it is between the Invocation of the HOLY GHOST and the LORD'S Prayer.

_ (2.) In the Alexandrian, it is before the Commemoration of the Institution. ·

(3.) In the Nestorian, it is between the Commemoration of Institution and the Invocation of the HOLY GHOST.

IV. *The Order of the Liturgies themselves.*

1. Every Liturgy may be divided into two parts :
  ′ The Pro-Anaphoral : and
  The Anaphoral portion.

The former extends to the *Sursum corda :* the latter from thence to the end.

2. The Pro-Anaphoral portion is divided into
  The Mass of the Catechumens : and
  The Mass of the Faithful.

3. The Anaphoral portion has these four divisions :
  The Great Eucharistic *Prayer :*
  The Consecration :

The Intercession for quick and dead : and
The Communion.

4. The Mass of the Catechumens consists of these
parts :

The *Prefatory Prayer* :
The Initial Hymn, Introit, Ingressa, Anti-
phon, or by whatever other name it may
be called :
The Little Entrance :
The Trisagion :
The Lections : (in some rites, *Prophecy*,
Epistle and Gospel; in others, only
Epistle and Gospel :)
The *Prayers* after the Gospel, and Expul-
sion of the Catechumens.

5. The Mass of the Faithful consists of
The *Prayers* of the Faithful : or, After the
unfolding the Corporal.
The Great Entrance :
The Offertory :
The Kiss of *Peace* :
The Creed.

5. Proceeding to the Anaphora : under the Great
Eucharistic *Prayer* we have

The *Preface* :
The Triumphal Hymn :
The *Prayer* of the Triumphal Hymn :
Commemoration of our LORD's Life :
Commemoration of Institution.

6. Under the Consecration we have
Words of Institution for the Bread:
Words of Institution for the Wine;
Oblation of the Body and Blood:
Prayer for the *D*escent of the HOLY GHOST:
Prayer for the change of Elements.

7. Under the Great Intercession we have
The *P*rayer for quick and dead:
The *P*rayer before the LORD's *P*rayer:
The LORD's *P*rayer:
The Embolismus; or *P*rayer against
Temptation.

8. Under the Communion we have
The *P*rayer of Intense Adoration:
The *Sancta Sanctis:*
The Elevation of the Host:
The Fraction:
The Confession:
The Communion:
The Antidoron:
The *P*rayer of Thanksgiving:
The *D*ismissal.

V. *Arrangement of an Oriental Church.*

1. The rubrics of the Liturgies are so closely connected with the parts of an Eastern Church, that **a**
short description of one is absolutely necessary.

The following is the ground-plan of S. Theodore
at Athens.

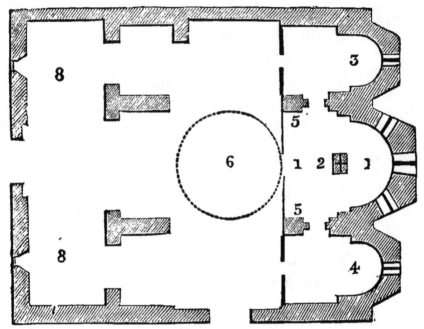

1. The ἅγιον βῆμα, or sanctuary.
2. The altar, in the centre of the chord of the apse.
3. The *prothesis* ⎫ which when divided, as here, by walls
4. The *diaconicon* ⎭ from the bema, are called *parabemata.*
5. The *iconostasis.*
6. The *trullus*, or dome: under it the choir.
7. The trapeza, or nave, not architecturally divided from the choir.
8. The narthex.

2. Every Eastern Church consists of **four** portions:

> *Bema* or Sanctuary:
> Choir:
> *Trapeza*, or Nave:
> Narthex, or Western Porch.

But, as in the West, the sanctuary and the choir have hardly any separation, and go together under the name of *chancel,* so in the East the choir and nave have hardly any separation, and go together under the name of *naos*.

3. The bema is separated from the naos by a solid screen—the *iconostasis;* so termed because of the icons on it.

This answers, *not* to the rood-screen of the Western, but to the altar-rails of the English, Church. Its doors are called the Holy *Doors.*

4. North of the altar—there is only one altar in every Eastern Church—is the chapel of the prothesis, with the table at which the preparation of the Elements takes place. Thence the Little and Great Entrances are made.

5. South of the altar is the diaconicon, skeuophylakion, or sacristy.

VI. *The Liturgies contained in the present volume are those of*

S. James,	S. Mark,
S. Chrysostom,	S. Clement, (²)
The Church of Malabar.	

The Anaphoræ of the first four have been translated by Dr. Brett; the whole of S. James by Dr. Rattray; and of S. Chrysostom by Dr. King and

(²) I am anxious to correct a mistake in my preface to the Greek edition of this Liturgy, into which I was led by too implicitly following an assertion of my friend Dr. Daniel. It is that the expression, "cleansing ourselves from all filthiness both of the flesh and spirit," is quoted seven times in the Clementine Liturgy. I ought to have said that the verse, which contains that expression, is *referred to five* times in that Liturgy.

Dr. Covel. I believe that the whole of these Liturgies has not appeared before in English : the whole of S. Chrysostom and the Anaphoræ of S. James and S. Mark may be found in my Introduction to the History of the Eastern Church. The Malabar Liturgy is given as a specimen of the family of S. Thaddeus, rather than one of the three Nestorian Liturgies, as not less valuable, and not having been before translated.

To these I add the office of the *P*rothesis; as now said all over the Eastern Church.

The Liturgy of S. Chrysostom is the normal Liturgy of the Eastern Church. That of S. Basil is said on all the Sundays in Lent, (except *P*alm Sunday,) Maundy Thursday, Easter Eve, the Vigils of Christmas and Epiphany, and the Feast of S. Basil (Jan. 1.) That of S. James is said in some of the Greek islands on the Festival of the Saint. That of S. Mark has been obsolete since the time of Theodore Balsamon. This prelate, a complete Oriental ultramontane, was for squaring everything according to " the most strictest " rule of the Great Church ; and procured the abolition of this Liturgy, more venerable than his own, just as Rome has abolished, and is still abolishing, the national Liturgies of other Churches.

The Malabar Liturgy I have never been able to see in the original ; and an *unadulterated* copy of the original does not seem to exist. *D*iligent inquiry, but in vain, was made for it in India by the late Dr. Mill. As it **is** now printed, it was revised by the *P*ortuguese Archbishop of Goa, Alexis de Menezes, and the Synod of Diamper, (1599)—a revision which, as even Roman Liturgists allow, shews utter ignorance of Oriental Liturgies. Raulin, in his edition, professes to point out all the alterations made by the Synod, and to give, in a note, the original: but the least study of his work will shew that some important changes pass without the least notice by him.

VII. *Mystical Interpretation of Oriental Liturgies.*

The best key to the mystical explanation of the Liturgy of S. Chrysostom is to be found in the Commentary of Symeon of Thessalonica—a translation of the latter part of which here follows. This prelate—a man of the highest character for learning and piety, and the stay of the whole Eastern Church in troublesome times—died in 1429. To his treatise should be added that of Theodore of Andida, a writer of uncertain age, first published by Cardinal Mai, in the sixth vol. of his Nova Bibliotheca, in 1855.

" The Bishop therefore who is about to celebrate, descending from the throne in which he has been stationed, figures the condescension of GOD the SON to us. And having put on the holy stole, ([3]) he

---

([3]) The stole, used by Priests in the Eastern Church, is also called epitrachelion and horarion, or orarion: it differs in shape from that of the West. It is merely a long piece of silk or other stuff, something more than double the width of the Western stole, and with a hole in the middle of the upper part, through which the celebrant puts his head. As, however,

figures the LORD's most holy Incarnation ; and going
out to the gates of the temple, His presence and
manifestation on earth, even till His death and
descent into hell. This is signified by the *P*riest
going towards the West and as far as the Church
doors.

" Now when the holy Liturgy is begun, which is
when the Bishop gives the sign—for no one can
attempt to commence anything without him—the
*P*riests within the bema commence the prayers, and
the singers modulate the Antiphons and divide them
into three portions, and those things which are
taken from the *P*salms : (⁴) to these they add the
hymns which pertain to the time of grace. By the
*P*salms, the prediction of the Incarnation of the
Word to those of old time is set forth : by the
hymnody which follows, the perfect completion of
grace is typified to the bystanders, and the SON of
GOD incarnate, and all the things which He worked
for our sakes. Wherefore also, first of all, we
honour her who virginally bare Him, and beseech
her mediation for us, saying: *By the intercession of
the Mother of God, O Saviour, hear us.* Then, commemorating the Saints, who, agonising for the
mystery of faith, died a holy death, we beseech their
supplications also ; and last of all, venerating

---

it has an embroidered seam down the middle, its appearance
is much the same as that to which we are accustomed.—
Symeon on the Liturgy.

(⁴) The three Antiphons of the Constantinopolitan rite will
be seen in the Liturgy of S. Chrysostom, where an explanation
of them is given.

CHRIST, the author and finisher of our salvation, we cry out with a loud voice, *Save us, O Son of God.* ([5]) But when the Bishop has finished his holy prayers without the bema, the *Deacons* stand by him, who typify, not only the Apostles, but also the Angels, who minister also in the mysteries of CHRIST. But when the *Priests* within the bema have also finished their own prayers, and come forth, the descent of the holy Angels, which took place in the Ascension of CHRIST, is signified. And when the torches are borne forth, and the *Deacons* advance by two and two, and the Holy Gospel is carried in procession, and the Bishop, supported on either side by *Deacons*, advances, and the other *Priests* follow behind, and sing out clearly, *O come let us worship* CHRIST, and the acclamations of good wishes to the Bishop resound, and the *Deacon* after the prayer of the Entrance, while he holds the Gospel in his hands, exclaims: *Wisdom; stand up:* ([6]) the Resurrection and Ascension of the Saviour is shadowed forth. For the *Deacon*, while he thus cries out, announces the Resurrection of CHRIST; and the choir of *Priests* and *Deacons*, as we said before, typify the Apostles present with the LORD and beholding Him, and the most holy Angels. But the Bishop is a type of the LORD Himself made manifest to the disciples, and

---

([5]) The reader is recommended to follow the Liturgy of S. Chrysostom, as given below, while he reads the explanation of Symeon, comparing it at the same time with the ground-plan of S. Theodore, above.

([6]) This refers to the ceremonies of the Little Entrance, of which more at length hereafter.

taken up from earth to heaven. Wherefore, as we have said, the whole of the exterior *naos* is a type of earth; the most holy bema represents heaven. Wherefore, as *David* also prophesies, when the LORD ascended, the Angels assisted in His triumph; and cried out to them that were above, Lift up your doors, and they named Him King of Glory and LORD, and confessed Him the Mighty. Thus too doth the Church, while she honours the celebrant entering with the pomp of a procession into the Holy of Holies: and the holy doors of the bema, shut before that procession enters, and opened that it may enter, signify the same thing.

But when the celebrant has entered and has censed the holy table around, the advent of the

HOLY GHOST is signified by him. For the SPIRIT came to us from heaven, when CHRIST went up into heaven. Furthermore, the Bishop, signing the Gospel crosswise by a certain double taper, *dikerion,*

typifies the illumination brought to pass both in heaven and earth by the Incarnation of JESUS in His two natures. For by the Incarnation of the WORD of GOD, He not only gave light to men, but also to the Angels.

The Trisagion, which is forthwith said, manifests the mystery of the TRINITY; which the Incarnation of one person of the TRINITY manifested to men; ([7]) and also the sympathy and union of Angels and men. Wherefore also it is sung within the bema by the *Priests*, and without it by the clerks and laity: for one Church of Angels and men hath been formed through CHRIST. It is this which the Pontiff proclaims, while he signs the Gospel crosswise with a three-headed taper, (*trikerion,*) and shews that the

([7]) The expression "One of the TRINITY" is not used accidentally by Symeon, but is a profession of the faith of the writer with respect to the phrase so much controverted in the Monophysite discussions, "One of the TRINITY suffered for man."

preaching of the TRINITY is contained in the same, and
prays that by it we may be confirmed and established.

But also while he advances to the divine synthronus, ([8]) which typifies the session of CHRIST at
the Right Hand of the FATHER; and then blesses
the people crosswise with the trikerion, he assures
us of the sanctification which is through the TRINITY,
and reminds us that CHRIST, having ascended into
heaven, sent down upon us the splendour of the
TRINITY, typified by the light, and the blessing.
And sitting down in the synthronus, where he is a
type of CHRIST, and where he has, as his fellow-
assessors, his brother Bishops and *Priests*, who represent the figure and the similitude of the Apostles,
he gives peace to all; and this is a symbol of Christian union. For it is CHRIST, saith *Paul*, Who hath
put an end to enmity in His Flesh, and hath made
both one, both things in heaven and things in earth.
Then follows the lection of the Apostolic words,
which allegorises the mission of the Apostles to the
nations. And the Bishops and *Priests* sit while
these are read, but the *Deacons* do not; because the
former also possess the grace of the Apostolate.
Then follows the hymn Alleluia, ([9]) which manifests
the praise of GOD, and the advent of the *Divine*

([8]) The synthronus is the seat in the depth of the Eastern
apse, in the centre of which the Bishop sat with his face west-
ward towards the altar,—the altar itself occupying the central
position in the chord of that apse,—and having his Clergy on
his right and left hand.

([9]) See the note on this Alleluia in the **Liturgy of S. Chrysostom** between the Epistle and Gospel.

grace, which is the lection of the Gospel. Now this lection sets forth the preaching of the Gospel throughout the whole world, which was brought to pass after the Ascension of the LORD, by the hands of His Disciples. Wherefore also, we first read the Epistle, then the Gospel; because the Disciples were first invigorated and sent forth, and afterwards, performing their circuit throughout the world, preached the Gospel. And before the Gospel, incense is offered on account of the grace of the HOLY GHOST, which by means of the Gospel was given to the whole world.

But while the Gospel is being read, the Bishop lays aside his omophorion, ([10]) thereby making profession of his service to the LORD. For since it is the LORD Who is represented as speaking by the Gospel, and is, as it were, Himself present, the Bishop at that time ventures not to be arrayed with the symbol of His Incarnation—I mean the omophorion; but taking it off from his shoulders he gives it to the Deacon, who holds it folded in his right hand, himself standing near the Bishop, and preceding the holy gifts. He also holds the trikerion in his hand: and this signifies that in the world to come, JESUS, Who was Incarnate and wounded for us, and being one of the TRINITY shining upon us with the rays of Godhead, will be manifestly revealed to all. Then the Pontiff, descending from the syn-

---

([10]) This omophorion, which is worn by every Eastern Bishop, resembles the Latin pallium, except that it is broader and tied round the neck in a knot.

thronus, and after the Gospel and the prayer for the Emperors, blessing the people with the trikerion, makes manifest that the pious empire and the priesthood exist by means of the Gospel, and prays that they may remain by the grace of the TRINITY.

And now, approaching the altar, he begins the work of prayers, manifesting himself to be the minister of the mystery. And forthwith the catechumens are dismissed, and the faithful are exhorted to remain; because that moment represents the season of the end of the world. "For," saith he, "the Gospel must first be preached throughout all the world, and then shall the end be." And again he saith, "He shall send forth His Angels, and they shall sever the wicked from the good." Thus also the Church doth when she commands the catechumens to depart, and the faithful alone to remain. Whence also we may learn how careful the faithful ought to be that they communicate not with them with whom there ought to be no communion; and this is more particularly the duty of *Priests*. For if it is unlawful to associate in prayer, how much more in the Sacrifice? Neither ought they to receive the oblations for the sacrifice of those faithful who are open and notorious sinners, but first to require from them penitence. For mutual communion arises from the oblations that are brought to the altar; and it is not meet that the unworthy should partake in the sacrifice. And when the *Divine* gifts are about to be offered, the Pontiff first washes his hands before all, thereby manifesting his purity and irreprehensibleness in this hierurgy; and that it is right to approach that which is so pure without any manner of pollution, so far as is possible for man, and thus to minister in those most pure mysteries.

But the procession, after these things, of the Divine gifts, is with great pomp of *Readers*, *Deacons*, and *Priests*, with the lamps and holy vessels preceding and following: ([11]) because this symbolises the last Advent of CHRIST, when He shall come with glory. Whence the omophorion marked with the Cross goes before, which sets forth the sign of the SON of MAN, which will appear from heaven, and the SON of MAN Himself. And after this follow the *Deacons* in order, symbolising the ranks of Angels; and this also the Fans, ([12]) as they are

---

([11]) That is the Great Entrance, for which see pages 10, 108; and also the frontispiece.

([12]) These Fans are a not unimportant part of the plate of an Oriental Church ; they are now generally made of silver, and in the shape of the heads and wings of cherubim. The Clementine Liturgy, (see page 65) orders them to be made of silk or peacock's feathers, or some other light material: they were originally intended to prevent flies and the like insects from settling on the Holy Mysteries, and in process of time came to signify mystically the vibration of the wings of the Seraphim before the throne of GOD. Under the name of Flabella or Muscaria, they were employed in early Western ritual. Hildebert of Le Mans has an elegant and playful letter to a friend who presented him with a pair. S. Udalric, in his Constitutions of Cluny, book ii. chap. 29, thus writes : "And one of the Deacons, of whom there always ought to be two, shall stand with a fan near the Priest, from the time that flies begin to be troublesome, till the end of the service, that he may drive them away from the sacrifice and from the altar." Durandus thus writes, iv. 35—8 : " But lest flies

called, set forth, which S. Dionysius names wings.
Then come they who carry the Holy Gifts, after
whom follow the rest, and they who bear on their
head the holy veil, which represents the veil that
was wrapped about the Body of the LORD JESUS.
These then, going round the Temple processionally,
and praying for the people, enter in to the altar,
and all of them pray for the Pontiff; and they give
heed to no other prayer, but only for the kingdom
of GOD. Now all these things teach that, in the
end of the world, after the departure of the wicked,
when the SAVIOUR shall have appeared, there shall
be no other heritage for the faithful, save the Kingdom of GOD. Now CHRIST Himself is the Kingdom
of GOD, and the contemplation of His dispensation:
His having been humbled even to death; His having
been sacrificed for us; to behold that sacrificed and
divine and quickening Body, manifesting its wounds
—the Body That indeed tasted of death, but is the
earnest to us of victory over death; the Body which
bestows on us, out of its wounds, immortality and
life and the Beatific Vision with the Angels, and
food and drink, and life and light, the very Bread
of Life, the True Light, eternal life, CHRIST JESUS.
Wherefore this entrance symbolises, at the same
time, both the Second Advent of CHRIST and His

---

should come and spoil the sweetness of the ointment, that is,
lest troublesome thoughts should arise and destroy the devotion
of prayer, they are to be driven away by the *fan* of the spirit.
And to signify this, in summer time, a material fan should be
used while the *secreta* is being said."

sepulture : for it is He, as we have said before, Who will be our Beatific Vision in the life to come. Then all the faithful, as is meet, fall down before the Priests, partly as desiring their prayers, and to be remembered in their hierurgy, and partly venerating the Divine gifts. For although they have not yet been sanctified, yet they have been dedicated to God in the prothesis ; and the Priest there presented them to God, and besought that they might be received upon the heavenly altar. Although then their sanctification is not yet complete, yet they are prepared for completeness, and are dedicated to God, and an antitype of the Lord's Body and Blood. If then we attribute honour and adoration to holy images, how much more do these gifts which, as the great Basil says, are the antitypes of, and are brought in to the end that they may become, the Body and Blood of Christ. ([18]) . . . . And the people saith not *Kyrie Eleison,* but, *For many years, O Lord* ; asking, as it were, that he should proceed prosperously in his hierurgy, and should continue his sacrificial functions for a long time. When he has entered in, the doors are shut ; because it is not fitting that the Mystery should be beheld by all, but only by those who have been invested with the priesthood. Furthermore, in the same way that

---

([18]) Symeon is replying to the objections brought by Latin writers against this anticipative adoration, which is common, as we shall see, to all the Eastern Communions, heterodox as well as Catholic, and which is even defended by many Roman writers. Some sentences in the text which dilate on this subject are omitted.

there is order and rank in the blessed Angels: for
they that are highest enjoy the Beatific Vision without any intermediation, the second rank through
the first, ([14]) and the third through the second, as
Dionysius, ([15]) endowed with heavenly wisdom,
teaches, so also is the case in the Church. The
Pontiff approaches the Divine altar without any
intermediary; the Priests and other ecclesiastics,
by means of him. And by the Priests and the
Ministers the people is admitted to a participation
in the tremendous Communion and the sacred
hymns. But when, after the first set of prayers,
the Creed has been recited, comes the Kiss of Peace,
because by the true confession of the TRINITY, and
of the One of the TRINITY That was Incarnate, we
are united with each other, and that confession
associates us with the Angels. And because we
ought to love each other, since CHRIST became an
oblation through love, and whoever is about to communicate, ought to present himself without any
feeling of anger; and because all, in the world to
come, are in union with each other, and no one
there can be an enemy. But they keep the sacred
veil over the gifts until the holy Creed is finished;
because we must first make a true and sincere confession about the LORD, before we can behold Him
without any veil. After this, the Pontiff who is to

([14]) See this idea worked out with greater fulness in the
Liturgy of Joseph Bar-Vahib: Renaudot, tom. ii. p. 525.

([15]) The writer is of course referring to the Treatise of Pseudo-
Dionysius the Areopagite on the Heavenly Hierarchy.

celebrate approaches the altar, and praises the works of GOD, and giving thanks for all, associates himself with the Angels, and vociferates with them the triumphal hymn, the Holy, Holy, Holy: and the people also recite it, typifying the equality of peace which we shall hereafter enjoy with the Angels, and our union with them. Then the Pontiff having praised the greatest of the works of GOD, the Incarnation of the Only-Begotten, and again the greatest act of His dispensation, His *Death* for us, goes on to the commencement of the Mysteries, and utters the holy words, the same which our LORD used when Himself sacrificing. Then, having given thanks for all things, and offering the gifts on account of all, he invokes upon himself, and upon the Mysteries laid on the altar, the divine grace of the SPIRIT. By which, having accomplished the rite by the seal of the Cross, and the invocation of the HOLY GHOST, he forthwith beholds the living JESUS lying before him, and Him in His very essence, being truly the Bread and the Cup. For His is that saying, This Bread is My Body; and His again is this saying, That which is in the cup is My Blood. And the sacrifice for the whole world, and the common propitiation, and the living delicacy, and the infinite joy, and the kingdom of the heavens, and the only essential good, is set before all on the *Divine* table; wherefore also the celebrant prays with the greater boldness on behalf of all. For he takes confidence when he beholds Him Who is the patient Lover of men, lying before him a sacrifice; and he offers

praise and makes supplication for all, and remem-
bers those that are absent, and more especially the
Maiden Mother of GOD, who virginally bare Him.
Testifying also in this how we are one with the
Saints, and by this sacrifice are partakers with
them, and that they, having boldness with Him
Who loves and is loved, have the power to reconcile
and unite us with Him. At last, having exhorted
us with one mind and one mouth to praise our GOD,
and having called down upon us the mercies of our
great GOD JESUS CHRIST, He leads us up to our
adoption by our heavenly FATHER, and prays that
we, being purged from sin by Him Who is His Son
according to nature, may become His sons according
to grace; and that we may be able rightly to call
Him our FATHER, Who is the Father of heaven.
And this is the sign of the union in the future
world, and of our being united to GOD, through the
Only-Begotten by the HOLY GHOST. Whence the
Pontiff, having prayed for peace and returned
thanks, calls upon JESUS that He would make him
partaker of the Holy Mysteries, that the rest may
be counted worthy to become partakers of them
through Him.

When he has finished the Liturgy, and comes to
the Communion, he again assumes the omophorion,
manifesting that, before this, he was one of the
ministers, and was afraid to put upon himself that
holy garment. But when the work is accomplished,
and he goes on to elevate the Bread and to divide it
into parts, and to receive it himself and distribute

it to others, it is necessary that he should put on all the sacred symbols of his dignity : and since the omophorion is the principal vest of a Pontiff, he necessarily assumes that, and in that is partaker of the most divine Things. Having, therefore, put it on, and having made the elevation, and having proclaimed the Holy Things for Holy Persons, he in vites all holy persons to that divine and living food of the Holy Table. And the people with one mind cry out, One Holy, One LORD, JESUS CHRIST, to the glory of GOD the FATHER. And this, as S. Paul saith, shall be preached in the Last Day, when every knee shall be bowed to JESUS, and every tongue shall confess that JESUS CHRIST is LORD, to the glory of GOD the FATHER. Hence, then the common union of all the faithful is published, and the consent of all concerning the preaching of the Incarnate SON of GOD, Who shall reign over all, and of HIS Kingdom there shall be no end, as it is written. But the answer made to the Holy Things to Holy Persons, namely, There is One Holy, &c., first signifies to us the essential sanctity of GOD Himself, and that from Him is the sanctification of all things that are hallowed. And it is, as it were, an expression of humility; and if we said, Who of us is holy, or who of us is pure ? One only is holy, One only is the LORD JESUS CHRIST, Who will of His mercy sanctify us.

Now the elevation of the Bread sets forth to us the elevation of JESUS on the Cross ; wherefore also the cup itself lies before our eyes containing the

b 2

Blood and Water which flowed from His Holy Side.
The bread then he divides into four parts, and places
them crosswise, and in this he sees JESUS crucified.
Nor can there be any greater spectacle than the
vision of the Most High GOD humbled for our sakes.
Then taking the upper portion, and with it making
the sign of the Cross, he dips it in the chalice, and
makes the union of the mysteries; and then he
pours the warm water into the cup. ([16])   And this
he does to signify that the LORD's Body, even when
dead, and when the *Divine* Soul was separated from
it still remained possessed of its quickening powers:
the *Divinity* never being separated from it, as
neither any of the energies of the *Divine* Spirit.
Since then warm water affords by its heat a type of
life, it is then employed in the time of Communion
that when our lips touch the chalice and participate
in the Blood, we may be so affected as if we received
it from that quickening side.   There are other
reasons also, and that of marvellous depth, assigned
by writers far superior to ourselves; but that which
we have mentioned may suffice for us.   For we may
understand from the words that accompany the
injection of warm water, that this which we have
mentioned is the intention of Church.   For he
saith, " The fervour of the HOLY GHOST." And a
still clearer proof is, that this admixture also takes
place in the Liturgy of the Presanctified.([17])   For

([16]) See all these rites more fully explained at page 120.
([17]) The Liturgy of the Pre-sanctified, or of S. Gregory, is
employed by the whole Eastern Church, and has been so at

there would be no use in this, were the reason of the rite any other than that we have assigned; seeing that in the previous Liturgy it had already been mixed with the Gifts. But the Pontiff, dividing the Bread into many particles, intimates in that action the sacrifice of JESUS CHRIST. For it is written, He took bread and brake and gave to His disciples. He first then himself communicates in the Bread, and participates in the tremendous Chalice. For no one else administers it to him, except it be some one of his own rank, namely another Pontiff. Then he imparts the Communion to all the rest, who kiss his hand and cheek, by which he proclaims the communion of the Body of JESUS, even in the future world, which shall be for ever and ever. But the hand and cheek receive the kiss—the former as the agent in those tremendous mysteries—the latter as the instrument of speech, by which prayers are offered, and because of love and communion in CHRIST; which is confirmed by that which is then said—CHRIST is in the midst of us. Furthermore, because the LORD was smitten on the cheek, so that the Pontiff may be reminded of how great humility the LORD showed Himself to be possessed of, and may never be lifted up in functions so divine and so great.

Those then of the altar communicate at the altar,

---

least since the time of the Council in Trullo, on every day of Lent except the Saturdays, the Sundays, the Annunciation, and Maundy Thursday.

and analogously with their order, as Paul also teaches of the future life: Every man, saith he, in his own order: taking the divine Bread in their own hands, and receiving the Chalice with their lips; and after this he exhibits to the people the Holy Gifts veiled. This teaches that it is not lawful, as hath been said before, for all men to see them unveiled. But if any one is in a proper state to communicate, he then, advancing with reverence and fear, participates of them, but mediately: for he receives the mysteries at the hand of the Pontiff by the spoon. ([18]) And thus, when prayer has been offered for the heritage of GOD and His innumerable people, the *Pontiff* goes and censes the gifts, and adds that which signifies the Ascension of the LORD, and the glory of the subsequent preaching of Him to all creation. As if he thus spake to the SAVIOUR, and said: Thou didst descend even to us and wast seen amongst us, and didst ascend again into heaven; and being taken up from the earth, Thou

---

([18]) The mystical reference is to the tongs by which the live coal from the altar was laid on the prophet's lips. The laity in the Eastern Church receive the Body and Blood of our LORD together, the former having been dipped in the latter. The more ancient way was to receive the latter by means of a tube which they held in their own hands and put into the Chalice for themselves. This was also the custom in the West, till the introduction of the present corruption of the disuse of the Chalice in the eleventh and twelfth centuries. I have seen, in the French cathedrals, as many as four of these tubes, or reeds as they were called: one of gold, the other three of silver-gilt. At present, the united elements are administered in the East by a spoon.

didst with Thy glory fill the earth ; by which we, performing the hierurgy of these Thy mysteries, are both partakers of Thee, and without intermission hold Thee. After this, the sacred Gifts being carried back to the prothesis, the *Deacon* holding the paten on his head, and the *Priests* the chalices, he giveth thanks, and having washed his hands, goeth forth to give that which is called the Antidoron to the people. ([19]) For since the Pontiff, as we have said, expresses the character of Christ, and has both offered Him and received Him, and has distributed Him to them that are sanctified, it is necessary also that the people should partake of sanctification, that is to say, as far as it can be intellectually conveyed to them by prayer and the tremendous hierurgy. And since we, who are endued with a body, must of necessity receive sanctification by sensible things, it is given us by the Antidoron. This is the sanctified bread, over which, on the table of prothesis, prayers have been poured forth, and the uppermost part has been cut out and has been consecrated. This, after being signed with the spear, ([20]) and hallowed by the divine words said over it, is distributed instead of the tremendous

---

([19]) *Antidoron.* See note at page 125.
([20]) For an explanation of the spear, by the means of which the Lamb is cut out and stabbed, see the office of prothesis, at the end of the book. The oblation serves two uses: the seal or Lamb stamped with IC XC NIKA serves for the Sacrament ; the remaining part, as here, for the antidoron.

Gifts to those who have not communicated.   Which,
when the *P*ontiff has done, and has prayed over
the people, he puts an end the Liturgy. . . .([21])

([21]) The rest of the treatise is taken up by the author's
apology and by a few remarks on the Prothesis, which will
better be given under that rite.

THE DIVINE LITURGY

OF

S. Mark.

THE PRIEST. Peace be with all.
    People. And with thy spirit.
Deacon. Pray.
People. LORD, have mercy. LORD, have mercy.
LORD, have mercy.

Priest (secretly). We yield Thee thanks, we yield Thee exceeding thanks, O LORD our GOD, FATHER of our LORD and GOD and Saviour JESUS CHRIST, for all things, and through all things, and in all things: for that Thou hast sheltered, assisted, defended, and brought us through the past time of our life, and hast guided us to this hour, vouchsafing again to set before Thee, in Thy holy place, us who ask pardon of our sins, and propitiation for all Thy people. And we pray and beseech Thee, O Lover of men, O good GOD, give us to accomplish ([1]) this holy day ([2]) and all the time of our life sinlessly, with all joy, health, safety, and with all sanctification and Thy fear. But all envy, all fear, all temptation, every Satanic operation, every plot of wicked

---

([1]) I know not but that the word ἐπιτέλεσαι may here partly retain its religious signification, "to offer as a sacrifice:" thus Ælian in his Various History: Καὶ καθ᾽ ἕκαστον ἔτος ἐπετέλουν αὐτῷ. (Lib. 12, cap. 61.)

([2]) It is a mistake to conclude from this expression that this Liturgy was only used on the Sunday; since we know from the replies of Timotheus, Patriarch of Alexandria, (A.D. 380—385,) that it was said daily.

men, repel from us, O GOD, and from Thy holy
Catholic and Apostolic Church. That which is
good and profitable, do Thou supply to us: if we
have at all sinned against Thee in word or deed, or
by thought, do Thou, as good and the Lover of men,
vouchsafe to overlook it, and forsake not us, O GOD,
who put our trust in Thee, nor lead us into temptation, but deliver us from the evil one, and from his
works, through the grace and pity and benignity of
Thine Only-Begotten SON: (*aloud*) through Whom
and with Whom, be to Thee the glory and the
might, in Thine all-holy and good and life-giving
SPIRIT, now and ever, and to ages of ages.

People. Amen.

Priest. Peace be with all.

People. And with thy spirit.

Deacon. Pray for the king.

People. LORD, have mercy. LORD, have mercy,
LORD, have mercy.

Priest (secretly). Master, LORD, and GOD, FATHER
of our LORD and GOD and Saviour JESUS CHRIST, we
beseech and supplicate Thee that Thou wouldest
perpetually keep our king in peace and fortitude
and righteousness. Subject to him, O GOD, every
enemy and adversary: lay hand upon the shield
and buckler, and stand up to help him. Grant to
him, O GOD, victories, and that he may be peaceably
disposed towards us, and towards Thy holy Name. (³)
That we also in the tranquillity of his days, may

(³) This is a clear proof that this prayer was composed before
the beginning of the great Tenth Persecution; *during* which it
would have been differently worded, and *after* which, it would
have been inappropriate. In fact there is no doubt that these
three prayers are of the most remote antiquity; and this particular clause, with its singularly crabbed construction, may,
not improbably, contain the original words of the Apostle.

lead a quiet and peaceable life in all godliness and honesty, (⁴) through the grace and mercies and benignity of Thine Only-Begotten Son : (*aloud*) through Whom and with Whom, be to Thee the glory and the might, in Thine all-holy and good and life-giving Spirit, now and ever, and to ages of ages.

People. Amen.

Priest. Peace be with all.

People. And with thy spirit.

Deacon. Pray for the Pope and the Bishop. (⁵)

People. Lord, have mercy. Lord, have mercy. Lord, have mercy.

Priest. Master, Lord, and God, the Almighty, (⁶) the Father of our Lord and God and Saviour Jesus Christ, we beseech and supplicate Thee, O Lover of men, O good God, preserving our most holy and blessed Pontiff, the Pope N., and the most sacred Bishop N., preserve them to us peacefully many years, executing the holy Arch-priesthood intrusted by Thee to them according to Thy holy and blessed word, rightly dividing the word of truth, with all orthodox Bishops, Priests, Deacons, Sub-deacons, Readers, Singers, and laymen, with the whole fulness of Thy holy and only Catholic Church, granting to them peace and health and salvation. And their prayers which they make for us, and we for them,

---

(⁴) Notice the coincidence of these expressions, with those in the First Epistle to Timothy ; and remember that it is quite as likely that the Apostle was quoting from the Liturgy, as the Liturgy from the Apostle.

(⁵) By the Pope is of course meant the Patriarch of Alexandria, Pope being his specific title, as Patriarch was that of the Metropolitan of Antioch, and Archbishop that of him of Constantinople. Probably the original bidding prayer was simply,—Pray for the Bishop.

(⁶) I take the epithet by itself, as more in accordance with the structure of the commencement of the second prayer.

receive, O LORD, unto Thy holy and heavenly and reasonable altar. And every enemy of Thy holy Church subdue speedily under their feet, through the grace and mercies and benignity of Thine Only-Begotten SON : (*aloud*) through Whom and with Whom, be to Thee the glory and the might, in Thine all-holy and good and life-giving SPIRIT, now and ever, and to ages of ages.

People. Amen.

Priest. Peace be with all.

People. And with thy spirit.

Deacon. Stand for prayer.

People. LORD, have mercy. LORD, have mercy. LORD, have mercy.

The Priest subjoins the Prayer of the Entrance (⁷) *and for the Incense ;*

Master, LORD, and our GOD, Thou Who didst elect the twelve-lighted lamp of the twelve Apostles, and didst send them into the whole world, to preach and to teach the Gospel of Thy kingdom, and to heal every sickness and every infirmity in the people ; and didst breathe into their faces, and didst say to them, Receive the HOLY GHOST, the Comforter : whose sins ye remit, they are remitted unto them ; whose sins ye retain, they are retained ; thus do Thou also upon us Thy servants that stand around in the Entrance of our holy ministry * * * * with the Bishops, *Priests*, *Deacons*, Readers, Singers, and laity, together with all the fulness of Thy holy Catholic and Apostolic Church. *Preserve us, O*

(⁷) That is to say the Little Entrance, or the bringing in of the Gospel—a ceremony of considerable pomp. Preceded by tapers and incense, the Priest and Deacon carry the Holy Gospels from the Prothesis, and so through the Holy Doors to the Altar.

LORD, from curse, and ban, and from anathema, and binding, and excommunication, and from the part of the adversary, and purify our lips and our heart from all pollution and from all iniquity ; that with a pure heart, and pure conscience, we may offer to Thee this sacrifice for a sweet-smelling savour, and for the remission of our sins, and of the sins of Thy people : through the grace and mercies and benignity of Thine Only-Begotten SON : (*aloud*) through Whom and with Whom, be to Thee the glory and the might, with Thine all-holy and good and life-giving SPIRIT, now and ever, and to ages of ages.

Priest. Amen.

Deacon. Stand up. (⁸)

And they sing the Only-Begotten SON.

Priest. Only-Begotten SON and WORD of GOD, immortal, Who didst vouchsafe for our salvation to take flesh of the holy Mother of GOD, and Ever-Virgin Mary, and didst without mutation become man, and wast crucified, CHRIST, our GOD, and by death didst overcome death, being one of the Holy Trinity, and glorified together with the FATHER and the HOLY GHOST, save us. (⁹)

And the Entrance of the Gospel takes place.

Deacon. For prayer.

Priest. Peace be with all.

People. And with thy spirit.

Deacon. For prayer.

(⁸) This word, ὀρθοί, has, like other short speeches of the Deacon, been retained untranslated in other Liturgies : thus the Armenian gives it *orti*.

(⁹) This anthem, which is in the original simply referred to, is clearly of later date than the Council of Ephesus, and is one of the four employed in the Oriental Liturgies.

People. LORD, have mercy.

The Priest saith the Prayer of the Trisagion. (¹⁰)

Master, and LORD JESUS CHRIST, co-eternal WORD of the self-existent FATHER, Who didst become like us in all respects, sin excepted, for the salvation of our race: Who didst send forth Thy holy disciples and Apostles to preach and teach the Gospel of Thy kingdom, and to cure all sickness and all infirmity among Thy people, do Thou Thyself, O LORD, send out thy light and Thy truth, and enlighten the eyes of our understanding to the comprehension of Thy *D*ivine oracles ; and enable us to be hearers of them, and not hearers only, but also doers of the word, that we may bring forth fruit and produce good fruits, thirty-fold, and an hundred-fold, that we may be counted worthy of the kingdom of heaven. (*Aloud.*) And let Thy mercies speedily prevent us, O LORD, for Thou art the good tidings, Saviour, and guardian, of our souls and of our bodies, LORD our GOD ; and to Thee we send up glory and giving of thanks and the hymn of the Trisagion, FATHER, SON, and HOLY GHOST, now and ever, and to ages of ages.

People. Amen. Holy GOD, Holy and Mighty, Holy and Immortal, have mercy upon us.

And after the Trisagion, the Priest signs (¹¹) *the people, saying,* Peace be with all.

(¹⁰) This prayer is said in a low voice, while the people are singing the Trisagion, as presently. This little anthem is usually ascribed to a miraculous origin, in the time of S. Proclus (434—437), but it is probably far older, and if not Apostolic, is at least Isapostolic. The troubles excited by the addition made by Peter the Fuller, '' Thou That wast crucified for us,'' are well known.

(¹¹) That is, makes the sign of the Cross towards or on them.

People. And with thy spirit.

And the Attend; ([12]) the Apostle; the *Prologue of* the Alleluia. *The Deacons, according as they are enjoined, say—*

Sir, give the blessing. ([13])

Priest. The LORD bless and minister with you by His grace, now and ever, and to ages of ages.

The Priest before the Gospel offers incense and saith thus:

We offer incense before Thy glory, O GOD: do Thou receive it ([14]) to Thy holy and super-celestial and intellectual altar. Do Thou, in its stead, send down the grace of Thy HOLY SPIRIT, for Thou art blessed, and do Thou send forth Thy glory.

When the Deacon is about to read the Gospel, the Priest saith:

The LORD bless and strengthen, and make us to be hearers of His holy Gospel,—Who is GOD That is blessed, now and ever, and to ages of ages. Amen.

Deacon. Stand: let us hear the holy Gospel.

Priest. Peace be with all.

People. And with thy spirit.

([12]) This Rubric requires explanation. *Attend,* is a not unfrequent exclamation of the Deacon in the Oriental rites. The πρόσχωμεν of the Greek is literally retained in the Armenian, *Proschume.* The *Apostle* is the more usual title in the Oriental, as it was in the Gallican, Liturgy, for the *Epistle.* The Prologue of the Alleluia seems to have been some prayer recited by the Priest, while the Alleluia was recited by the people.

([13]) This might also be translated, *Lord, bless:* but, by the analogy of the Western Church, I prefer the version which I have given.

([14]) The reading seems rather corrupt, but its sense is manifest.

The Deacon saith the Gospel. The Priest subjoins the Collect : ([15])

Visit, O Lord, in thy pity and mercies, those of Thy people that are sick : those of our brethren that have departed, or are about to depart, give to each a prosperous journey in his place, and seasonably. Send down rains on the places that want and stand in need of them. Raise the waters of the river to their measure, through Thy grace. ([16]) Increase the fruits of the earth, to seed-time and to harvest; guard the kingdom of Thy servant, whom thou hast appointed to rule over the land, in peace and courage and righteousness and tranquillity. This humble and poor and CHRIST-loving city, preserve it, O GOD, from evil days, from famine, plague, and incursion of the heathen, as Thou didst spare the city of Nineveh : because Thou art full of mercy and pity, and keepest not in remembrance the iniquities of man. Thou, by Thy prophet Isaiah, hast said, I will protect this city, and save it for My sake, and for My servant *David's* sake. Wherefore we beseech Thee, and supplicate Thee, O Lover of men, O good GOD, guard this city for the sake of Thy Martyr and Evangelist, Mark, who showed to us the way of salvation, through the grace and mercies and benignity of Thine Only-Begotten SON : (*aloud*) through Whom and with Whom, be to Thee the glory and the might, in Thine all-holy and good

([15]) *Synapte.* literally Collect ; but in no way responding to the prayer so called in the Western Church, to which, indeed, the East offers no parallel. This answers much more nearly to the Ectene, or Missal Litany—perfect examples of which will be found in the Liturgies of S. James and S. Chrysostom.

([16]) The rise of the Nile being a point of such vital importance to the Egyptian harvest, is a subject put prominently forward in all the Coptic Liturgies.

and life-giving SPIRIT, now and ever, and to ages of ages. (17)

Deacon. Begin.

And they say the Stichos. The Deacon saith the Three. (18)

Priest. Master and LORD, GOD the Almighty, the FATHER of our LORD JESUS CHRIST, we pray and beseech Thee, assign the peace which is from heaven to the hearts of all of us, and also bestow on us the peace of this world. Our most holy and blessed Pope N., and our most sacred Bishop N., guard to us for many years, peacefully accomplishing the holy Arch-priesthood, intrusted by Thee to them, according to Thy holy and blessed will, rightly dividing the word of truth; with all orthodox Bishops, Priests, Deacons, and Sub-deacons, Readers, Singers, with all the fulness of Thy holy Catholic and Apostolic Church. Bless, O LORD, our assemblies; grant them to be without let and without hindrance, according to Thy holy will. Grant them to be houses of prayer, houses of blessing, to us and to Thy servants after us for ever. Arise, O LORD, and let Thine enemies be scattered; let them also that hate Thee flee before Thee. And bless Thy faithful and orthodox people; increase them to myriads of myriads, and let not the death of sin prevail

---

(17) It is almost unnecessary to remark that the reference to the Evangelist is of far later date than the original Liturgy: and the whole prayer, as perhaps the next also, seems to me made up from the Great Intercession for quick and dead, to which we shall presently come.

(18) The *Stichos*, or Versicle, was no doubt some varying anthem for different festivals. What is intended by *the Three*, is not agreed. Some take it to mean three collects to be recited in this place: others, a verse beginning, " The Three Persons and One Essence," or something of a similar kind

against us, nor against all Thy people, through the
grace and mercies and benignity of Thine Only-
Begotten Son : (*aloud*) through Whom and with
Whom, be to Thee the glory and the might, in
Thine all-holy and good and life-giving Spirit, now
and ever, and to ages of ages.

People. Amen.

Priest. Peace be with all.

People. And with thy spirit.

Deacon. Look lest any of the Catechumens...([19])

Here they sing the Cherubic Hymn.

Let us, who mystically represent the Cherubim,
and sing the holy hymn to the quickening Trinity,
lay by at this time all worldly cares, that we may
receive the King of Glory, invisibly attended by the
angelic orders. Alleluia. Alleluia. Alleluia. ([20])

*The Priest offers Incense for the Entrance, and
prays.* ([21])

Priest. Lord our God, Who hast no need of any

([19]) Here followed the expulsion of the Catechumens and
penitents, preceded probably in this, as in the Constantinopolitan ritual, by the Priest unfolding the Corporal. We shall
find a fuller form for this expulsion in other Liturgies.

([20]) This, one of the four Liturgical hymns, is not earlier
than the time of Justinian ; and accordingly does not occur in
any of the heretical Liturgies except the Armenian. It is
found in all the great rites, except the Clementine.

([21]) This is the Great Entrance ; the carrying the Elements
from the Prothesis to the altar. It is the most imposing
ceremony in the Eastern Church. The anticipative worship
paid to these Elements by the congregation, who fall down in
the very path of the Priest, is defended with difficulty by Greek
ritualists; but at all events proves thus much, with how true
and real a worship they must adore those Elements after
Consecration, which before it were counted worthy, as they
themselves seem to say, of anticipative *latria*.

gift, accept this incense offered by an unworthy hand, and count us all worthy of the blessing which is from Thee; for Thou art our sanctification, and to Thee we ascribe glory.

And the Holy Things enter to the Altar, and the Priest prayeth thus.

Holy, Most High, terrible, Thou Who restest in the holies, O LORD, Thyself sanctify us, and count us worthy of Thy fearful Priesthood, and cause us to approach to Thy venerable altar with all good conscience: and purify our hearts from every pollution: chase away from us every evil sensation: hallow our mind and our soul, and grant us to accomplish the worship of our holy fathers with Thy fear, propitiating Thy Face at all times; for Thou art He that blessest and sanctifiest all things, and to Thee we ascribe the glory and the giving of thanks.

Deacon. Kiss one the other.

The Priest saith the prayer of the Kiss.

Master, and LORD Almighty, look down from heaven upon Thy Church, and upon all Thy people, and all Thy flocks, and save all of us Thine unworthy servants, the creatures of Thy fold; and grant to us Thy peace, and Thy love, and Thy help, and send down upon us the gifts of Thy most HOLY SPIRIT, that, in a pure heart, and with a good conscience, we may salute one another with an holy kiss, not in hypocrisy, not taking part with the Alien, (22), but blameless and unspotted, in one spirit, in the bond of peace and of love, one body and one spirit, in one faith, as we have also been

---

(22) There is something here corrupt.

called in one hope of our calling, that we may all of us arrive at the *Divine* and boundless affection, in CHRIST JESUS our LORD, with Whom Thou art blessed.   •

Then the Priest offers Incense, saying :

Incense is offered to Thy Name. Let it ascend, we pray Thee, out of the poor hands of us sinners, to thy super-celestial altar, for a sweet-smelling savour for the propitiation of all Thy people. For to Thee is due all glory, honour, worship, and giving of thanks, the FATHER, the SON, and the HOLY GHOST, now and ever, and to ages of ages.

And after the Kiss of Peace, the Deacon, aloud :

Stand to make your offerings according to your order. ([23])   .

The Priest signing with the Cross the patens and the chalices, saith with a loud voice—

I believe in one GOD the FATHER Almighty, Maker of heaven and earth, and of all things visible and invisible : and in one LORD JESUS CHRIST, the Only-Begotten SON of GOD, begotten of His FATHER before all words, Light of Light, very GOD of very GOD, begotten, not made, being of one substance with the FATHER ; by Whom all things were made : Who for us men, and for our salvation, came down from heaven, + and was Incarnate by the HOLY GHOST of the Virgin Mary, and was made man, and was crucified + also for us under *Pontius Pilate.* He suffered and was buried, and the third day He rose again according to the Scriptures, and ascended into heaven, and sitteth on the right hand of the

---

([23]) This I take to be the meaning of κατὰ τρωπόυς. Renaudot translates it *modestly.*

Father. And He shall come again with glory to judge both the quick and the dead : Whose kingdom shall have no end. And I believe in the + Holy Ghost, the Lord and Giver of Life, Who proceedeth from the Father, Who with the Father and the Son together is worshipped and glorified, Who spake by the Prophets. And I believe one Catholic and Apostolic Church. I acknowledge one Baptism for the remission of sins : and I look for the Resurrection of the dead, and the life of the world to come. Amen.

Deacon. Stand for prayer.

Priest. Peace be with all.

Deacon. Pray for them that offer.

The Priest saith the prayer of the Offertory.

Our Master, Jesus Christ, Lord, co-eternal Word of the self-existent Father and of the Holy Ghost, Thou that art the Great High Priest, the Bread that comest down from heaven, and bringest up our life from corruption, That didst give Thyself, a spotless Lamb, for the life of the world, we pray and beseech Thee, O Lord, Lover of men, cause Thy face to shine upon this bread and upon these chalices, which the most holy table receives, through the ministry of angels, and the surrounding choir of archangels, and the priestly hierurgy, to Thy glory and the renovation of our souls ; through the grace and mercies and love to men of Thine Only-Begotten Son, through Whom and with Whom, be to Thee the glory and the might. ([24])

([24]) Observe the corruption which affixes such an ending to a prayer addressed to the Son ; unless by a most violent construction we leave the former part of the prayer without any apodosis, and conceive the clause that begins, " We pray and beseech Thee," to be addressed to the Father.

At the end of the Creed, the Priest signs the people with the Cross, saying aloud—

The LORD be with all.
People. And with thy spirit.
Priest. Lift we up our hearts.
People. We lift them up unto the LORD.
Priest. Let us give thanks to the LORD.
Priest. It is meet and right.

The Priest begins the Oblation.

It is verily meet and right, holy and becoming, and advantageous to our souls, I AM, LORD GOD, FATHER Almighty, to worship Thee, to hymn Thee, to give thanks to Thee, to return Thee praise, both night and day, with unceasing mouth, and lips that keep not silence, and heart that cannot be still: Thee Who madest the heaven and the things that are in heaven, the earth and the things that are in the earth, the sea, the fountains, the rivers, the lakes, and all things that are in them: Thee Who didst make man after Thine own image and likeness, and also gavest him the delights that were in paradise, and didst not overlook him when he fell, nor desert him, O good GOD, but didst call him back by the Law, didst educate him by the Prophets, didst reform him, and renew him by this tremendous and life-giving and heavenly mystery. All which things Thou hast done by Thy Wisdom, the true Light, Thine Only-begotten SON, our LORD and GOD and SAVIOUR JESUS CHRIST, by Whom, rendering thanks to Thee with Himself and the HOLY GHOST, we offer to Thee this reasonable and unbloody sacrifice, which all nations offer to Thee, O LORD, from the rising of the sun unto the going down of the same; from the north and the south; for Thy name is great among the Gentiles, and in every place incense is offered to Thy name, and a pure offering.

And we pray and beseech Thee, O Lover of men, O good GOD :

Remember, O LORD, the holy and only Catholic and Apostolic Church, which is from one end of earth to the other end of it, all peoples and all Thy flocks. Vouchsafe to all our hearts the peace which is from heaven, and also bestow on us the peace of this life.

The king, the military orders, the princes, the councils, the boroughs, every neighbourhood, our comings in and our goings out, set in order in all peace.

O King of peace, give to us Thy peace in concord and love : possess us, O GOD ; beside Thee we know none other : we are called by Thy Name : quicken all our souls, and the death of sin shall not have dominion over us, nor over all Thy people.

Them that are sick, O LORD, of thy people, visit in Thy pity and mercies, and heal.

Avert from them and from us all sickness and infirmity, drive away from them the spirit of weakness : raise up again them that are lying in long sickness ; heal them that are vexed of unclean spirits, them that are in prisons, or in mines, or in courts of justice, or with sentence given against them, or in bitter slavery, or tribute, have mercy on all, free all : for Thou art our GOD, He that sets free the bound, He that raises those that are in misery, the hope of the hopeless, the succour of the defenceless, the resurrection of the fallen, the harbour of the tempest-tost, the avenger of the afflicted. To every Christian soul that is in trouble, and that is a petitioner to Thee, give mercy, give remission, give refreshment. Furthermore, O LORD.

heal the diseases of our souls, cure our bodily weak-nesses, O *P*hysician of souls and bodies; overseer of all flesh, oversee and heal us by Thy salvation.

To our brethren that have departed from us, or are about to depart, in whatever place, give a fair journey, whether by land or rivers, or lakes, or highways, or in whatever way they may be travel-ling, restore them all everywhere to a tranquil harbour, to a safe harbour: vouchsafe to be their fellow-voyager and fellow-traveller. Give them back to their friends, rejoicing to the rejoicing, healthful to the healthful.

And preserve, O Lord, to the end, our sojourning also in this life, without harm, and without storm.

Send down richly good showers on the places that need them and desire them; rejoice and renew by their descent the face of the earth, that in their drops it may be made glad, and may spring up. Raise up the waters of the river to their full measure; rejoice and renew by their ascent the face of the earth: water her furrows, multiply her increase. Bless, O Lord, the fruits of the earth. *P*reserve them continually whole and unhurt; pre-serve them to us for seed and for harvest. Bless also now, O Lord, the crown of the year of Thy goodness, for the poor of Thy people, for the widow, and for the orphan, for the proselyte, ([25]) for all of us who hope in Thee, and who are called by Thy holy Name: for the eyes of all wait upon Thee, and Thou givest them their meat in due season. Thou That givest meat to all flesh, fill our

---

([25]) If this word, as is probable, is to be taken in its Jewish meaning, it must fix the date of this intercession to a period of the most remote antiquity, prior to the destruction of Jerusalem.

hearts with joy and gladness, that we always, having all sufficiency in all things, may abound unto every good work, in CHRIST JESUS our LORD.

King of kings, and LORD of Lords, * * * * * the kingdom of Thy servant, the orthodox and CHRIST-loving king, whom Thou hast vouchsafed to rule over the land in peace and might and justice. * * * * O GOD, every enemy, both native and foreign. Lay hand upon the shield and buckler, and stand up to help him; bring forth the spear, and stop the way against them that persecute him. Cover his head in the day of battle: cause them that spring from his loins to sit on [his throne] * * * * (26) [speak good things to his heart] for Thy holy Catholic and Apostolic Church, and all the people that loveth CHRIST; that we also in his tranquillity may lead a quiet and peaceable life in all godliness and honesty. Give rest to the souls of our fathers and brethren that have heretofore slept in the faith of CHRIST, O LORD our GOD, remembering our ancestors, fathers, patriarchs, prophets, Apostles, martyrs, confessors, Bishops, holy and just persons, every spirit that has departed in the faith of CHRIST, and those whom to-day we keep in memory [and our holy father Mark, the Apostle and Evangelist, who made known to us the way of salvation.]

[Hail, thou that art full of grace, the LORD is with thee; blessed art thou among women, and blessed is the fruit of thy womb, because thou didst bring forth the Saviour of the world,] (aloud) especially the most holy, stainless, blessed, our Lady, Mother of GOD, and ever-Virgin.

---

(26) We may, I think, see in the broken and corrupted state of the petitions for the Emperor, that they formed no part of the original Liturgy, but were a later edition, when the Government had become Christian.

C

Deacon. Sir, pray for a blessing.

Priest. The LORD shall bless thee with His grace, now and ever, and to ages of ages.

The Deacon reads the Diptychs of the departed. ([27])
The Priest bows down and prays:

And to the spirits of all these give rest, our Master, LORD and GOD, in the Tabernacles of Thy Saints, vouchsafing to them in Thy kingdom the good things of Thy promise, ([28]) which eye hath not seen, and ear hath not heard, and it hath not entered into the heart of man, the things which Thou hast prepared, O GOD, for them that love Thy holy Name. Grant rest to their souls, and vouchsafe to them the kingdom of heaven; and to us grant that the end of our lives may be Christian and well-pleasing to Thee, and without sin, and grant to us to have a

---

([27]) That is to say, the names of the former Prelates of the See, and of celebrated benefactors to the Church. The name is derived from their being inscribed on a board with two leaves, like a modern book: just as Triptych is a board with three leaves, two of which overlap and cover the third. The insertion of a name in the Diptychs, or its erasure from them, was equivalent to a declaration that its possessor died in, or out of, the Communion of the Church; and hence fierce contests in the earlier ages, especially between Rome and Constantinople, on this subject. The only rite which at present retains the lection of the Diptychs as a part of the Liturgy, is the Mozarabic.

([28]) Observe here, (1) one of the many examples of prayers for the dead as an Isapostolic practice; (2) that, nevertheless, every single expression contained in them militates against the doctrine of a purgatory,—*i.e.* in the sense of a place of pain. As this is a subject of such great importance, I have thrown together in an Appendix the prayers for the departed contained in the principal Liturgies not here translated; the exceeding beauty of the language will render them acceptable to those who have no need of a proof of the doctrine.

portion and a lot with all Thy saints. **The thank-**offerings of them that offer sacrifices and oblations receive, O GOD, to Thy holy and super-celestial and spiritual altar, to the height of the heavens, by Thy arch-angelic ministry; of them that offered much or little, secretly and with open boldness, of them that desired and had not wherewithal to offer : and of them that have brought this day their oblations : as Thou didst receive the gifts of Thy righteous servant Abel; [*and the Priest offers incense and saith,*] the sacrifice of our father Abraham, the incense of Zacharias, the alms of Cornelius, and the two mites of the widow, receive also their thank-offerings, and give to them instead of things earthly, things heavenly; instead of things temporal, things eternal. The most holy and blessed *P*ope N., whom Thou didst foreknow and * * * to take in hand the government of Thy holy Catholic and Apostolic Church, and our most sacred Bishop N., guard them by Thy care, for many years, in peaceful time, accomplishing Thy holy Archpriesthood intrusted to them by Thee, according to Thy holy and blessed will, rightly dividing the word of truth. And remember also all orthodox Bishops everywhere, *P*resbyters, *D*eacons, Sub-deacons, Readers, Singers, Monks, ever-virgins, widows, laymen. Remember, O LORD, the holy city ([29]) of CHRIST our GOD, and

([29]) Notice the extreme antiquity of this collocation, which places Jerusalem first. I am inclined to think that the "reigning city" is not Constantinople, but Rome : since it is hardly likely that, were this clause posterior to the time of Constantine, three of the Patriarchal thrones should be mentioned without that which was by universal consent, the first. Anyhow it is remarkable, that Rome is either omitted altogether, or is preceded by Jerusalem; and that, too, in the Liturgy of Alexandria, the Church which, of all in the East clung most closely to the Latin See.

c 2

the reigning city, and this our city, every city and
region, and those that dwell in it in the orthodox
faith of CHRIST, their peace and safety. Remember,
O LORD, every Christian soul in affliction and
trouble, that needs the mercy and succour of GOD,
and the conversion of them that have wandered.
Remember, O LORD, our brethren that are in
bonds; grant them to find mercy and pity in the
sight of all those that have carried them captive.
Remember, O LORD, also us, as sinners and Thy
unworthy servants, and blot out our sins as the good
GOD, and Lover of men. Remember, O LORD, also
me, Thy humble and sinful and unworthy servant,
and blot out my sins, as the GOD that is the Lover
of men. Be present with us who are ministering
to Thy all-holy Name. Bless, O LORD, our congre-
gations. Root out idolatry wholly from the world:
bruise Satan and all his power and wickedness
beneath our feet. The enemies of Thy Church, O
LORD, as at all times, so now also humble. Lay
bare their pride, speedily make manifest their weakness: bring to nought their plots and their villany
which they employ against us. Arise, O LORD, and
let Thine enemies be scattered, and let all them
that hate Thy holy Name flee backward. ([30]) [Bless]
Thy faithful and orthodox people, them that do Thy·
holy will, with a thousand thousand and ten thousand times ten thousand blessings.

Deacon. Ye that are sitting, stand up.

Priest. Free them that are bound, bring forth
them that are in necessities. Satisfy the hungry,
comfort the pusillanimous, convert them that have
strayed, enlighten them that are in darkness, raise
the fallen, establish those that are wavering, heal

([30]) The passage is manifestly corrupt: but this is the sense.

the sick: direct all, O good GOD, into the way of salvation, and unite them to Thy holy flock; and preserve us from our iniquities, being in all things our guard, and our defender.

Deacon. To the East.

The Priest bows down and prays.

Thou art above all power and dominion, and might, and principality, and every name that is named not only in this world but also in that which is to come. Round Thee stand thousand thousands, and ten thousand times ten thousand armies of holy angels and archangels. Round Thee Thy two most honourable creatures, the Cherubim, with many eyes, and the Seraphim with six wings, with twain whereof they cover their feet, with twain their face, and with twain they do fly: and cry one to the other with incessant voices and perpetual praise, singing, vociferating, glorifying, crying, and saying to the Majesty of Thy glory, the triumphal Trisagion: Holy, Holy, Holy, LORD of Sabaoth: heaven and earth are full of Thy holy glory. (*Aloud.*) Thou ever sanctifiest all: but with all that glorify Thee, receive, O LORD, our praise also, who with them laud Thee and say,

People. Holy, Holy, Holy, LORD.

The Priest signs the Holy Mysteries with the Cross, saying,

Verily earth and heaven are full of Thy holy glory, through the manifestation of our LORD and GOD and SAVIOUR JESUS CHRIST: fulfil also, O GOD, this sacrifice with Thy heavenly blessing, by the coming down on it of Thy most HOLY GHOST. For the LORD Himself and our GOD and universal King,

JESUS CHRIST, in the night wherein He surrendered Himself for our sins, and . . . . [underwent] death in the flesh for all, sitting down at supper with His holy *D*isciples and Apostles, took bread (³¹) in His holy and pure and spotless hands, looked up to Thee His own Father, our GOD and the GOD of all, and gave thanks, and blessed, and hallowed, and brake, and distributed to His holy and blessed *D*isciples and Apostles, saying, (*aloud*) Take, **eat**.

Deacon. Pray earnestly.

Priest. For this is My Body which is broken for you, and distributed for the remission of sins.

Choir. Amen.

Priest. Likewise also the cup after supper, having taken, and mingled with wine and water, and looking up to heaven to Thee His own Father, our GOD, and the GOD of all, He gave thanks, He blessed, He filled with the HOLY GHOST, He distributed it to His holy and blessed Apostles and *D*isciples, saying, (*aloud*) *D*rink ye all of this.

Deacon. Yet pray earnestly.

Priest. This is My Blood of the New Testament, which is shed and distributed for you and for many for the remission of sins.

People. Amen.

Priest. Do this in remembrance of Me. For as often as ye eat this bread and drink this cup, ye

---

(³¹) The points dwelt on in the Oriental Liturgies with respect to the institution of the Blessed Eucharist are principally these. Of the Bread; that our LORD (1) looked up to Heaven: (2) took *leavened* bread: (3) blessed: (4) brake: (5) Himself received: (6) distributed to His Apostles. Of the Chalice: (1) that He mingled it with wine and water: (2) looked up to heaven: (3) blessed: (4) Himself received: (5) distributed to His Apostles. In Appendix II., I give the words of institution from all known Liturgies.

shew forth My death, and confess My Resurrection
and Ascension till I come.

O Almighty Lord and Master, King of heaven,
we, announcing the death of Thine Only-begotten
Son, our Lord and God and Saviour Jesus Christ,
and confessing His blessed Resurrection from the
dead on the third day, confess also His Ascension
into heaven, and His session on Thy right hand,
His God and Father, looking also for His second
and fearful and dreadful coming, when He shall
come to judge the quick and the dead in righteousness, and to render to every man according to his
works :

O Lord our God, we have set before Thee Thine
own of Thine own gifts.

And we pray and beseech Thee, (32) O good God

---

(32) We now come to the Invocation of the Holy Ghost, by
which, according to the doctrine of the Eastern Church, and
not by the words of institution, the bread and wine are
"changed," "transmuted," "transelemented," "transubstantiated," into our Lord's Body and Blood. This has always
been a point of contention between the two Churches—the
time at which the change takes place. Originally, there is no
doubt that the Invocation of the Holy Ghost formed a part
of all Liturgies. The Petrine has entirely lost it: the Ephesine
(Gallican and Mozarabic,) more or less retains it : as do also
those mixtures of the Ephesine and Petrine,—the Ambrosian
and Patriarchine or Aquileian. To use the words of the au-
thorized Russian catechism : "Why is this (the Invocation) so
essential ? Because, at the moment of this act, the bread and
wine are changed or transubstantiated into the very Body of
Christ, and into the very Blood of Christ. How are we to
understand the word Transubstantiation? In the exposition
of the faith by the Eastern Patriarchs, it is said that the word
is not to be taken to define the manner in which the bread and
wine are changed into the Body and Blood of our Lord ; for
this none can understand but God ; but only this much is
signified, that the bread, truly, really, and substantially
becomes the very true Body of the Lord, and the wine the
very Blood of the Lord."

and Lover of men, to send down from Thy holy
height, and appointed habitation, and incircumscript bosom, the very PARACLETE, the SPIRIT of
truth, the Holy, the LORD, the Life-giving: Who
spake in the Law and by the *P*rophets and the
Apostles; Who is everywhere present, and filleth
all things, and works of His own free will, and not
as a minister, according to Thy good pleasure, in
those in whom He wills, sanctification.   One in
His nature, manifold in His energies, fountain of
*D*ivine graces; consubstantial with Thee, proceeding from Thee, fellow-sharer in the Throne of Thy
kingdom, and of Thine Only-Begotten SON, our
LORD and GOD and SAVIOUR, JESUS CHRIST.   Send
down then on us, and on these loaves, and on these
cups, Thy HOLY GHOST, that He may sanctify and
perfect them, as GOD Almighty. (*Aloud.*)   And
make this bread the Body.

People. Amen.

Priest. And this cup the Blood of the New Testament, of our very LORD and GOD and SAVIOUR and
universal King, JESUS CHRIST.

Deacon. Come down, ye *D*eacons.

Priest. That they may be to all of us who participate in them for faith, for sobriety, for healing, for
temperance, for sanctification, for renovation of
soul, body, and spirit, for participation of the
blessedness of eternal life and immortality, for the
glory of Thy holy Name, for the remission of sins,
that Thy most holy and precious and glorious Name
may here, as also in every place, be hallowed, and
hymned and sanctified with JESUS CHRIST and the
HOLY GHOST.

People. As it was and is.

Priest. Peace be with all.

Deacon. Pray.

Priest. GOD of light, Father of life, Author of grace, Framer of the worlds, Founder of knowledge, Giver of wisdom, Treasure of holiness, Teacher of pure prayers, Benefactor of the soul, Who givest to the weak-hearted who trust in Thee those things into which the angels desire to look : Who hast raised us from the abyss to light, hast given us life from death, hast granted us freedom from slavery, hast dissolved in us the darkness of sin by the coming of Thine Only-Begotten SON ; now also, O LORD, illuminate the eyes of our understanding by the visitation of Thy HOLY SPIRIT, that we may without condemnation partake of this immortal and heavenly food ; and sanctify us wholly, soul, body, and spirit, that with Thy holy *Disciples* and Apostles we may say to Thee this prayer, Our FATHER, &c. And make us worthy, O LORD and Lover of men, with boldness, without condemnation, with a pure heart, with an enlightened soul, with a countenance that needeth not to be ashamed, with hallowed lips, to dare to call upon Thee our holy GOD and FATHER, Which art in heaven, and to say,

People. Our FATHER, &c. ([33])

Priest. Even so, LORD, LORD, lead us not into temptation, but deliver us from the evil one : for Thy great mercy knoweth that we are unable to bear up through our much infirmity ; but make with the temptation also a way of escape, that we may be able to bear it ; for Thou hast given us power to tread on serpents and scorpions, and on all the might of the enemy : (*aloud*) for Thine is the kingdom, and the power.

([33]) The LORD'S Prayer, as is well known, forms a part of every Liturgy, except the Clementine ; and is always followed by the short supplication against temptation, technically known as the *Embolismus.*

People. Amen.

Priest. Peace be with all.

Deacon. Bow your heads to JESUS.

People. To Thee, O LORD.

Priest. ([34]) Master, LORD, and GOD Almighty, Who sittest upon the Cherubim, and art glorified by the Seraphim ; Who didst prepare the heaven from the waters, and didst adorn it with the choirs of the stars ; Who hast arranged the bodiless armies of angels in the highest, to sing Thy praise everlastingly, to Thee we have bowed the neck of our souls and bodies, signifying the outward appearance of service ; and we pray Thee, disperse the dark attacks of sin from our understanding, and enlighten our soul with the divine rays of Thy HOLY SPIRIT, that we, being filled with the knowledge of Thee, may worthily participate in the good things that are set before us, the spotless Body and precious Blood of Thine Only-Begotten SON, our LORD and SAVIOUR JESUS CHRIST, forgiving us every kind of sin, through Thy great and unsearchable goodness, through the grace and mercies and benignity of Thine Only-Begotten SON ; (*aloud*) by Whom and with Whom, be to Thee the glory and

---

([34]) This is the prayer of Intense Adoration, which has its place in all Oriental Liturgies, and answers to the worship paid by the Western Church to our LORD's Sacramental Body and Blood at the Elevation of the Host. An attempt has been made to prove that the East does not agree with the West in paying the worship of *latria* to that Body and that Blood, from the long interval which separates the prayer of Intense Adoration (in all Liturgies except the present one) from the Invocation of the HOLY GHOST. Nothing can be more futile : the obvious tangible reason being, that during the consecration, the holy doors were closed, or, in the Armenian Church, the veil was drawn ; so that the people could hardly be called on to worship that which was not presented to their eyes, as they can be and are in the Western Church, where it is so presented. But now the holy doors are opened ; hence the reason of the position of this prayer.

the might, in Thine all-holy and good and life-giving
SPIRIT.

Priest. Peace be with all.

Deacon. With the fear of GOD.

Priest. Holy, most high, tremendous LORD, Who
restest in the holies: sanctify us, LORD, by the word
of Thy grace and the visitation of Thy most HOLY
SPIRIT. For Thou, LORD, hast said, Be ye holy,
for I am holy. O LORD our GOD, incomprehensible
WORD of GOD, consubstantial and co-eternal, and
ruling ([35]) with the FATHER and the HOLY GHOST,
receive the pure hymn, with Cherubim and Seraphim,
and from me a sinner and Thine unworthy servant,
crying and saying from my unworthy lips,

People. LORD, have mercy, (*thrice.*)

Priest. HOLY THINGS FOR HOLY PERSONS. ([36])
One holy FATHER, one holy SON, one HOLY GHOST;
in the unity of the HOLY GHOST. Amen.

Deacon. For salvation and succour, &c.

*The Priest, signing the people with the sign of the
Cross, saith,*

The Lord be with all.

He breaks the bread, and saith,

O praise GOD, (Ps. cl.)

The Priest divides it among the assistants, and saith,

The LORD shall bless and minister with you,
through His great mercy,

([35]) σύναρχε: unless, indeed, the true reading be rather
συνάναρχε, *together with Them without origin.*

([36]) The famous exclamation which makes a part of all
Eastern Liturgies, and is accompanied with the Elevation of
the Host. These words are no doubt of Apostolic origin and
are quoted over and over again by the Eastern Fathers. It is
the more wonderful that, to carry out a novel theory, an emi-
nent scholar should lately have attempted to translate them:
" The holy things are lifted up to the holy places."

Priest. Command.

The Clerks. The HOLY GHOST commands and sanctifies.

Priest. Behold, they are sanctified and consecrated.

The Clerks. One HOLY FATHER, &c. (*thrice*).

Priest. The LORD be with all.

The Clerks. And with thy spirit.

Priest. Himself hath blessed it.

> *And the Priest saith either the prayer,*

According to Thy mercy. ([37])

Or else Psalm xlii.   *Quemadmodum*

> *And he communicates. And when he gives the Communion to any one, he saith,*

The Holy Body.

> *And when he gives the Chalice, he saith,*

The precious Blood of our LORD and GOD and SAVIOUR.

> *When all is ended, he saith,*

Stand for prayer.

Priest. Peace be with all.

Deacon. Pray,

Priest. We give Thee thanks, Master, LORD, and our GOD, for the reception of Thy holy, spotless, immortal, and heavenly mysteries, which Thou hast given us for the well-doing and sanctification and salvation of our souls and bodies; and we pray and beseech Thee, good LORD, and Lover of men, to grant that the participation of the holy Body and precious Blood of Thine Only-Begotten SON, may be to faith that shall not be ashamed, to love unfeigned, to the

---

([37]) This prayer, as so much else of the ritual of S. Mark, appears to be lost.

fulfilment of piety, to the turning away the enemy, to the keeping Thy Commandments, to a provision on our way to eternal life, to an acceptable defence before the fearful tribunal of Thy CHRIST: (*aloud*) by Whom and with Whom, &c.

Then the Priest turns to the people, and saith,

Mighty King and co-sharer of Thy Father's rule, Who didst by Thy might spoil hell, and trample on death, and didst raise Adam from the tomb, by Thy god-like might, and by the illuminative splendour of Thine ineffable Godhead, do Thou, O LORD, by the participation of Thy spotless Body and precious Blood, send forth Thine invisible right hand, that is full of blessings, and bless us all ; pity and strengthen by Thy divine power, and destroy in us the vicious and sinful working of fleshly lust : enlighten the eyes of our souls from the darkness of sin that lies around them ; unite us to the all-blessed company that is well-pleasing to Thee : for through Thee and with Thee, to the FATHER and the HOLY GHOST, every hymn is due, honour, might, adoration, and giving of thanks, now and ever, and to ages of ages.

Deacon. Depart in peace.

People. In the name of the LORD.

Priest, (*aloud.*) The love of GOD and the FATHER, the grace of the SON and our LORD JESUS CHRIST, the communion and gift of the HOLY GHOST, be with us all, now and ever, and to ages of ages.

People. Amen. Blessed be the Name of the LORD. (38)

---

(38) In the printed copies there is another prayer " to be said in the Sacristy :" which, as clearly having no business in this place, I have omitted.

THE DIVINE LITURGY

OF

S. James.

Priest. Master, Lord, and our God, reject me not utterly, though polluted with the multitude of my sins; for, behold, I have come to this Thy divine and heavenly mystery. Not as being worthy, but looking up to Thy goodness, I address my voice unto Thee. O God, be merciful to me a sinner: I have sinned against heaven and before Thee, and am not worthy to present myself before this Thy sacred and spiritual Table, whereon Thine Only-Begotten Son, and our Lord Jesus Christ, is mystically set forth as a sacrifice for me a sinner, and marked with every stain. Therefore I offer unto Thee this supplication and thanksgiving, in order to the sending down upon me Thy Spirit of consolation, to confirm and prepare me for this service; and do Thou make me worthy to declare, without condemnation, the word delivered by me to Thy people from Thee, through Jesus Christ our Lord; with Whom Thou art blessed, together with Thy most holy, and good, and quickening, and consubstantial Spirit, now and ever, and to ages of ages. Amen.

Prayer of Standing before the Altar.

Glory to the Father, and to the Son, and to the Holy Ghost, the Trinal and only light of Godhead, existing, one Substance in Trinity, and undividedly: for the one Almighty God is the Trinity, Whose glory the heavens relate, and the earth His power, and the sea His might, and every sentient and intelligent creature heralds everywhere His greatness : for Him befits all glory, honour, might, greatness, and magnificence, now and ever, and to ages of ages. Amen.

Prayer of the Incense.

Master and LORD, JESUS CHRIST, O WORD of GOD, Who didst voluntarily offer Thyself, a spotless sacrifice, upon the Cross to GOD and the FATHER, the coal of two natures, Who didst kindle with the tongs the prophet's lips, and didst take away his sins, kindle also the perceptions of us sinners, and purify us from every spot, and cause us to stand pure before Thy holy altar, that we may offer to Thee the sacrifice of praise : and receive from us, Thine unprofitable servants, for a sweet-smelling savour, and make sweet that which is unsavoury both in our souls and our bodies ; and sanctify us with the sanctifying power of Thy most HOLY SPIRIT : for Thou only art holy, Who sanctifiest, and art distributed to, Thy faithful people ; and glory befits Thee with Thy self-existent FATHER, and Thy most holy and good and quickening SPIRIT, now and ever, and to ages of ages. Amen.

Introductory Prayer.

O Beneficent King of Ages, and Maker of the whole Creation, accept Thy Church approaching Thee through Thy CHRIST ; fulfil that which is profitable to each ; bring all to perfection ; and make us worthy of the grace of Thy sanctification ; gathering us together in Thy holy Church, which Thou hast purchased by the precious Blood of Thine Only-Begotten SON, our LORD and Saviour JESUS CHRIST ; with Whom Thou art blessed and glorified, together with the most holy and good and quickening SPIRIT, now and ever, and to ages of ages. Amen.

Deacon. Let us yet pray to the LORD.

Priest. O GOD, Who didst receive the gifts of Abel, the sacrifice of Noah and Abraham, the incense of Aaron and Zacharias, receive also out of the hand of us sinners this incense for a sweet-smelling savour, and for the remission of our sins, and of all Thy people; for Thou art blessed, and to Thee glory is due, FATHER, SON, and HOLY GHOST, now and ever.

Deacon. Sir, give the blessing.

Priest. JESUS CHRIST, our LORD and GOD, Who, through the exceeding greatness of Thy goodness, and Thy love not to be restrained, wast crucified, and didst not refuse to be pierced by the spear and the nails; Who didst provide this mysterious and fearful rite as an eternal remembrance to us continually; bless thy ministry in CHRIST our GOD, and bless our Entrance, and accomplish perfectly the ministration of this our Liturgy by His ineffable loving-kindness, now and ever, and to ages of ages.

Responsory prayer from the Deacon.

The LORD bless and vouchsafe to us to bring presents to Him seraphically, and to sing the widely-celebrated hymn of the divine Trisagion, by the measureless fulness of all the completeness of sanctification, now and ever. ([1])

The Deacon sings in the Entrance.

Only-Begotten SON and WORD of GOD, immortal, Who didst vouchsafe for our salvation to take flesh of the holy mother of GOD, and ever-Virgin Mary, and didst without mutation become man, and wast crucified, CHRIST, our GOD, and by death didst over-

---

([1]) These Prayers except the first and fourth, have a comparatively later origin, and cannot be considered more ancient than the time of S. Proclus.

come death, being one of the HOLY TRINITY, and glorified together with the FATHER and the HOLY GHOST, save us.

The Priest saith this prayer from the gates to the Altar.

O GOD, the Almighty and glorious LORD, Who hast given to us an Entrance to the Holy of Holies, by the sojourning on earth of Thine Only-Begotten Son, our LORD, and GOD, and Saviour, JESUS CHRIST, we beseech and supplicate Thy goodness, seeing that we are full of fear and trembling, when about to stand before Thy holy Altar, send down upon us, O LORD, Thy good grace, and sanctify our souls and bodies and spirits, and change our dispositions to piety, that we, with a pure conscience, may offer to Thee gifts, presents, fruits, to the putting away of our transgressions and for the propitiation of all Thy people, through the grace, and mercies, and love to man of Thine Only-Begotten Son, with Whom Thou art blessed to ages of ages. Amen.

And after entering to the Altar, the Priest saith—

Peace be with all.

People. And with thy spirit.

Priest. The LORD bless us all, and hallow us in the entrance and hierurgy of the divine and spotless Mysteries, giving peace also to the blessed souls with the holy and the just, through His grace and love to man, now and ever, and to ages of ages. Amen.

Then the Deacon saith the Collect.—In peace let us make our supplication to the LORD.

For the peace that is from above, and the loving-kindness of GOD, and the salvation of our souls, let us make our supplication to the LORD.

For the peace of the whole world, and the union of all the holy Churches of God, let us make our supplication to the Lord.

For the forgiveness of our sins, and the remission of our transgressions, and that we may be preserved from all affliction, wrath, danger, and necessity, and the insurrection of our enemies, let us make our supplication to the Lord.

Then the Singers sing the hymn of the Trisagion.

Holy God, Holy and Mighty, Holy and Immortal, have mercy upon us.

Priest (bowing down). Merciful and pitiful, long-suffering, and gracious, and very Lord, look upon us from Thy prepared habitation, and hear us Thy suppliants, and preserve us from all temptation whether of the devil or of man, and set not Thy help far from us, nor bring upon us chastisements heavier than we can bear: for we are not able to conquer the things which are adverse to us: but Thou art able, O Lord, to save us from all adversities. Save us, O God, from the difficulties of this world, according to Thy goodness; that we, entering with a pure conscience to Thy holy Altar, may without blame send up to Thee, together with the heavenly powers, the blessed hymn of the Trisagion; and, accomplishing the Liturgy, well-pleasing to Thee and divine, may be counted worthy of everlasting life.

Exclamation. For Thou art holy, O Lord, our God, and Thou dwellest and restest in the Holies, and to Thee we ascribe glory, and the hymn of the Trisagion, Father, Son, and Holy Ghost, now and ever, and to ages of ages.

People. Amen.

Priest. Peace be with all.
People. And with thy spirit.
The Singers. Alleluia!

Then are read consecutively ([2]) the sacred oracles of the Old Testament and the Prophets; and the Incarnation of the Son of Man, His sufferings and Resurrection from the dead, His Ascension into heaven, and His Second Coming with glory, are set forth. And this is done every ([3]) day in the holy and Divine Service. And after the reading and teaching, the Deacon says,

Let us all say, LORD, have mercy.

LORD, Almighty, GOD of our Fathers, we beseech Thee to hear us.

For the peace that is from above, and the salvation of our souls, let us make our supplication to the LORD.

For the peace of the whole world, and the unity of the holy Churches of GOD, let us make our supplication to the LORD.

For the salvation and succour of all the CHRIST-loving people, we beseech Thee to hear us.

That we may be delivered from all affliction, wrath, danger, and necessity, bondage, bitter death, and our iniquities, we beseech Thee to hear us.

For the people that is standing round about, and expecting the rich and great mercy that is from Thee, we beseech Thee, be compassionate and have mercy.

([2]) διεξοδικώτατα. So they usually interpret the word, though others will have it to mean *at very great length.* The Rubric is of the most venerable antiquity.

([3]) Καθ' ἑκάστην. It is most natural to understand ἡμέραν. This passage is another proof that the Primitive Liturgies were not confined to Sunday only.

Save, O LORD, Thy people, and bless Thine inheritance.

Visit Thy world in mercy and loving-kindnesses.

Raise the horn of Christians, by the might of the
precious and quickening Cross.

We beseech Thee, O LORD of many mercies, hear
us who supplicate Thee, and have mercy.

People (thrice.) LORD, have mercy.

Deacon. For the forgiveness of our sins, and the
remission of our offences, and that we may be preserved from all affliction, wrath, danger, and
necessity, let us make our supplication to the LORD.

Let us beseech from the LORD, that we may pass
through this whole day in perfectness, holiness,
peace, and sinlessness.

Let us beseech from the LORD, an Angel of peace,
a faithful guide, guardian of our souls and bodies.

Let us beseech from the LORD, pardon and remission of our sins and transgressions.

Let us beseech from the LORD, such things as are
good and convenient to our souls, and peace to the
world.

Let us beseech from the LORD, that we may
accomplish the remainder of our lives in peace and
health.

Let us beseech that the ends of our life may be
Christian, without pain, and without shame, and a
good answer at the dreadful and fearful judgment-
seat of CHRIST.

Priest. For Thou art the good tidings, and the
illumination, the Saviour and the Guardian of our
souls and bodies, GOD, and Thy Only-Begotten SON,
and Thy all-holy SPIRIT, now and ever.

People. Amen.

Priest. Commemorating our all-holy, spotless,
exceeding glorious Lady, the Mother of GOD, and

ever-Virgin Mary, with all Saints, and just men, let us commend ourselves, and each other, and all our life to CHRIST, our GOD.

People. To Thee, O LORD.

Priest. O GOD, Who hast sounded into our ears Thy divine and salutary oracles, illuminate the souls of us sinners to the comprehension of that which has been before read, so that we may not only be seen to be hearers of spiritual things, but doers of good works, following after faith without guile, blameless life, conversation without charge of guilt.

Exclamation. In CHRIST JESUS our LORD, with Whom Thou art blessed, with Thy most holy and good and quickening SPIRIT, now and ever, and to ages of ages.

People. Amen.

Priest. Peace be with all.

People. And with thy spirit.

Deacon. Let us bow our heads to the LORD.

People. To Thee, O LORD.

Priest. LORD and Giver of Life, Supplier of good things, Thou That didst give to men the blessed hope of everlasting life, our LORD JESUS CHRIST, vouchsafe that we may in holiness accomplish this divine Liturgy to Thee, to the enjoyment of future blessedness.

Exclamation. To the end that we, ever guarded by Thy might, and conducted to the light of truth, may send up to Thee glory and thanksgiving, FATHER, SON, and HOLY GHOST, now and ever.

People. Amen.

Deacon. Let none of the Catechumens, let none of the uninitiated, let none of those who are not able

to join with us in prayer;—look upon ([4]) one another. The doors! All upright! Let us pray yet
to the LORD.

Prayer of the Incense.

Priest. Master, Almighty, King of Glory, Who
knowest all things before their origin, be Thyself
present with us who call upon Thee in this holy
hour, and ransom us from the shame of our falls.
Purify our mind and our thoughts from impure con-
cupiscences and worldly deceit, and every diabolic
influence; and receive from the hands of us sinners
this Incense, as Thou didst receive to Thyself the
offering of Abel and Noe, and Aaron and Samuel,
and all Thy Saints; defending us from every evil
thing, and preserving us to the being evermore well-
pleasing to Thee, and worshipping Thee, the FATHER
and Thine Only-Begotten SON, and Thy most Holy
SPIRIT, now and ever, and to ages of ages.

And the Readers begin the Cherubic Hymn.

Let us, who mystically represent the Cherubim,
and sing the thrice-holy hymn to the quickening
TRINITY, lay by at this time all worldly cares, that
we may receive the King of Glory, invisibly attended
by the angelic orders.   Alleluia.([5])
Priest. Let all mortal flesh keep silence, and
stand with fear and trembling, and ponder nothing
earthly in itself; for the King of Kings, and LORD
of Lords, CHRIST our GOD, cometh forward to be
sacrificed and to be given for food to the faith-

([4]) So as to be sure that none, whom any worshipper knew
to be a Catechumen or heretic, might conceal himself in the
church.

([5]) See this hymn in the Liturgy of S. Mark.

ful; and He is preceded by the choirs of the Angels, with every *Domination* and *Power*, the many-eyed Cherubim, and the six-winged Seraphim, that cover their faces, and vociferate the hymn, Alleluia, Alleluia, Alleluia.

The Priest brings in the Holy Gifts, and saith this prayer.([6])

O God, our God, Who didst send forth the heavenly Bread, the nourishment of the whole world, our Lord Jesus Christ as our Saviour and Ransomer and benefactor, blessing and sanctifying us, Thyself bless this offering, and receive it to Thy super-celestial Altar. Remember, as good and the Lover of men, them that brought it, and them for whom they brought it: and continually guard us without condemnation, in the hierurgy of Thy divine mysteries. For hallowed and glorified is Thine all-honourable and majestic Name, of Father, and Son, and Holy Ghost, now and ever, and to ages of ages.

Priest. Peace be with all.

Deacon. Sir, give the blessing.

Priest. Blessed be God, Who blesseth and halloweth us all at the offering of the divine and spotless mysteries, and giveth rest to the blessed souls with the Saints and the just, now and ever, and to ages of ages.

Deacon. Let us attend in wisdom.

The Priest begins—

I believe in one God the Father Almighty, Maker of heaven and earth, and of all things

---

([6]) The Great Entrance: for which see the parallel passage in the Liturgy of S. Mark.

visible and invisible : and in one LORD JESUS CHRIST, the Only-Begotten SON of GOD, begotten of His FATHER before all worlds. Light of Light, very GOD of very GOD, begotten, not made, being of one substance with the FATHER ; by Whom all things were made : Who for us men, and for our salvation came down from heaven, and was Incarnate by the HOLY GHOST of the Virgin Mary, and was made man, and was crucified also for us under *Pontius Pilate.* He suffered and was buried, and the third day He rose again according to the Scriptures, and ascended into heaven, and sitteth on the right hand of the FATHER. And He shall come again with glory to judge both the quick and the dead : Whose kingdom shall have no end. And I believe in the HOLY GHOST, the Lord and Giver of Life, Who proceedeth from the FATHER : Who with the FATHER and the SON together is worshipped and glorified, Who spake by the *P*rophets. And I believe one Holy Catholic and Apostolic Church. I acknowledge one Baptism for the remission of sins. And I look for the Resurrection of the dead, and the life of the world to come. Amen.

Then he prayeth, bowing the neck.

GOD and Master of all things, make us, the unworthy, O Lover of men, worthy of this hour, that we, remaining pure from all guile and all hypocrisy, may be united together by the bond of peace and of love, being stablished by the sanctification of Thy divine knowledge, through Thine Only-Begotten SON, our LORD and SAVIOUR JESUS CHRIST : with Whom.

Deacon. Let us stand well : let us stand piously; let us stand with the fear of GOD, and compunction of heart. In the peace of the LORD, let us pray.

Priest. For the GOD of peace, mercy, love, bowels of compassion, and love to man, art Thou and Thine Only-Begotten SON, and Thine all-holy SPIRIT, now and ever.

People. Amen.

Priest. Peace be with all.

People. And with thy spirit.

Deacon. Let us kiss one another ([7]) with an holy kiss. Let us bow our heads to the LORD.

The Priest bowing down, saith this prayer.

Thou Who alone art LORD and merciful GOD, on them that bow down their necks before Thine holy Altar, and seek the spiritual gifts that are from Thee, send forth Thy good grace; and bless us all with every spiritual blessing, that cannot be taken away, Thou Who dwellest on high, and regardest things that are humble.

Exclamation. For laudable and adorable and exceeding glorious is Thy most holy Name, of FATHER, SON, and HOLY GHOST, now and ever, and to ages of ages.

Deacon. Sir, give the blessing.

Priest. The LORD shall bless, and shall minister with all of us in His grace and love to men. *And again.* The LORD shall bless, and make us worthy of standing before His holy Altar, always, now and ever, and to the ages. *And again.* Blessed be GOD, Who blesseth and sanctifieth all of us in our presence at, and hierurgy of, His spotless mysteries, now and ever, and to the ages.([8])

([7]) Observe that the Kiss of Peace follows the Creed in this Liturgy—precedes it in that of S. Mark.

([8]) It is not easy to say whether these are different versions of the same blessing, or whether they bear any reference to the Blessed Trinity.

The Deacon makes the universal Litany.

In peace let us make our supplication to the LORD.

People. LORD have mercy.([9])

For the peace that is from above and the love of GOD, and the salvation of our souls, let us make our supplication to the LORD. [*Each clause ends in the same way.*]

For the peace of the whole world, and the unity of all the holy Churches of GOD.

For them that bear fruit and do good deeds in the holy Churches of GOD, that remember the poor, the widows and the orphans, the strangers, and them that are in need; and for them that have desired us to make mention of them in our prayers.

For them that are in old age and infirmity, the sick, the distressed, and that are vexed of unclean spirits, their speedy healing from GOD and salvation.

For them that lead their lives in virginity, and purity, and asceticism, and in venerable marriage, and them that carry on their struggle in the caves and dens ([10]) and holes of the earth, our holy fathers and brothers.

For Christians that sail, that journey, that are strangers, and for our brethren that are in bonds and exiles, and imprisonment and bitter slavery, their peaceful return.

For the forgiveness of our sins and remission of

([9]) The Deacon in the printed texts, continues, *Preserve, have pity, and guard us, O God, by Thy grace.* This petition is clearly mis-placed here: it may have belonged to the end. Compare this " Catholic Synapte " with the Ectene of the Liturgy of S. Chrysostom.

([10]) A clause probably added in the 4th century.

our offences, and that we may be preserved from all affliction, wrath, danger and necessity, and the insurrection of enemies.

For good temperature of the atmosphere, peaceful showers, pleasant dews, abundance of fruits, fulness of a good season, and for the crown of the year.

For those, our fathers and brethren, that are present and pray together with us in this holy hour and at all seasons, their diligence, labour, and readiness.

And for every Christian soul in affliction and distress, and needing the mercy and succour of God, and for the conversion of the erring, the health of the sick, the rescue of the prisoners, and the rest of them that have departed afore, our fathers and brethren.

That our prayer may be heard and acceptable before God, and that His rich mercies and pities may be sent down upon us.

Let us commemorate the most holy, spotless, exceedingly glorious, blessed Lady, the Mother of God and Ever-Virgin Mary, with all the Saints together, that we may obtain mercy through their prayers and intercessions.

And for the proposed, precious, heavenly, ineffable, spotless, glorious, fearful, terrible, divine gifts, and the salvation of the Priest that stands by and offers them, let us supplicate the LORD our GOD.

People. LORD have mercy.

Then the Priest signs the Gifts with the Cross, and standing saith secretly thus—

Glory to God in the highest, and on earth peace, good-will to men. (*Thrice.*)

O LORD, open Thou my lips, and my mouth shall shew forth Thy praise. (*Thrice.*)

Let my mouth be filled with Thy praise, O Lord, that I may set forth Thy glory, and Thy majesty all the day long. (*Thrice.*)

Of the Father. Amen. And of the Son. Amen. And of the Holy Ghost. Amen. Now and ever, and to ages of ages. Amen.

And bowing to this side and that, he saith—

O magnify the Lord with me, and let us exalt His Name together.

And they answer, bowing down.

The Holy Ghost shall come upon thee, and the power of the Highest shall overshadow thee.

And the Priest at length.

Lord and Master, Thou That dost visit us with mercies and loving-kindnesses, and hast freely given boldness to us Thy humble and sinful and unworthy servants, to stand before Thy holy Altar, and to offer to Thee the fearful and unbloody sacrifice for our sins and for the ignorance of the people, look upon me, Thine unprofitable servant, and blot out my sins by Thy tender mercy: and cleanse my lips and heart from all pollution of flesh and spirit; and remove from me every unseemly and foolish thought, and make me fit, by the might of Thine all-holy Spirit, for this Liturgy; and receive me by Thy goodness, approaching to Thy holy Altar; and vouchsafe, O Lord, that these gifts, brought to Thee by our hands, may be acceptable, condescending to my weaknesses: and cast me not away from Thy Face, neither abhor Thou mine unworthiness: but pity me according to Thy great mercy, and according to the multitude of Thy loving-kindnesses pass by my transgressions: that I, coming blamelessly into the presence of Thy glory, may be counted worthy of the protection of Thine Only-Begotten Son, and of the illumination of the most HOLY SPIRIT; and may not, as a slave of sin, be rejected, but, as Thy servant, may find grace and mercy and remission of sins before Thee, in this world, and in that which is to come. Yea, all-ruling Master, Almighty LORD, hear my supplication; for Thou art He That workest all in all, and we all seek in all things after the succour and assistance that is from Thee and Thine Only-Begotten Son, and the good and quickening and consubstantial SPIRIT, now and for ever.

O GOD, Who through Thy great and ineffable love to man didst send Thine Only-Begotten Son into the world, that He might turn back again the sheep that had gone astray; turn not back us sinners, that take hold of Thee in the fearful and unbloody sacrifice : for we trust not in our own righteousness, but in Thy good mercy, by which Thou redeemest to Thyself our race. We supplicate and beseech Thy goodness that this Mystery planned for our salvation may not be for condemnation to Thy people, but for the blotting out of sin, for the renewal of souls and bodies, for the well-pleasing of Thee, our GOD and FATHER, in the mercy and love to men of Thine Only-Begotten Son, with Whom Thou art blessed, with, &c.

LORD GOD, Thou That didst form us and bring us to life, Thou That hast manifested to us ways to salvation ; Thou That hast vouchsafed to us the revelation of celestial Mysteries, and didst place us in this ministry in the might of Thine all-holy SPIRIT : vouchsafe, Master, that we may be servants of Thy New Testament, ministers of Thy spotless mysteries, and according to the multitude of Thy mercy receive us who approach to Thy holy Altar, that we may be worthy to offer to Thee gifts and sacrifices for our own ignorances and for those of the people; and grant us, O Lord, with all fear and with a good conscience to set before Thee this spiritual and unbloody sacrifice, receiving which unto Thy holy and super-celestial and rational Altar, for a savour of spiritual sweetness, send down to us in its stead the grace of Thine all-holy Spirit. Yea, O God, look upon us, and have regard to this our reasonable sacrifice, and receive, as Thou didst receive the gifts of Abel, the sacrifices of Noe, the priestly offerings of Moses and Aaron, the peace-offerings of Samuel, the repentance of David, the incense of Zacharias: as Thou didst receive from the hand of Thine Apostle this true worship, thus receive also from the hands of us sinners, in Thy goodness, these gifts that are laid before Thee. And grant that our oblations may be well-pleasing to Thee and hallowed by the Holy Ghost, for a propitiation of our transgressions, and of the ignorances of the people, and for the repose of the souls that have fallen asleep; that we also, Thy humble and sinful, and unworthy servants, being counted worthy to minister without guile at Thy holy Altar, may receive the reward of faithful and wise stewards, and may find grace and mercy in the fearful day of Thy just and good recompense.

Prayer of the Veil. ([11])

We render thanks to Thee, Lord our God, for that Thou hast given us boldness to the entrance in of Thy holy places, the new and living way which Thou hast consecrated for us through the veil of the Flesh of Thy Christ. We therefore, to whom it

---

([11]) Because the Veil is now raised, and the Holy Mysteries exposed to view.

hath been vouchsafed to enter into the place of the tabernacle of Thy glory, and to be within the veil, and to behold the Holy of Holies, fall down before Thy goodness: Master, have mercy upon us: since we are full of fear and dread, when about to stand before Thy holy Altar, and to offer this fearful and un-bloody sacrifice for our sins and for the ignorances of the people. Send forth, O God, Thy good grace, and hallow our souls, and bodies, and spirits ; and change our disposition to piety, that in a pure con-science we may present to Thee the mercy of peace, the sacrifice of praise. (¹²)

Exclamation. Through the mercy and love to men, and Thine Only-Begotten Son, with Whom, &c.

People. Amen.

Priest. Peace be with all.

Deacon. Let us stand with piety ; let us stand with the fear of God and compunction of heart ; let us attend to the holy Anaphora, to offer peace [*i.e.* a peace-offering] to God.

People. The mercy of peace, the sacrifice of praise.

Priest. And do Thou, uncovering the veils of enigmas which mystically surround this holy rite; make them gloriously manifest to us: and fill our intellectual eyes with incomprehensible light; and, having cleansed our poverty from every pollution of flesh and speck, make it worthy of this fearful and dread ministration: for Thou art the God of ex-ceeding tender mercy : and to Thee we send up the glory and giving of thanks to the FATHER, the SON, and the HOLY GHOST, now and for ever.

(¹²) Notice the sublime depth of this prayer, which seems perfectly apostolic. Did the writer quote S. Paul, (*Heb.* x. 19, 20,) or did S. Paul, in writing to the Hebrews, quote their own Liturgy?

Then he exclaims—

The love of the LORD and FATHER, the grace of the LORD and SON, the communion and gift of the HOLY GHOST, be with us all.

People. And with thy spirit.

Priest. Lift we up our mind and our hearts.

People. It is meet and right.

Priest. It is verily meet and right, fitting and due, to praise Thee, to hymn Thee, to bless Thee, to worship Thee, to glorify Thee, to give thanks to Thee, Who madest all creation visible and invisible; the Treasure of eternal good things, the Fountain of life and immortality, the GOD and Master of all Things, Whom heaven, and the heaven of heavens, hymn, and all their powers: the sun and the moon and all the choir of the stars; the earth, the sea, and all that is in them; Jerusalem the celestial assembly, the Church of the First-born written in heaven: the spirits of just men and of Prophets; the souls of Martyrs and Apostles; Angels, Archangels, thrones, dominations, principalities, virtues, and the tremendous powers; the Cherubim of many eyes, and the Seraphim that have six wings, with twain whereof they cover their faces, and with twain their feet, and with twain they do fly, crying one to the other, with ceaseless tongues and perpetual doxologies, the triumphal hymn to the majesty of Thy glory, singing with a loud voice, crying, praising, vociferating, and saying,

Choir. Holy, Holy, Holy LORD of Sabaoth; heaven and earth are full of Thy glory. Hosanna in the highest: blessed is He that cometh in the Name of the LORD: Hosanna in the highest.

Holy art Thou, King of ages, and LORD and Giver

of all holiness : holy also Thine Only-Begotten Son, our LORD JESUS CHRIST, by Whom Thou didst make all things : holy also the HOLY GHOST, Who searcheth all things, yea, even the deep things of GOD : holy art Thou, O Omnipotent, Almighty, Good, Tremendous, Long-suffering, and of great compassion towards Thy creatures : Thou Who didst make man from the earth after Thine image and likeness : and didst give him the delight of *Paradise*, and when he transgressed Thy commandment and fell, Thou didst not disregard nor leave him, O good GOD : but didst correct him as a tender Father, didst call him by the Law, didst educate him by the *Prophets*; and lastly didst send forth into the world Thine Only-begotten SON, our LORD JESUS CHRIST, that He might come and renew and restore in us Thine image : Who descended from heaven, and being incarnate of the HOLY GHOST and Mary the Virgin and Mother of GOD, and having had His conversation with men, accomplished all the dispensation for the salvation of our race, and Who being about to endure His voluntary and life-giving death on the Cross, the sinless, for us sinners, in the night wherein He was betrayed, or rather surrendered Himself for the life and salvation of the world (*here the Priest takes the bread in his hands*), taking bread in His holy and spotless and pure and immortal hands, and looking up to heaven, and shewing it to Thee, His GOD and FATHER, He gave thanks, and hallowed, and brake, and gave to us His Apostles and *D*isciples ([18]), saying,

The Deacons. For the remission of sins and eternal life.

([18]) Notice the word *us*, which is found in this connection in no other Liturgy, however ancient, .or bearing the name of any other Apostle. It seems to denote the authorship of one who was present at the Last Supper.—I,.

E

Priest (aloud.) Take, eat: this is My Body which is broken for you, and is given for the remission of sins.

People. Amen.

Then he takes the cup, and saith,

Likewise also the cup after supper, having taken, and mixed it with wine and water, and having looked up to heaven, and displayed it to Thee, His GOD and FATHER, He gave thanks, and hallowed, and blessed, and filled with the HOLY GHOST, and gave it to us, His *Disciples*, saying,

Drink ye all of this:

This is My Blood of the New Testament, which for you and for many is shed and distributed for the remission of sins.

People. Amen.

Priest. Do this in remembrance of Me. For as often as ye eat this bread, and drink this cup, ye set forth the death of the Son of Man, and confess His resurrection, till He come.

Deacon. We believe and confess.

People. We set forth Thy death, O LORD, and confess Thy resurrection.

Priest. We therefore also, sinners, remembering His life-giving *Passion*, His salutary Cross, His *Death*, and Resurrection from the dead on the third day, His Ascension into heaven, and session on the right hand of Thee, His GOD and FATHER, and His glorious and terrible coming again, when He shall come with glory to judge the quick and the dead, and to render to every man according to his works, offer to Thee, O LORD, this tremendous and unbloody sacrifice, beseeching Thee that Thou wouldst not deal with us after our sins, nor reward us according to our iniquities: but according to Thy gentleness

and ineffable love, passing by and blotting out the
hand-writing that is against us, Thy suppliants,
wouldst grant us Thy heavenly and eternal gifts,
which eye hath not seen, nor ear heard, neither
hath it entered into the heart of man to conceive
the things which Thou, O GOD, hast prepared for
them that love Thee.([14]) And set not at nought
Thy people, O LORD and Lover of men, for me and
for my sins. (*He repeats thrice.*) For Thy people
and Thy Church supplicate Thee.

People. Have mercy upon us, LORD GOD, FATHER
Almighty.

Priest. Have mercy on us, GOD Almighty.

Have mercy on us, GOD our SAVIOUR.

Have mercy on us, O GOD, according to Thy
great goodness, and send upon us, and upon these
proposed gifts, Thy most HOLY GHOST, (*he bends his
head,*) the LORD and Life-giving ; sharer of the throne
and of the kingdom with Thee, GOD and FATHER,
and Thine Only-Begotten SON, consubstantial and
co-eternal, Who spake in the Law, and the *P*rophets,
and Thy New Testament, Who descended in the form
of a dove on our LORD JESUS CHRIST in the river
Jordan, and rested on Him, Who descended upon
Thy holy Apostles in the likeness of fiery tongues in
the upper room of the holy and glorious Sion, at the
day of *P*entecost: send down the same most HOLY
GHOST, LORD, upon us, and upon these holy and
proposed gifts, (*he raises himself, and saith aloud,*)
that coming upon them with His holy and good and

([14]) This is the famous passage which is found in 1 Cor. ii.
9, but which is there a quotation, and irregular in grammatical
construction. It is commonly referred to Isaiah lxiv. 4, but
when tested by the LXX. proves to have only a superficial
resemblance to it. The inference is that this is the original
context, and that S. Paul quotes the Liturgy.--L.

glorious presence, He may hallow and make this bread the holy Body of Thy CHRIST.

People. Amen.

Priest. And this cup the precious Blood of Thy CHRIST.

People. Amen.

Priest, rising up, in a low voice,

That they may be to those that partake of them, for remission of sins, and for eternal life, for sanctification of souls and bodies, for bringing forth good works, for the confirmation of Thy Holy Catholic Church, which Thou hast founded upon the rock of faith, that the gates of hell may not prevail against it; freeing it from all heresy and scandals, and from them that work wickedness, and preserving it till the consummation of all things. (*Bending his head, he continues.*) We offer them also to Thee, O LORD, for Thy holy places which Thou hast glorified by the divine apparition of Thy CHRIST, and by the advent of Thine All-Holy SPIRIT: especially for the glorious Sion, the mother of all Churches. And for Thy holy Catholic Apostolic Church throughout the world. Supply it, O LORD, even now, with the plentiful gifts of Thy HOLY GHOST. Remember also, O LORD, our holy fathers and brothers in it, and the Bishops that in all the world rightly divide the word of Thy truth. Remember, also, O LORD, every city and region, and the Orthodox that dwell in it, that they may inhabit it with peace and safety. Remember, O LORD, Christians that are voyaging, that are journeying, that are in foreign lands, in bonds and in prison, captives, exiles, in mines, and in tortures, and bitter slavery, our fathers and brethren. Remember, LORD, them that are in sickness or travail, them that are vexed of unclean spirits, that they may speedily be healed and rescued by Thee, O God. Remember, Lord, every Christian soul in tribulation and distress, desiring the pity and succour of Thee, O God, and the conversion of the erring. Remember, Lord, our fathers and brethren that labour and minister to us through Thy holy Name. Remember, Lord, all for good; have pity, Lord, on all; be reconciled to all of us; give peace to the multitude of Thy people; dissipate scandals; put an end to wars; stay the rising up of heresies. Give us Thy peace and Thy love, O God our Saviour, the succour of all the ends of the earth. Remember, Lord, the healthfulness of the air. gentle showers, healthy dews, plenteousness of fruits, the crown of the year of Thy goodness, for the eyes of all wait upon Thee, and Thou givest them their meat in due season; Thou openest Thine hand, and fillest all things living with plenteousness. Remember, Lord, them that bear fruit and do good deeds in Thy holy Churches, and that remember the poor, the widows, the orphans, the stranger, the needy; and all those who have desired us to remember them in our prayers. Furthermore, O Lord, vouchsafe to remember those who have this day brought these oblations to Thy holy Altar; and the things for which each brought them, or which he had in his mind; and those whom we have now commemorated before Thee. Remember also, O Lord, according to the multitude of Thy mercy and pities, me Thy humble and unworthy servant; and the Deacons that surround Thy holy Altar. Grant them blamelessness of life, preserve their ministry spotless, keep in safety their goings for good, that they may find mercy and grace with all Thy Saints that have been pleasing to Thee from one generation to another, since the beginning of the world, our ancestors, and fathers, Patriarchs, Prophets, Apostles, Martyrs, Confessors, Teachers, Holy Persons, and every just spirit made perfect in the faith of Thy CHRIST.

(15) Hail, Mary, full of grace; the LORD is with thee; blessed art thou among women, and blessed is the fruit of thy womb, because thou hast brought forth the SAVIOUR of our souls. (*Aloud.*) Especially the most holy, spotless, excellently laudable, glorious Lady, the Mother of GOD, and Ever-Virgin Mary.

Choir. It is very meet to bless thee, the Mother of GOD, the ever blessed, the entirely spotless, (16) more honourable than the Cherubim, and infinitely more glorious than the Seraphim, thee, who didst bear without corruption GOD the Word, thee, verily the Mother of GOD, we magnify.

In thee, O full of grace, all creation exults, and the hierarchy of Angels, and the race of men; in thee, sanctified temple, spiritual paradise, glory of virgins, of whom GOD took flesh; our GOD, That was before the world, became a child. For He made thy womb His throne, and rendered it more extended than the heavens. In thee, O full of grace, all creation exults: glory to thee.

The Deacons. Remember, LORD our GOD.

Priest (*bowing*). Remember, LORD, the GOD of the spirits and all flesh, the Orthodox whom we have commemorated, from righteous Abel unto this day.

---

(15) The introduction of the angelical salutation is clearly a later interpolation, as interrupting the sequence of the prayer. And so is the ἐπὶ σοὶ χαίρει, the thoughts in which seem borrowed from the magnificent sermon of S. Proclus, delivered at Constantinople, March 25, A.D. 429.

(16) It is impossible in English, without tautology, to repeat the ημτέρα τοῦ Θεοῦ ἡμῶν, after having already given the Θεοτόκον

Give them rest there, in the land of the living, in
Thy kingdom, in the delight of paradise, in the
bosom of Abraham, Isaac, and Jacob, our holy
fathers, whence pain, sorrow, and groaning is exiled,
where the light of Thy countenance looks down, and
always shines. And direct, LORD, O LORD, in peace
the ends of our lives, so as to be Christian, and well-
pleasing to Thee, and blameless; collecting us under
the feet of Thine elect, when Thou wilt, and as Thou
wilt, only without shame and offence: through
Thine Only-Begotten SON, our LORD and GOD and
SAVIOUR JESUS CHRIST; for He alone hath appeared
on the earth without sin.

Deacon. And for the peace and stability of the
whole world, and of the holy Churches of GOD, and
for that for which each hath brought his offering,
or hath in his mind: and for the people that stand
around, and for all both men and women.

People. For all, both men and women.

Priest. For which things' sake, to us also, as being
good, and the Lover of men.

People. Remit, forgive, pardon, O GOD, our
offences, voluntary and involuntary, in deed and
word, by knowledge and ignorance, by night and by
day; in mind and intention: forgive us all, as being
good, and the Lover of men.

Priest. Through the grace, and pity and love of
Thine Only-Begotten SON, with Whom Thou art to
be blessed and glorified, together with the most holy
and good and life-giving SPIRIT, now and ever, and
to all ages.

People. Amen.

Priest. Peace be with all.

People. And with thy spirit.

Deacon. Again and always in peace, let us make
our supplications to the LORD.

For the oblations, and hallowed, precious, celestial, ineffable, stainless, glorious, terrible, tremendous, divine gifts to the LORD GOD.

That the LORD our GOD having received them to His holy, heavenly, intellectual and spiritual Altar, for the odour of a sweet-smelling sacrifice, would send down in their stead to us divine grace, and the gift of the most HOLY GHOST.

Having prayed for the unity of the faith, and the participation of the HOLY GHOST, let us commend ourselves and each other and all our life to CHRIST our GOD.

People. Amen.

Priest. GOD, the Father of our LORD and GOD and SAVIOUR JESUS CHRIST, the mighty LORD, blessed nature, ungrudging goodness, the GOD and LORD of all, Who art blessed for evermore : Who sittest upon the Cherubim, and art glorified by the Seraphim : before Whom stand thousand thousands, and ten thousand times ten thousand armies of holy Angels, and Archangels. Thou hast received in Thy goodness the gifts, presents, fruits that have been offered before Thee for a sweet-smelling savour, and hast been pleased to sanctify and perfect them by the grace of Thy CHRIST, and the visitation of Thy most HOLY SPIRIT : sanctify also, O LORD, our souls, bodies, and spirits ; touch the powers of our minds, search out our consciences, and cast out from us every evil thought, every impure imagination, every base lust, every unfitting motion, all envy and pride and hypocrisy, all falsehood and guile, every worldly distraction, all avarice, all vainglory, all idleness, vice, anger, passion, remembrance of wrongs, blasphemy, all motion of body and soul at variance with the will of Thy holiness. (*Aloud.*) And grant us, LORD, and Lover of men, with boldness, without condemnation, with a pure heart, with a broken spirit, with a face that needeth not to be ashamed, with hallowed lips to dare to call upon Thee, our holy GOD and FATHER in the heavens, and to say,

People. Our FATHER, &c.

Priest (bowing). And lead us not into temptation,([17]) LORD GOD of Hosts, Who knowest our infirmity, but deliver us from the evil one, and his works, and all his insults, and devices, for Thy holy Name's sake, by which our humility is called.

Aloud. For Thine is the kingdom, the power, and the glory, FATHER, SON, and HOLY GHOST, now and ever.

People. Amen.

Priest. Peace to all.

People. And with thy spirit.

Deacon. Let us bow our heads to the LORD. ([18])

People. To Thee, O LORD.

Priest. To Thee, O LORD, we Thy servants have bowed our necks before Thy holy Altar, waiting for the rich mercies that are from Thee : send down upon us, O LORD, Thy rich grace and blessing ; and sanctify our souls, bodies, and spirits, that we may become worthy partakers and communicants of Thy holy mysteries : to the forgiveness of our sins and eternal life.

Aloud. For Thou art to be worshipped and glorified, O our GOD, and Thine Only-Begotten SON, and Thy most HOLY SPIRIT, now and ever.

People. Amen.

([17]) This is the Embolismus, or Prayer against Temptation, which follows the LORD's Prayer in every Liturgy. *See* S. Mark, p. 25.

([18]) In the printed Greek Liturgy of S. James there is a double proclamation by the Deacon, and a double prayer of inclination ; but one of these is so clearly a second edition of the other, that I have ventured to omit it.

Priest, (aloud). And the grace and mercies of the Holy and consubstantial and uncreated and adorable TRINITY shall be with us all.

People. And with thy spirit.

Deacon. With the fear of GOD let us attend.

The Priest saith secretly.

Holy LORD, That restest in the holies, hallow us by the word of Thy grace, and by the visitation of Thine All-holy SPIRIT, for Thou, O LORD, hast said, be ye holy, for I am holy. LORD our GOD, incomprehensible Word of GOD, consubstantial, co-eternal, indivisible, with the FATHER and the HOLY GHOST, receive the pure hymn, in Thy holy and spotless Sacrifice, with the Cherubim and Seraphim, and from me a sinner, crying and saying,

Then he elevates the gifts, and saith,

Holy things for holy persons.

People. One holy, one LORD, JESUS CHRIST, in the glory of GOD the FATHER, to Whom be glory for ever and ever.

Deacon. For the remission of our sins, and the propitiation of our souls, and for every afflicted and distressed soul, that needeth the pity and help of GOD ⁚ and for the conversion of them that have strayed, the healing of them that are sick, the liberation of them that are in captivity, the rest of our fathers and brethren that have fallen asleep before us, let us pray earnestly and say, LORD, have mercy.

People. LORD, have mercy. (*Twelve times.*)

Then the Priest breaks the bread, and holds the half in his right hand, and the half in his left; and dips in the chalice that which he holds in his right hand, saying,

The union of the most holy Body and precious Blood of our LORD and GOD and SAVIOUR JESUS CHRIST.

Then he signs that which he holds in his left hand: then with that which is signed the other half: then he begins to divide before all, and to distribute one part into each chalice, saying,

It hath been united and sanctified and accomplished in the Name of the FATHER, and of the SON, and of the HOLY GHOST, now and ever.

And when he signs the bread, he saith,

Behold the LAMB of GOD, the SON of the FATHER, That taketh away the sin of the world, sacrificed for the life and salvation of the world.

And when he distributes one part into each chalice, he saith,

A holy portion of CHRIST, full of grace and truth, of the FATHER and the HOLY GHOST, to Whom be the glory and the might, for ever and ever.

Then he begins to break, and to say,

Psalm xxiii.
Psalm xxxiv.
Psalm cxlv.
Psalm cxvii.

Deacon. Sir, bless.

Priest. The LORD shall bless us and keep us without condemnation for the communion of His spotless gifts, now and ever, and to all ages.

Deacon. Sir, bless.

Priest. The LORD shall bless us and make us to receive with the pure tongs of our fingers the burning coal, and to place it in the mouths of the faithful, for the purification and renewal of their souls, and bodies, now and ever.

O taste and see that the LORD is good: He That

is broken, and not divided, distributed to the
faithful, and not consumed, for the remission of
their sins and eternal life, now and ever, and to
all ages.

Deacon. In the peace of CHRIST let us sing.

Choir. O taste and see that the LORD is good.

Priest (before communicating). LORD our GOD, the
Heavenly Bread, the Life of the world, I have
sinned against heaven and before Thee, and am not
worthy to partake Thy spotless mysteries : but do
Thou, Who art a compassionate GOD, make me
worthy by Thy grace to communicate without condemnation in the holy Body and precious Blood, for
the remission of sins, and eternal life.

[*The Priest communicates.*]

*But when the Deacons take up the patens and chalices
to communicate the people, the Deacon that takes
the first paten, says,*

Sir, bless.

Priest. Glory to GOD, Who hath sanctified, and
sanctifieth us all.

Deacon. Set up Thyself, O GOD, above the heavens,
and Thy glory above all the earth ; and Thy kingdom remaineth for ever and ever.

And when the Deacon is about to take it up from ([19])
the side table, the Priest saith,

Blessed be the Name of the LORD our GOD for ever.

([19]) All the editions read below, ἐπαίρει τὸν δίσκον ἀπό τοῦ
παρατραπέζου, and here, ὅτε μέλλει ὁ διάκονος τίθεναι εἰς τὸ
παρατράπεζον. It is nearly certain that the rubrics have been
misplaced. The point is one of great difficulty, but the commentators entirely neglect it. The first question is, what is
the παρατράπεζον · Du Cange will have it to be that on which
the sacred portions were lying, the μερίδες of the office of
prothesis. But it is clear that the Deacons are now in the

Deacon. With the fear of GOD, and faith, and love, draw near.

People. Blessed be he that cometh in the Name of the LORD.

[*The Communion.*]

And again, when the Deacon puts the paten down on the side table, he saith,

Sir, bless.

Priest. O LORD, save Thy people : and bless Thine heritage.

Glory to our GOD Who hath sanctified us all.

Deacons and people. Fill our mouths with Thy praise, O LORD, and fill our lips with thankfulness, that we celebrate Thy glory and Thy majesty all the day long.

---

naos, or just on the point of leaving the bema. The antidoron then is out of the question, for the Communion has not yet taken place. We must imagine the παρατράπεζον *in this instance* to be a side table placed in the bema, on which the chalices, &c., were set down (by the rubric before, ὅταν διδῷ μερίδα ἁπλῆν εἰς ἕκαστον κρατῆρα, λέγει, it is clear that several were contemplated) in order that the Deacons might take them thence, and not from the Altar. By the transposition of the rubrics, all is now clear : when the Deacon takes the paten up, for the purpose of administering to the people, he says, "Blessed be the Name," &c. He then desires the people to approach ; and they accordingly communicate. After this he returns to the παρατράπεζον, and *setting down* the paten or chalice, says, " Sir, bless," &c., as below. But if the alteration in the rubrics be not allowed, the only possible way of making sense is the arrangement which I adopted in another place, where I did not feel justified in making the change. (Tetralog. Liturgic. p. 192.) The Deacon, receiving the chalice from the Priest to set it on the side table, says, " Blessed be the Name," &c. He sets it down. He calls the people to approach. He then lifts it up, and says, " Sir, bless : " but the Priest does not bless till after the Communion is finished. The great awkwardness of this is clear.

We give Thee thanks, CHRIST our GOD, that Thou
hast vouchsafed to make us partakers of Thy Body
and Blood, for the remission of sins, and eternal
life.   Keep us, we beseech Thee, without condemnation, because Thou art good, and the LOVER of
men.

The Prayer of Incense at the last Entrance.

Priest. We thank Thee, GOD and SAVIOUR of all,
for all the good things which Thou hast bestowed
on us ; and for the participation of Thy holy and
spotless mysteries.   And we offer to Thee this incense, praying Thee to keep us under the shadow of
Thy wings ; and vouchsafe that, till our last breath,
we may receive Thy sanctifications ; for the sanctification of souls and bodies, for the inheritance of
the kingdom of heaven : for Thou, O GOD, art
our sanctification, and to Thee we ascribe glory and
thanks, &c.

The Deacon begins in the Entrance.

Glory to Thee, glory to Thee, glory to Thee,
CHRIST the King, Only-Begotten Word of the FATHER,
for that Thou hast vouchsafed us sinners and Thy
unworthy servants to enjoy Thy spotless mysteries,
for the forgiveness of sins and for eternal life : glory
to Thee. ([20])

([20]) Here, in the editions, follows this :

And when he makes the entrance the Deacon begins to say
thus,

Again and again, and evermore in peace, let us make our
supplications to the LORD.

That the participation of His sanctification may be to us
for the turning away of every evil thing, for a viaticum
of eternal life, for the participation and gift of the HOLY
GHOST.

And when he puts down the chalice on the holy table, the Priest saith,

([21]) Blessed be the Name of the LORD for ever and ever.

Priest. Peace be with all.
People. And with thy spirit.

Deacon. In the peace of CHRIST let us chant.
And again. In the peace of CHRIST let us depart.
People. In the Name of the LORD; LORD, bless us.

Priest. Commemorating the most holy, &c.
People. To Thee, O LORD.
Priest. GOD, Which through Thy great and ineffable love to man didst condescend to the weakness of Thy servants and hast vouchsafed that we should partake of this heavenly Table, condemn us not in the participation of Thy spotless mysteries, but guard us, good GOD, by the sanctification of Thy HOLY GHOST; that, being holy, we may find part and inheritance with all Thy Saints who have pleased Thee from the beginning of the world, in the light of Thy countenance, through the mercies of Thine Only-Begotten SON, our LORD and GOD and SAVIOUR JESUS CHRIST; with Whom Thou art blessed, with Thy most holy and good and quickening SPIRIT, &c.
People. Amen.

But, in all probability, this is nothing but a second edition of the two last prayers; it is hardly possible to conceive that both the Deacon and the Priest would say over again, in other words, what each of them has just been already saying; and the more so as the time is limited to that of the entrance. It will be seen that, as we at present have the Liturgy of S. James, the Priest remains at the Altar, while the Deacons distribute to the people.

([21]) Here I have made another change. In the editions, the rubric precedes the prayer of incense at the last entrance. But as it is clear that the Deacon must have entered the bema before he can set down the chalice on the Altar, I have reversed the order.

Prayer of Dismissal said by the Deacon.

From glory to glory advancing, we hymn Thee, the Saviour of our souls. Glory to the FATHER, and to the SON, and to the HOLY GHOST. We hymn Thee, the Saviour of our souls.

The Priest saith this prayer as he goes from the Altar to the Sacristy.

From might to might advancing, and having accomplished all the *Divine Liturgy* in Thy temple, we now also pray Thee, vouchsafe to us Thy full mercy; rightly divide our paths: root us in Thy fear; and count us worthy of Thy heavenly kingdom, in CHRIST JESUS our LORD: with Whom, &c.

Deacon. Again and again and evermore in peace, let us make our supplications to the LORD.

Prayer said in the sacristy after the dismissal.

Thou hast given us, O LORD, sanctification, &c. *As in the Liturgy of S. Mark.* ([22])

([22]) It cannot be parallelised with that prayer, because this follows, that precedes, the dismissal.

THE DIVINE LITURGY

OF

S. Clement.

And after the reading of the Law and the Prophets, and our Epistles and Acts, and the Gospels, let him that hath been elected salute the Church, saying,

The grace of our LORD JESUS CHRIST, the love of GOD and our FATHER, and the Communion of the HOLY GHOST, be with you all.

And let all answer: And with thy spirit.

And after this, let him address to the People words of exhortation, and when he hath accomplished the Word of Teaching, I, Andrew, the brother of Peter, say: All standing up, let the Deacon ascending to some high place, proclaim: Let none of the auditors: let none of the unbelievers. *And when quiet hath been made, let him say:*

Ye that are Catechumens, pray.

And let all the faithful, as they will, pray for them, saying,

LORD, have mercy.

And let him minister on their behalf, saying:

Let us all beseech GOD([1]) for the Catechumens,

([1]) S. Chrysostom, in his third homily on the incomprehensible nature of GOD, refers to this prayer, when he says—" Immediately after this exhortation follows the prayer." And the same thing is to be found in the nineteenth canon of the Council of Laodicea. (A.D. 363 or 365.)

F

that He Who is good and the Lover of men, may mercifully hear their prayers and supplications, and receiving their requests, may assist them and grant them their hearts' desire as may be expedient for them, and may reveal to them the Gospel of His . CHRIST, and may enlighten them and cause them to understand and may instruct them in Divine knowledge, and may teach them His commandments and judgments, and may implant in them His true and salutary fear, and may open the ears of their hearts to discover the things that are in His law day and night, may stablish them in piety, may unite and may number them together with His holy fold, may count them worthy of the laver of regeneration, of the vestment of immortality, of the true life; may preserve them from all impiety, and may give no place to the enemy against them; but may purify them from all pollution of flesh and spirit, may dwell in them and walk in them by His CHRIST, may bless their comings in and their goings out, and may direct that which lies before them as may be profitable. Furthermore, let us earnestly supplicate for them, that having obtained the remission of their transgressions through the initiation of baptism, they may be counted worthy of the holy mysteries, and of perseverance with the Saints. Ye that are Catechumens arise.

Ask for the peace of GOD through His CHRIST; that this day and all the time of your life may be peaceful and sinless; that your ends may be Christian; that GOD may be merciful and gracious; that your sins may be remitted; commend yourselves to the Only, Unbegotten GOD, through His CHRIST. Bow down and receive the blessing.

And for each of these whom the Deacon addresses, as

we have said before, let the people say, Lord, have
mercy: *and before all the children.* ([2]) *And while
they bow down their heads, let him that hath been
elected Bishop, bless them with this blessing:*

The Almighty God, the Unbegotten and Un-
approachable, the only true God, the God and
Father of Thy Christ, Thine Only-Begotten Son,
the God of the Paraclete, and the Lord of all:
Thou Who didst by Christ constitute Thy disciples
as teachers of piety;—do Thou Thyself also now
look upon these Thy servants, the Catechumens of
the Gospel of Thy Christ, and give to them a new
heart, and renew within them a right spirit, to
know and do Thy will with a full heart and willing
soul. Make them worthy of the holy initiation of
baptism, and unite them to Thy holy Church, and
make them participators of the *Divine* mysteries,
through Christ our Hope, Who died for them:
through Whom be to Thee the glory and the
worship, in the Holy Ghost, through all ages.
Amen.

And after this, let the Deacon say, Go forward,
ye Catechumens, in peace. *And after their having
gone forth, let him* s *ay:* Pray, ye that are troubled by
unclean spirits. Let us all earnestly pray for them,
that God, the Lover of men, may, through Christ,
rebuke the unclean and wicked spirits, and may pre-

([2]) It has been discussed what children are here intended.
Cotelerius would understand it of the choir; but I am inclined
to think that the words are spoken of all the children present;
the same who are afterward committed to the charge of their
mothers. The explanation, given by S. Chrysostom in his
seventy-second homily on S. Matthew, seems to make this in
terpretation clear; and I am glad to see that my friend
Dr. Daniel also adopts it.

serve His suppliants from the over-mastery of the
enemy: He that rebuked the legion of fiends, and
the primæval source of evil, the *D*evil, let Him
rebuke also now the apostates from piety, and preserve His own handiwork from the energy of Satan,
and purify them whom with much wisdom He made.
Furthermore, let us intently pray for them: Save
and raise them up, O GOD, in Thy might.   Bend
your heads, ye Energumens, and receive the blessing.
And let the Bishop pray over them, saying, Thou That
didst bind the strong man, and spoil all his goods:
Thou That didst give us power to tread upon
serpents and scorpions and all the might of the adversary: Thou That didst give over to us bound,
the man-slaying serpent, as a sparrow to children: (³)
Whom all things fear and tremble at from the face
of Thy power: Thou That didst break him as light-
ning from heaven, not with a local fracture, but
from honour to dishonour, through his own evil-
mindedness: Thou Whose look drieth up the
abysses, and Whose threat wasteth the mountains,
and Whose truth remaineth for ever; Whom infants praise, and sucklings bless: Who lookest upon
the earth, and makest it to tremble: Who touchest
the mountains, and they smoke: Who threatenest
the sea, and driest it up, and utterly destroyest all
the rivers: to Whom the clouds are the dust of Thy
feet: Thou That walkest upon the sea as upon a
foundation: Only-Begotten GOD, SON of the Mighty
FATHER, rebuke the evil spirits, and preserve the
works of Thine Hands from the energy of an adverse
spirit: for to Thee is glory, honour, and worship,

(³) The allusion is to Job xli. 5—" Wilt thou play with him
as with a bird, or wilt thou bind him for thy maidens?"

and by Thee to Thy FATHER, and the HOLY GHOST.
Amen.

And let the Deacon say: Pass forward, ye Energumens. *And after this let him exclaim:* Pray, ye
that are illuminated. Let us, the faithful, all pray
earnestly for them, that the LORD may count them
worthy, having been initiated into the death of
CHRIST, raise them up together with Him, and to
become partakers of His kingdom, and sharers of
His mysteries, that He may unite and may collect
them together with those that are saved in His
Holy Church. Save and raise them up in Thy
grace. Let them that have been sealed to GOD by
His CHRIST, bow down and be blest with this blessing from the Bishop. Thou That saidst aforehand
by Thy holy *Prophets* to the initiated, Wash you,
make you clean, and didst through CHRIST give
them the law of spiritual regeneration,—do Thou
Thyself now look upon the baptized, and bless them
and hallow them, and prepare them so as to be
worthy of Thy spiritual gift, and the true adoption
of Thy spiritual mysteries, the gathering together
with them that are saved, through CHRIST our
Saviour: ([4]) through, &c.

And let the Deacon say: Pass forward, ye that
are illuminated. *And after this, let him proclaim:*
Pray, ye that are in penitence. Let us earnestly
supplicate for our brethren that are in penitence,
that GOD, the very pitiful, may point out to them
the way of repentance, may receive their recantation
and their confession, and may bruise Satan under
their feet shortly, and may ransom them from the

([4]) This prayer would appear, from the Council of Laodicea,
and from the silence of S. Chrysostom, to be of later date than
the others.

snare of the devil, and the insult of demons, and
may deliver them from every unlawful word, and
every unseemly deed and wicked imagination ; may
pardon them all their falls, voluntary and involuntary ; and may blot out the handwriting that is
against them, and may write them in the Book of
Life, and may cleanse them from every pollution of
flesh and spirit, and may restore them so as to unite
them to His holy flock : for He knoweth our frame.
For who can boast that he hath a pure heart ?   Or
who can be confident that he is pure from sin?
For we are all subject to penalty.   Let us yet pray
more earnestly for them, because there is joy in
heaven over one sinner that repenteth, that they,
turning away from every unlawful work, may be
made familiar with every good deed, to the end that
GOD, the Lover of men, may speedily receive their
prayers with favour, may give them the joy of His
salvation again, and may stablish them with His
Princely Spirit, that they may be no more shaken :
that they may become partakers of His holy things,
and sharers of the *D*ivine mysteries, and being
manifested as worthy of adoption, may attain eternal
life.   Let us yet say earnestly for them : LORD,
have mercy : save them, O GOD, and raise them up
by Thy mercy.   Rise up and bend your heads to
GOD, through His CHRIST, and receive the blessing.
   Then let the Bishop pray after this fashion. Almighty, everlasting GOD, Master of all, Creator and
Governor of all things, Thou Who didst through
CHRIST consecrate man to be the ornament of the
world, (⁵) and didst give him a law implanted in
him and written, to the end that he might live

(⁵) *Ornament of the world.* It is of course impossible to
preserve the paronomasia, κόσμον τοῦ κόσμου.

according to Thy statutes, as is reasonable: and
didst by Thy goodness give to him when he had
sinned a warning to repentance ; look down upon
these that have bowed to Thee the necks of their
souls and their bodies : for Thou willest not the
death of a sinner, but his conversion, so as to turn
him from his evil ways that he may live. Thou
That didst receive the repentance of the Ninevites ;
Thou That willest that all men should be saved and
come to the knowledge of the truth ; Thou That
didst, through Thy fatherly pity, receive the son who
devoured his substance in riotous living, because of
his repentance ; do Thou Thyself now receive the
repentance of Thy suppliants ; for there is none
who sinneth not before Thee ; for if Thou, LORD,
shalt be extreme to mark what is done amiss, O LORD,
who may abide it ? for with Thee there is mercy.
And restore them to Thy holy Church in reputation
and honour, through CHRIST, our GOD and Saviour :
through Whom, &c.

And let the Deacon say : Depart, ye that are in
penitence. *And let him add :* Let none of those that
are not able to pray with us, pass forward : let as
many as are faithful kneel with us. Let us all with
one accord call upon GOD through His CHRIST. For
the peace and good condition of the world, and the
holy Churches, let us make our supplication ; that
He, Who is the GOD of all, may bestow peace on
us, eternal, and that cannot be taken away, to the
end that He may preserve us perseveringly in the
fulness of that virtue which is according to godliness. For the Holy Catholic and Apostolic Church,
which is from one end of the earth to the other, let
us make our supplication ; that the LORD would
preserve it and guard it continually, unshaken and
without storm, unto the consummation of all things,

founded upon the rock. (⁶) And for the holy parishes here, let us make our supplication, that He Who is the LORD of all may vouchsafe to give us a share in His heavenly hope, and to bestow unceasingly the reward of our prayers.

For every Episcopate under heaven of those who rightly divide the word of Thy truth, let us make our supplication : and for our Bishop James and his parishes, let us make our supplication : for the Bishop Clement and his parishes, let us make our supplication : for our Bishop Euodius and his parishes, let us make our supplication. (⁷) That the merciful GOD may vouchsafe them to their holy Churches safe, honourable, full of length of days, and may afford them an honourable old age in piety and righteousness.

And for their Presbyters let us make our supplication : that the LORD would preserve them from every unseemly and wicked thing, and afford to them their priestly office, safe and honourable. For all the diaconate, and ministry in CHRIST, let us make our supplication, that the LORD may preserve their services blameless.

For Readers, Singers, Virgins, Widows, and Orphans, let us make our supplication : for them that are in the yoke of marriage, and the production of children, let us make our supplication : that the LORD may have mercy on them all.

For Eunuchs, walking holily, let us make our

(⁶) Observe that the reference is not to S. Matthew xvi. 18, but to S. Matthew vii. 25.

(⁷) These names are manifestly an insertion by way of a pious fraud on the part of the compiler of the Apostolic Constitutions. In some MSS. instead of Euodius, Anianus, the first Bishop of Alexandria after S. Mark is mentioned.

supplication : for those that are in continence and piety, let us make our supplication : for them that bring forth fruit in the holy Church, and do alms to the poor, let us make our supplication; and for them that bring offerings and first-fruits to the LORD our GOD, let us make our supplication : that the all-good GOD may recompense them with His heavenly gifts, and may give them a hundred-fold more in the present world, and in the world to come, life everlasting, and may grant to them of His grace, for things earthly, things heavenly.

For our newly-illuminated brethren, let us make our supplication that the LORD may confirm and stablish them.

For our brethren that are exercised by sickness, let us make our supplication; that the LORD may preserve them from all diseases and infirmity, and may restore them safely to His holy Church.

For them that sail and that journey, let us make our supplication : for them that are in mines and exiles and prisons and bonds for the Name of the LORD, let us make our supplication : for them that travail in bitter slavery, let us make our supplication : for our enemies, and them that hate us for the LORD's sake, let us make our supplication : that the LORD may soften their mind, and disperse their passion against us.

For them that are without and wandering, let us make our supplication : that the LORD may convert them.

Let us remember the little ones of the Church, that the LORD, perfecting them in His fear, may bring them to the full measure of age : for each other, let us make our supplication; that the LORD may guard us and preserve us by His grace to the end, and may defend us from the wicked one, and all the scandals of them that work iniquity, and may save us to His heavenly kingdom.

For every Christian soul, let us make our supplication. *Preserve and raise us up, O God, by Thy pity.*

Let us rise up.

Having earnestly made our supplication, let us commit ourselves and each other to the Living God, through His Christ. *Then let the Bishop pray over them and say:* Lord Almighty, Most Highest, Thou That dwellest in the highest, Thou Holy One That restest in the Holies, Thou That art without beginning, Thou That art only Ruler: Thou Who through Christ didst give us the preaching of knowledge for the acknowledgment of Thy glory and of Thy Name which He manifested to our comprehension : do Thou Thyself now look down through Him upon this Thy flock : and free it from all ignorance and evil practices, and grant that it may entirely fear Thee and perfectly love Thee, and may be endued with the glory of Thy countenance : be Thou propitious to them, and merciful, and ready to hear their supplications, and keep them without turning, without blame, without accusation ; that they may be holy in body and soul, not having spot nor wrinkle, nor any such thing : but that they may be perfect, and not one of them may be imperfect or incomplete. Thou That art the Helper, the Mighty, Thou That respectest not the persons of men, become Thou the assistance of this Thy people, whom Thou didst purchase with the precious Blood of Thy Christ. Defender, Guardian, Steward, Most secure Wall, Fence, Security, for none can pluck out of Thine Hands : nor is there any other God like Thee, for in Thee is our trust. Sanctify them in Thy truth, for Thy word is truth. Thou That art not to be flattered, Thou That canst not be deceived, preserve them from all sickness and all infirmity, from every fall, from all injury and deceit, from the fear of the enemy, from the arrow that flieth by day, from the thing that walketh in darkness: and vouchsafe to them the eternal life, which is in CHRIST Thine Only-Begotten SON, our GOD and Saviour, through Whom.

And after this let the Deacon say : Let us attend.

And let the Bishop salute the Church, and say : Let the peace of GOD be with you all.

And let the people answer, And with thy spirit.

And let the Deacon say to all, Salute one another with an holy kiss.

And let the Clergy kiss the Bishop ; and of the Laity, the men the men, and the women the women. And let the children stand by the Bema. And let a Deacon preside over them, that they may not be disorderly. And let other Deacons walk about and observe the men and the women that there may be no disturbance, and that no one nod, or whisper, or wink. And let the Deacon stand at the doors of the men, and the Sub-Deacons at those of the women, that no one may go out, and that the door may not be opened even though it may be by one of the faithful, during the time of the Anaphora. And let one Sub-Deacon give water to the Priests to wash their hands, the symbol of the purity of the souls devoted to GOD.

The order of James, the brother of John, the son of Zebedee.

And I, James, the brother of John, the son of Zebedee, command that forthwith the Deacon say,

Let none of the Catechumens, none of the hearers, none of the unbelievers, none of the heterodox, stay. Ye who have prayed the former prayer, depart. Mothers, take up your children. Let no one have ought against any man. Let none be in hypocrisy. Let us stand upright, to present unto the LORD our offerings with fear and trembling.

When this is done, let the Deacons bring the gifts to the Bishop at the Altar; and let the Priests stand on his right hand, and on his left, as disciples by their Master. But let two of the Deacons on each side of the Altar hold a fan made up of thin membranes, or peacock's feathers, or fine cloth, and let them silently drive away flies and gnats, that they may not fall into the cups. Then the Bishop, after having prayed secretly, (and likewise the Priests,) and having put on his splendid vestment, ([8]) and standing at the Altar, and signing himself with the sign of the Cross upon his forehead, let him say,

The grace of the Almighty GOD, and the love of our LORD JESUS CHRIST, and the fellowship of the HOLY GHOST, be with you all.

And let all with one voice say, And with thy spirit.
Bishop. Lift up your mind.
People. We lift it up unto the LORD.
Bishop. Let us give thanks to the LORD.
People. It is meet and right.
Bishop. It is indeed meet and right before all things to sing praises to Thee, the true GOD, from everlasting, of Whom the whole family in heaven and earth is named; Who alone art unbegotten, without beginning, the supreme LORD, Almighty King, and self-sufficient; the Author and Giver of all good things, without cause, without generation, self-existing; the same yesterday, to-day, and for ever. At Thy Word, as from a necessary original, all things started into being. For Thou art everlasting knowledge, sight before all objects, hearing

---

([8]) This very ancient rubric establishes the use of a special Eucharistic robe at an exceedingly early date. It is unlikely to be an interpolation, because there is no trace of this Liturgy having ever been actually employed in public worship.—L.

before all sounds, wisdom without instruction; the first in nature, the law of being, exceeding all number. Thou createdst all things out of nothing by Thine Only-Begotten Son, begotten before all ages by no other means than Thy will, Thy power, and Thy goodness; God the Word, the Only-Begotten Son, the Living Wisdom, the First-born of every creature, the Angel of Thy great counsel, Thy High Priest, but Lord and King of all sensible and intellectual creatures, Who was before all things, and by Whom all things were made. Thou, O eternal God, didst make all things by Him, and by Him too dispensest Thy providence over them; for by the Same that Thou didst graciously bring all things into being, by Him Thou continuest all things in well-being. The God and Father of Thine Only-Begotten Son; Who by Him didst make first the Cherubim and Seraphim, the Ages, Thrones, Archangels, and Angels, and after these didst by Him create this visible world, and all things which are therein. For it is Thou Who hast fixed the heaven like an arch, and stretched it out like the covering of a tent; and didst establish the earth upon nothing by Thy will alone; Who hast established the firmament, and prepared the night and the day, bringing light out of Thy treasures, and darkness to overshadow it, that under its covert the living creatures of this world might take their repose. Thou hast appointed the sun to rule the day, and the moon to govern the night; and moreover hast inscribed in the heavens a choir of stars for the honour of Thy glorious majesty. Thou hast made water for drink, and for cleansing, the vital air for respiration, and conveyance of sounds by the tongue's striking of it, and the hearing which co-operates with it, so as to perceive the voice when it

is received by it, and falls upon it. Thou madest
fire for our consolation in darkness, and for the
relief of our necessities, that we might be both
warmed and enlightened by it. Thou didst divide
the great sea from the land, making the one naviga-
ble, and the other a basis for our feet in walking;
the former Thou hast replenished with small and
great beasts, the latter too both with tame and wild;
and hast moreover furnished it with various plants,
crowned it with herbs, beautified it with flowers,
and enriched it with seeds. Thou didst constitute
the great deep, and didst set about it a mighty hollow; (⁹) seas of salt waters stand as an heap bounded
on every side with barriers of sand; sometimes
Thou dost swell it by the wind, so as to equal the
high mountains, and sometimes smooth it into a
plain; now making it rage with a tempest, then
stilling it with a calm, for the ease of mariners in
their voyages. The earth, which was made by
Thee, through CHRIST, Thou hast encompassed with
rivers, watered with currents, and moistened with
springs which never fail; Thou hast girt it about
with mountains, that it may not be moved at any
time; Thou hast replenished and adorned it with
fragrant and medicinal herbs, with many and various
kinds of living creatures, strong and weak,.for food
and for labour, tame and wild; with the dull harsh
noises of those creatures which move upon the
earth, and the soft sprightly notes of the gaudy
many-coloured birds which wing the air; with the

(⁹) Brett translates "didst cast a mound about it." But I
cannot see what is the authority for this signification of κῆτος.
It is best to take it in the sense of a great hollow or chasm.
See Buttman's Lexilogus, under the word κητώεσσα. Had
that distinguished scholar been acquainted with Patristic
writings, he would have been glad to find in this passage a
corroboration of his hypothesis.

revolution of years, the number of months and days, the regular succession of the seasons; with the courses of the clouds big with rain, for the production of fruits, the support of living creatures: where also the winds take their stand, which blow at Thy command, and for the refreshment of trees and plants. And Thou hast not only created the world, but man likewise the citizen of it; manifesting in him the beauty and excellency of that beautiful and excellent creation. For Thou saidst to Thine Own Wisdom, Let us make man in Our Own Image, and after Our likeness, and let them have dominion over the fish of the sea, and over the fowl of the air. Wherefore Thou madest him of an immortal soul, and perishable body, the soul out of nothing, the body of the four elements; this endued with five senses, and a power of motion; that with reason, and a faculty of distinguishing between religion and irreligion, the just and the unjust. Thou, O Almighty GOD, didst also by CHRIST plant a garden eastward in Eden, adorned with every plant that was meet for food; into this Thou didst put him, a rich and magnificent habitation; having given him a law in his nature, and such powers that without the assistance of other means, even in himself he might have the principles of divine knowledge. And when Thou didst put him into this paradise of pleasure, Thou gavest him the privilege of enjoying all its delights, with this only exception, that he should not out of vain curiosity in hopes of bettering his condition, taste of one tree, and immortality was to be the reward of his obedience to this command; but when he had broken through it, and eaten of the forbidden fruit, over-reached by the subtilty of the serpent, and the counsel of the woman, Thou didst justly drive him out of paradise ; but in Thy goodness didst not despise him, nor suffer him wholly to perish ; for he was the work of Thine own hands : but Thou gavest him dominion over all things, and by his labour, and the sweat of his face, to procure his food, Thy providence co-operating with him, so as to make the fruits of the earth to spring up, increase, and ripen. And having subjected him for a while to a temporary death, Thou didst bind Thyself by an oath to restore him to life again ; loosing the bands of that death, by the promise of a resurrection to the life which is eternal. Nor was this all ; but Thou didst likewise multiply his posterity without number, glorifying as many of them as were obedient unto Thee, and punishing those who rebelled against Thee. Thou didst accept the sacrifice of Abel on account of his righteousness, and reject the offering of Cain who slew his brother, because of his unworthiness. And besides these, Thou didst receive Seth and Enos, and translate Enoch. For Thou art the creator of men, the author of life, the supplier of our wants, the giver of laws, the rewarder of those who keep them, and the avenger of those who transgress them ; Who didst bring the great flood upon the world because of the multitude of the ungodly, but didst deliver righteous Noah from it with eight souls in the ark, the last of the foregoing, and the first of the succeeding generations ; Who didst kindle a dreadful fire in the five cities of Sodom, and turn a fruitful land into a salt lake for the wickedness of them that dwelt therein ; but didst snatch holy Lot out of the conflagration. Thou art He, Who didst preserve Abraham from the idolatry of his forefathers, and appoint him the heir of the world, manifesting unto him Thy CHRIST ; Who didst ordain Melchisedeck an high priest for Thy worship; Who didst approve Thy servant Job by his patience and long suffering, the conqueror of that serpent, who is the author and promoter of all wickedness; Who madest Isaac the Son of the promise, and Jacob the father of twelve sons, whom Thou didst multiply exceedingly, bringing him into Egypt with seventy-five souls. Thou, O LORD, didst not overlook Joseph, but gavest him, as the reward of his chastity for Thy sake, the government over the Egyptians. Neither didst Thou, O LORD, overlook the Hebrews when in bondage under the Egyptians, but according to Thy promises made to their fathers, Thou didst deliver them, and punish the Egyptians. And when men corrupted the law of nature, and esteemed the creation, sometimes as the effect of chance, and sometimes to be worthy of honour equal to Thine, Who art the GOD of all, Thou didst not suffer them to wander in error; but didst raise up Thy holy servant Moses, and by him give a written law to strengthen the law of nature, and shew the creation to be Thy work, and that there were no other Gods besides Thee. Thou didst adorn Aaron and his posterity with the honour of the priesthood. Thou didst punish the Hebrews when they sinned, and receive them again when they returned to Thee. Thou didst torment the Egyptians with ten plagues, and divide the sea for the Israelites to pass through, overwhelming the Egyptians in their pursuit after them with the waves thereof. Thou didst sweeten the bitter water with wood, and bring water out of the precipitous rock. Thou didst rain manna from heaven, and quails out of the air for food. Thou madest a pillar of fire to give them light in the night, and a pillar of a cloud to shadow them from the heat in the day. Thou didst raise up Joshua to be a general of

their armies, and by him destroy seven nations of
the Canaanites. Thou didst divide Jordan, and dry
up the rivers of Etham. Thou didst overthrow
walls without engines, or any assistance of human
force. For all these things, glory be to Thee, O
LORD Almighty; Thee the innumerable hosts of
angels, archangels, thrones, dominions, principalities, virtues, powers, Thine everlasting armies
adore. The Cherubim and Seraphim with six wings,
with twain they cover their feet, with twain their
heads, and with twain they fly, and say, together
with thousand thousands of archangels, and ten
thousand times ten thousand of angels, crying
incessantly with uninterrupted shouts of praise ;

And let all the People say with them :

Holy, holy, holy, is the LORD of Sabaoth, heaven
and earth are full of His glory. Blessed be He for
evermore. Amen.

After this, let the Bishop say,

Thou art indeed holy, and most holy; the highest,
and most highly exalted for ever. Holy also is
Thine Only-Begotten SON JESUS CHRIST our LORD
and GOD. Who, always ministering to Thee His
GOD and FATHER, not only in the various works of
the creation, but in the providential care of it, did
not overlook lost mankind. But after the law of
nature, the admonitions of the positive law, the
prophetical reproofs, and the superintendency of
angels, when men had perverted both the positive
and natural law, and had forgotten the flood, the
burning of Sodom, the plagues of the Egyptians,
the slaughter of the nations of *Palestine*, and were
now ready to perish universally ; He, Who was
man's Creator, was pleased with Thy consent to

become man; the Lawgiver to be under the law; the *Priest* to be Himself the sacrifice; the Shepherd a sheep; to appease Thee His GOD and FATHER, to reconcile Thee (9) to the world, and deliver all men from the impending wrath. He was incarnate of a Virgin, GOD the WORD, the beloved SON, the First-born of every creature; and, as He Himself had foretold by the mouth of the prophets, of the seed of *David*, and of Abraham, and of the tribe of Juda. He, Who forms all that are born in the world, was Himself formed in the womb of a Virgin; He That was without flesh, became flesh; and He Who was begotten from eternity, was born in time. He was holy in His conversation, and taught according to the law; He cured diseases, and wrought signs and wonders amongst the people; He Who is the feeder of the hungry, and fills every living creature with His goodness, became partaker of His own gifts, and eat, and drank, and slept amongst us: He manifested Thy Name to them that knew it not; He dispelled the cloud of ignorance, restored piety, fulfilled Thy will, and finished Thy work which Thou gavest Him to do. And when He had regulated all these things, He was seized by the hands of a disobedient people, and wicked men abusing the office of *Priests* and High-*Priests*, being betrayed to them by one who excelled in wickedness; and when He had suffered many

(9) Notice here, and again presently, this "unscriptural" phrase. According to S. Paul's teaching, it is man that must be reconciled to GOD, not GOD to man. This appears to me a good argument in favour of the belief that S. Clement's Liturgy was never really employed by any Church. Such an error might easily escape the notice of an individual writer; but the marvellous theological accuracy of early Liturgies would not have allowed the phrase to remain in use.

things from them, and been treated with all manner of indignity, He was by Thy permission delivered to *P*ilate the governor ; the Judge of all the world was judged, and the Saviour of mankind condemned ; although impassible, He was nailed to the cross ; and although immortal, died. The Giver of Life was laid in the grave, that He might deliver those from the pains of death, for whose sake He came ; and that He might break the bands of the devil, and rescue man from his deceit. He arose from the dead the third day ; and after continuing forty days with His disciples, He was taken up into heaven, and is set down on the right hand of Thee His GOD and FATHER.

Calling therefore to remembrance those things which He endured for our sakes, we give thanks unto Thee, O GOD Almighty, not as we ought, but as we are able, to fulfil His institution. For in the same night that He was betrayed, taking bread into His holy and immaculate hands, and looking up to Thee His GOD and FATHER, and breaking it, He gave it to His disciples, saying, This is the Mystery of the New Testament ; take of it ; eat ; this is My Body, which is broken for many for the remission of sins. Likewise also having mingled the cup with wine and water, and blessed it, He gave it to them, saying : *D*rink ye all of it : this is My Blood, which is shed for many for the remission of sins ; do this in remembrance of Me ; for as often as ye eat of this bread, and drink of this cup, ye do shew forth My death till I come.

Wherefore having in remembrance His passion, death, and resurrection from the dead, His return into heaven, and His future second appearance, when He shall come with glory and power to judge the quick and the dead, and to render to every man according to his works; we offer to Thee, our King and our GOD, according to this institution, this bread and this cup; giving thanks to Thee through Him, that Thou hast thought us worthy to stand before Thee, and to sacrifice unto Thee. And we beseech Thee, that Thou wilt look graciously on these gifts now lying before Thee, O Thou self-sufficient GOD; and accept them to the honour of Thy CHRIST. And send down Thy HOLY SPIRIT, the Witness of the sufferings of the LORD JESUS, on this sacrifice, that He may make this bread the Body of Thy CHRIST, and this cup the Blood of Thy CHRIST. That all who shall partake of it may be confirmed in godliness, may receive remission of their sins, may be delivered from the devil and his wiles, may be filled with the HOLY GHOST, may be made worthy of Thy CHRIST, and may obtain everlasting life; Thou, ([10]) O LORD Almighty, being reconciled to them.

We further pray unto Thee, O LORD, for Thy holy Church, spread from one end of the world unto the other, which Thou hast purchased by the precious Blood of Thy CHRIST, that Thou wilt keep it stedfast and immovable unto the end of the world; and for every Episcopate rightly dividing the word of truth. Further we call upon Thee for my unworthiness, who am now offering; and for the whole *Pres*bytery; for the *D*eacons, and all the Clergy; that Thou wouldst endue them with wisdom, and fill them with the HOLY GHOST. Further we call upon Thee, O LORD, for the King and all that are in authority, for the success of the army, that they may be kindly disposed towards us; that leading our whole life in peace and quietness, we may glorify

---

([10]) Notice what is said before of this expression.

Thee through JESUS CHRIST our hope. Further we offer to Thee for all the saints, who have pleased Thee from the beginning of the world: the patriarchs, prophets, righteous men, apostles, martyrs, confessors, bishops, priests, deacons, sub-deacons, readers, singers, virgins, widows, laymen, and all whose names Thou knowest. We further offer to Thee for this people; that for the glory of Thy CHRIST Thou wilt render them a royal priesthood, an holy nation; for the virgins, and all that live chastely; for the widows of the Church; for those that live in honourable marriage, and child-bearing; for the young ones among Thy people; that Thou wilt not permit any of us to become castaways. Further we pray unto Thee for this city, and the inhabitants thereof; for the sick; for those that are in bitter slavery; for those that are in banishment; for those that are in prison; for those that travel by land or by water; that Thou wilt be to all of them an helper, strengthener, and supporter.

We further beseech Thee also for those who hate us and persecute us for Thy Name's sake; for those that are without, and wander in error; that thou wouldst convert them to that which is good, and appease their wrath against us. Further we pray unto Thee for the catechumens of the Church; for those who are under possession, and for those our brethren who are in the state of penance: that Thou wilt perfect the first in Thy faith, deliver the second from the power of the wicked one, accept the repentance of the last, and grant unto them and to us the remission of our sins. Further we offer unto Thee for seasonable weather, and that we may have plenty of the fruits of the earth: that receiving the abundance of Thy good things we may incessantly praise Thee Who givest food to all flesh. Further we pray unto Thee for all those who are absent upon a just cause; that Thou wilt preserve all of us in godliness, and gather us together in the kingdom of Thy CHRIST our king, the GOD of every sensible and intelligent being. And that Thou wilt keep us stedfast, unblameable, and unreproveable. For to Thee is due all glory, adoration, and thanksgiving, honour, and worship to the FATHER, and to the SON, and to the HOLY GHOST, both now and ever, and world without end.

And let all the People say, Amen.

And let the Bishop say, The peace of GOD be with you all.

And let all the people say, And with thy spirit.

And let the Deacon again proclaim,

Again and again let us pray to GOD through His CHRIST, in behalf of the gift that is offered to the LORD GOD; that the good GOD will receive it through the mediation of His CHRIST at His heavenly Altar for a sweet-smelling savour. Let us pray for this Church and people. Let us pray for every Episcopate, for the whole *P*resbytery, for all the *D*eacons and Ministers in CHRIST, for the whole congregation; that the LORD will preserve and keep them all. Let us pray for kings and all that are in authority, that they may be peaceable towards us; so that enjoying a quiet and peaceable life, we may spend our days in all godliness and honesty. Let us commemorate the holy martyrs, that we may be deemed worthy to be partakers of their trial. Let us pray for all those who have fallen asleep in the faith. Let us pray for the good condition of the air, and the ripening of the fruits. Let us pray for those that are newly-baptized, that

they may be confirmed in the faith, that all may be
mutually comforted by one another. Raise us up, O
GOD, by Thy grace. Rising up, let us devote our·
selves to GOD through JESUS CHRIST.

And let the Bishop say,

O GOD Who art great, great in name and counsel,
powerful in Thy works, the GOD and FATHER of Thy
holy SON JESUS CHRIST our Saviour, look upon this
Thy flock, which Thou hast chosen through Him to
the glory of Thy Name; sanctify us in body and
soul; and grant that we being purified from all
filthiness of flesh and spirit, may partake of the
mystic blessings now lying before Thee, and judge
none of us unworthy of them, but be Thou our
supporter, our helper, and defender, through Thy
CHRIST, with Whom glory, honour, laud, praise, and
thanksgiving be to Thee and the HOLY GHOST for
ever. Amen.

And after all have said Amen, *let the Deacon say,*
Let us attend.

*And the Bishop shall speak aloud to the People in
this manner;*
HOLY THINGS FOR HOLY PERSONS.

And let the People answer: There is one Holy,
one LORD, one JESUS CHRIST to the glory of GOD
the FATHER, blessed for evermore. Amen. Glory be
to GOD in the highest, and on earth peace, good will
towards men. Hosanna to the Son of David.
Blessed be He that cometh in the Name of the LORD:
GOD is the LORD, and He hath appeared unto us.
Hosanna in the highest.

*After this, let the Bishop receive; then the Pres-
byters, and Deacons, and Sub-Deacons, and Readers,*

and Singers, and Ascetics; and of the women, the Deaconesses, Virgins, and Widows. Afterwards the Children, and then all the People in order with fear and reverence, without tumult or noise. And the Bishop shall give the oblation, saying, The Body of CHRIST.

And let him that receives say, Amen.

And the Deacon shall hold the cup, and when he gives it, let him say, The Blood of CHRIST, the cup of life.

And let him that drinks say, Amen.

Let the Thirty-third Psalm be said while the rest are receiving; and when all, both men and women, have received, let the Deacons take up that which is over and carry them into the Sacristy. (¹¹)

And let the Deacon say, when the Singers have finished,

Having received the precious Body and precious Blood of CHRIST, let us give thanks to Him Who hath vouchsafed that we should receive His holy mysteries,—and let us beseech Him that they may not be to us to judgment, but to salvation ; to the advantage of soul and body, to the preservation of godliness, to the forgiveness of sins, to the life of the world to come. Let us rise. In the grace of CHRIST, let us commend ourselves to GOD, the only-unbegotten GOD, and to His CHRIST.

And let the Bishop give thanks.

Master, GOD Almighty, Father of CHRIST, Thy

(¹¹) Ἐις τὰ παστοφόρια. The word seems originally to have been used of that which was borne on a shrine : from παστόν, a small chapel; and that again from πάσσω, either in the sense of ornamental work generally, or of embroidery in particular, from the curtain hung before such a shrine.

Blessed Son, Who art ready to hear them that with
uprightness call upon Thee ; Who also knowest the
petitions of them that are silent ; we yield Thee
thanks that Thou hast vouchsafed us to receive Thy
holy mysteries, which Thou hast afforded us, to the
preservation of godliness, to the remission of sins,
because the name of Thy Christ has been called
upon us, and we have been made members of Thy
family.   Thou That hast separated us from fellowship with the wicked, unite us with them that are
hallowed to Thee : establish us in the truth by the
coming down of the Holy Ghost : that which we
know not do Thou reveal : that which is wanting in
us do Thou fill up ; in that which we know do Thou
strengthen us : guard continually Thy Priests blameless in Thy service : keep evermore kings in peace,
rulers in righteousness, the atmosphere in good
temperature, the fruits in abundance, the world in
all-powerful ([12]) forethought.   Soften the natures
that delight in war : turn again that which has
gone astray : hallow Thy people : continually preserve them that are in chastity : preserve in
faith those who are in marriage : fill with might
them that observe continence : bring the babes to
ripe age : confirm the newly-initiated : educate the
catechumens, and cause them to become worthy of
initiation ; and bring us all together to the kingdom
of heaven : through Christ Jesus our Lord : through
Whom.

And let the Deacon say,

To God, through His Christ, bow down and
receive the blessing.

([12]) I would propose to substitute for παναλκεῖ, which does
not seem to give any particular sense here, the word παναλθεῖ,
which is used by Nicander, in the sense of *all-healing*, and
which would better respond to the general sense.

And let the Bishop pray, saying,

GOD, the Almighty, the True and Incomparable, Who art ever existent, and all present, and existest in nothing; Thou Who art not circumscribed by places, Who art not aged by times, Who art not limited by ages, Who art not led aside by words; Who art not subject to generation, Who needest not guard, Who art superior to destruction, Who art unsusceptible of turning, Who art immutable by nature, Who inhabitest the light which no man can approach unto, Who art comprehensible to all rational natures that seek Thee with good feeling, Who art invisible by Thy nature, Who art comprehended of them that with good will seek Thee: the GOD of Israel, of him that truly ([13]) seeth Thee: of Thy people that believeth in CHRIST: be favourable and hear me for Thy Name: and bless them that have bowed down their necks to Thee, and give to them the desires of their hearts so far as may be expedient for them; and grant that none of them may be rejected from Thy kingdom; but sanctify them, guard, shelter, assist, preserve them from the enemy, and from every adversary. Guard their houses; preserve their comings in and their goings out: for to Thee is glory, laud, magnificence, worship, adoration, and to Thy Son JESUS, Thy CHRIST, our LORD and GOD and King, and to the HOLY GHOST, now and ever, and to ages and ages. Amen.

And let the Deacon say, Depart in peace.

These things we, the Apostles, enjoin concerning the Mystic Service to you, the Bishops, the Priests, and the Deacons.

([13]) Allusion is made to the derivation of Israel—"that sees GOD."

THE DIVINE LITURGY

OF

S. Chrysostom.

Deacon. Sir, give the blessing.

Priest. Blessed be the kingdom of the FATHER, the SON, and the HOLY GHOST, now and ever, and to ages of ages.

Choir. Amen.

Deacon. In peace let us make our supplications to the LORD.

Choir. LORD, have mercy: (*and so at the end of every petition.*)

Deacon. For the peace that is from above, and for the salvation of our souls, let us make our supplications to the LORD.

For the peace of the whole world, the stability of the holy Churches of GOD, and the union of all, let.

For this holy house, and them that in faith, piety, and the fear of GOD enter into it, let.

For our Archbishop N.; the venerable *P*resbytery, the *D*iaconate in CHRIST, all the Clergy and the laity, let.

For our most pious and divinely preserved kings, all their palace and their army, let.

That He would fight on their side, and subdue every enemy and adversary under their feet, let.

For this holy abode, the whole city and country, and them that inhabit it, in faith, let.

For healthfulness of air, plenty of the fruits of the earth, and peaceful times, let.

For them that voyage, that journey, that are sick, that labour, that are in bonds, and their safety, let.

That we may be preserved from all tribulation, wrath, danger, and necessity, let.

Assist, preserve, pity, and protect us, O GOD, by Thy grace.

Commemorating the all-holy, spotless, excellently laudable, and glorious Lady, the Mother of GOD and Ever-Virgin Mary, with All Saints, let us commend ourselves and each other and all our life to CHRIST our GOD.

Choir. To Thee, O LORD.

Priest (aloud). For all glory, worship, and honour befits Thee, FATHER, SON, and HOLY GHOST, now and ever, and to ages of ages. Amen.

The first Antiphon is sung by the Choir, and the Priest saith the Prayer of the first Antiphon. The Deacon, having made a reverence, leaves his place, and goes and stands before the Icon of the Mother of GOD,([1]) *looking towards the Icon of* CHRIST, *taking hold of the Orarion with three fingers of his right hand.*

[*First Antiphon.*([2])

Stichos. The heavens declare the glory of GOD: and the firmament sheweth His handywork.

By the intercession of the Mother of GOD.

([1]) This rubric is not given in the older editions. In the Russian Church it is worded differently, but with the same meaning. "The Deacon goes and stands before the icon of CHRIST." But both directions simply place him on the north side of the holy doors, under the icon of the Panaghia, there represented.

([2]) As an example of these Antiphons, I have given those for Pentecost; and shall do so in the succeeding Antiphons.

Stichos. One day telleth another: and one night certifieth another.

    By the intercession of the Mother of GOD.

Stichos. There is neither speech nor language : but their voices are heard among them.

    By the intercession of the Mother of GOD.

Stichos. Their sound is gone out unto all lands : and their words unto the end of the world.

    By the intercession of the Mother of GOD.

    Glory.   Both now.

    By the intercession of the Mother of GOD.]

Prayer of the first Antiphon.

LORD our GOD, of boundless might, and incomprehensible glory, and measureless compassion, and ineffable love to man, look down, O LORD, according to Thy tender love, on us, and on this holy house, and shew to us, and to them that pray with us, the riches of Thy mercies and compassions.

And after the Antiphon hath been sung, the Deacon comes and stands in the accustomed place, adores and says,

    Again and again in peace let us make our supplications to the LORD.

    Assist, preserve, pity, and protect us, O GOD.

    Commemorating the all-holy, undefiled, excellently laudable, glorious Lady, &c.

    Exclamation. For Thine is the strength, and Thine is the kingdom, the power and the glory, FATHER, &c.

In like manner the Choir sing the second Antiphon. The Deacon doth the same as in the former Prayer.

[*Second Antiphon.*

Stichos. The LORD hear thee in the day of trouble : the Name of the GOD of Jacob defend thee.

> Save us, O good PARACLETE, who chant to Thee Alleluia.

Stichos. Send thee help from the Sanctuary : and strengthen thee out of Sion.

> Save us, O good PARACLETE, who chant to Thee Alleluia.

Stichos. Remember all thy offerings ; and accept thy burnt sacrifice.

> Save us, O good PARACLETE, who chant to Thee Alleluia.

Glory. Both now.

The Only-Begotten SON and WORD of GOD.]

The Prayer of the Second Antiphon.

LORD our GOD, save Thy people, and bless Thine inheritance ; guard the fulness of Thy Church : hallow them that love the beauty of Thine house. Glorify them in recompence with Thy divine power : and forsake not them that put their trust in Thee.

Deacon. Again and again, in peace, &c.

Assist, preserve, &c.

Commemorating the most holy, &c.

Exclamation. For Thou art the good GOD, and the lover of men, and to Thee we ascribe, &c.

The Prayer of the Third Antiphon. ([8])

Thou, Who hast given us grace, at this time, with one accord, to make our common supplications unto

---

([8]) It would be curious to trace how this prayer came into our Prayer-Book : for there is no reason to suppose the Reformers intimately acquainted with the formularies of the Eastern Church.

Thee: and dost promise that, when two or three are gathered together in Thy Name, Thou wilt grant their requests : fulfil now, O LORD, the desires and petitions of Thy servants, as may be most expedient for them: granting us in this world knowledge of Thy truth, and, in the world to come, life ever-lasting.

And while the Third Antiphon is being sung by the Choir, or, if it be Sunday, the Beatitudes, ([4]) when they come to the Doxology, the Priest and Deacon make three reverences before the Holy Table. Then the Priest, taking the Holy Gospel, giveth it to the Deacon: and thus going through the north portion of the Sanctuary, preceded by lamps, they make the LITTLE ENTRANCE.

[*Third Antiphon.*

Stichos. The king shall rejoice in Thy strength, O LORD : exceedingly glad shall he be of thy salvation.

Blessed art Thou, CHRIST our GOD.

Thou hast given him his heart's desire; and hast not denied him the request of his lips.

Blessed art Thou, CHRIST our GOD.

Stichos. For Thou shalt prevent him with the blessings of goodness : and shalt set a crown of pure gold upon his head.

Blessed art Thou, CHRIST our GOD.

Stichos. He asked life of Thee, and Thou gavest him a long life : even for ever and ever.

Blessed be Thou, CHRIST our GOD.

([4]) It is strange that Goar should not have known that our LORD's Beatitudes were here intended; or at least should not have been certain of it. " Hymni," says he, " sanctorum beatitudinis memoriam recolentes : vel potius eæ beatitudines de quibus S. Matthæi v. : vel tandem pia viventium vota pro defunctorum requie."

Isodicon. (⁵) Be Thou exalted, LORD, in Thine own strength: so will we sing and praise Thy power.

Save us, O good PARACLETE, who sing to Thee Alleluia.]

Deacon (*in a low voice.*) Let us make our supplications to the LORD.

Priest secretly saith the Prayer of the Entrance.

Master, LORD, and our GOD, Who hast disposed in heaven troops and armies of Angels and Archangels, for the ministry of Thy glory: grant that with our entrance there may be an entrance of holy Angels, ministering together with us, and with us glorifying Thy goodness.

For to Thee is due all honour, &c.

The Prayer being finished, the Deacon pointing with his right hand to the east, and holding his Orarion with three fingers, saith to the Priest.

Sir, bless the Holy Entrance.

Priest. Blessed be the entrance of Thy Saints, always, now and ever, and to ages of ages.

Then the Deacon thus goes to the Hegumen, (⁶) *if any be present, who kisseth the Gospel; but if none be present, the Priest kisseth it.*

And when the Troparia are ended, the Deacon comes forth into the middle, and standing before the Priest, raiseth his hands a little, and showing the Holy Gospel, saith with a loud voice,

---

(⁵) The anthem accompanying the Little Entrance.
(⁶) That is, the Abbat. The rubrics of this Liturgy assume that celebration in a monastery, or in a parish church served by monks, is the rule.—L.

H

Wisdom, stand up. (⁷)

*Then he himself adores, and the Priest behind him:
and they both go to the holy Bema, and the Deacon puts
down the Holy Gospel on the Holy Table, and the Choir
sing the accustomed Troparia, and when they are singing
the last, the Deacon saith,*

Let us make our supplications to the LORD. (⁸)

Priest. For holy art Thou, our GOD; and we
ascribe glory to Thee, FATHER, SON, and HOLY
GHOST, now and for ever.

Deacon. And to ages of ages.

Choir. Amen.

The Choir sing the Trisagion.

Holy GOD, Holy and Mighty, Holy and Immortal,
have mercy upon us. (*Five times.*)

*In the meantime the Priest saith secretly the Prayer
of the Trisagion.*

GOD, Which art holy, and restest in the holies,
Who art hymned with the voice of the Trisagion by
the Seraphim, and glorified by the Cherubim, and
adored by all the heavenly powers; Thou Who
didst from nothing call all things into being; Who
didst make man after Thine image and likeness,
and didst adorn him with all Thy graces; Who
givest to him that seeketh wisdom and understanding, and passest not by the sinner, but dost give repentance unto salvation; Who hast vouchsafed that
we, Thy humble and unworthy servants, should
stand even at this time before the glory of Thy

(⁷) This seems the more natural reading; but many editions
read, σοφία, which must be interpreted to mean, " In wisdom
stand up;" and thus be a warning against the sin and folly of
now sitting.

(⁸) In the older copies this is thus given: " Sir, bless the
time of the Trisagion."

holy Altar, and should pay to Thee the worship and praise that is meet: receive, LORD, out of the mouth of sinners the hymn of the Trisagion, and visit us in Thy goodness. Forgive us every offence, voluntary and involuntary. Sanctify our souls and bodies, and grant that we may serve Thee in holiness all the days of our life; through the intercessions of the Holy Mother of GOD, and all the Saints who have pleased Thee since the beginning of the world. (*Aloud.*) For holy art Thou, our GOD, and to Thee.

When this Prayer is finished, the Priest also and Deacon say the Trisagion, making at the same time three reverences before the holy Table. Then the Deacon saith to the Priest,

Sir, give the order. *And they go towards the throne.*

And the Priest saith as he goes,

Blessed is he that cometh in the Name of the LORD.

Deacon. Sir, bless the throne.

Priest. Blessed art Thou upon the throne of Thy glory, Who sittest upon the Cherubim, always, now and ever, and to ages of ages.

And when the Choir have finished the Trisagion, the Deacon, coming before the holy doors, saith,

Let us attend.

Reader. Alleluia. ([9])

([9]) Here, as in the Rubric at the end of the Epistle, the Greek runs thus: Alleluia, a Psalm of David. But no Psalm is here sung; and therefore the question arises, what is the reason of the insertion. Some commentators receive it as an explanation of the Alleluia; as much as to say, that this ascription of praise was of the composition of David. But this seems very harsh. Were there any trace in Greek

Deacon. Wisdom.

The Reader saith the Prokimenon ([10]) *of the Apostle,*
   e. g. *on the Festival of S. Demetrius.*

The righteous shall rejoice in the LORD.
Stichos. Hear, O GOD, my voice.
Deacon. Let us attend.

The Apostle is read.

And the Apostle being ended, the Priest saith,
([11]) Peace be to thee.
Reader. Alleluia.

*While the Alleluia is being sung, the Deacon goes to
the Priest, and after asking for a blessing from him,
censes the holy Table in a circle, and the whole sanctuary,
and the Priest.   And the Priest saith the Prayer before
the Gospel.*

O LORD and lover of men, cause the pure light of
Thy Divine knowledge to shine forth in our hearts,
and open the eyes of our understanding, that we
may comprehend the precepts of Thy Gospel. Plant
in us also the fear of Thy blessed commandments,
that we, trampling upon all carnal lusts, may seek

---

ritualists of a psalm having anciently followed, I should
believe that after the rite was given up the Rubric remained.
The addition is not to be found in the Slavonic.

([10]) The *Prokimenon,* or short anthem before the Epistle,
consists of a verse and response: generally, but not always,
taken from the Psalms, but hardly ever consisting of consecu-
tive phrases. According to S. Germanus, the Prokimenon
signifies the previous proclamation by the Prophets of that
CHRIST of Whom the Epistle is about to tell.   And the versicles are chosen with that intent, *e.g.* in the festival of the
Expectation of the Nativity:
V. The LORD said unto Me, Thou art My Son.
R. Desire of Me, and I shall give thee the heathen for
Thine inheritance.

([11]) This is technically called εἰρηνεύειν τὸν Ἀπόστολον.

a heavenly citizenship, both saying and doing always such things as shall well please Thee. For Thou art the illumination of our souls and bodies, CHRIST our GOD ; and to Thee we ascribe, &c.

And the Deacon drawing nigh to the Priest, and laying aside his censer, and bowing to the Priest and holding the Orarion with the Holy Gospel with the tips of his fingers, in the place of the Holy Table whereon it lies, saith,

Sir, bless the preacher of the holy Apostle and Evangelist N.

And the Priest, signing him with the Cross, saith,

GOD, through the preaching of the holy and glorious Apostle and Evangelist, N., give the word with much power to thee who evangelizest, to the accomplishment of the Gospel of His beloved SON our LORD JESUS CHRIST.

Deacon. Amen.

And having adored with reverence the Holy Gospel, he takes it up; and going through the holy doors, preceded by tapers, he stands in the ambon, or in the appointed place. And the Priest standing before the holy Table, and looking towards the west, saith, with a loud voice,

Wisdom, stand up; let us hear the Holy Gospel Peace to all.

Deacon. The Lection from the Holy Gospel according to N.

Priest. Let us attend.

The Gospel is read.

When it is finished, the Priest saith to the Deacon,

Peace be to thee that evangelizest.

And the Deacon going to the holy doors, returns the Holy Gospel to the Priest; and standing in the accustomed place, begins thus:

Let us all say with our whole heart and soul,
Choir. LORD, have mercy. (*Thrice.*)
LORD Almighty, GOD of our fathers, we pray Thee, hear, and have mercy upon us.

Have mercy upon us, O GOD, after Thy great goodness: we pray Thee hear, and have mercy upon us.

Prayer of the Ectene.

LORD our GOD, we pray Thee to receive this intense supplication from Thy servants, according to the multitude of Thy mercy, and send down Thy compassions upon us, and upon all Thy people, which is expecting the rich mercy that is from Thee.

Deacon. Further we pray for pious and orthodox Christians.

People. LORD, have mercy. (*And so at the end of every petition.*)

Further we pray for our Archbishop N.

Further we pray for our brethren, Priests, Monks, and all our brotherhood in CHRIST.

Further we pray for the blessed and ever memorable founders of this holy abode, and for all our fathers and brethren that have fallen asleep before us, and lie here, and the orthodox that lie everywhere.

Further we pray for mercy, life, peace, health, safety, protection, forgiveness, and remission of sins of the servants of GOD, the brethren of this holy habitation.

Further we pray for them that bring forth fruit and do good deeds in this holy and all-venerable temple, that labour, that sing, and for the people that stand around, and are expecting the great and rich mercy that is from Thee.

Exclamation. For Thou art the merciful GOD and the lover of men, and to Thee we ascribe.

Deacon. Catechumens, pray unto the LORD. Let us, the faithful, pray for the Catechumens, that the LORD may have mercy upon them, and may teach them the word of truth.

People. LORD, have mercy. *And so at the end of each petition.*

That He may reveal to them the Gospel of right-eousness.

That He may unite them to His Holy Catholic and Apostolic Church.

Preserve, have mercy, support, and continually guard them, O GOD.

Catechumens, bow your heads to the LORD.

Prayer of the Catechumens before the holy Oblation.

LORD our GOD, Who dwellest on high, and be-holdest the humble, Who didst send forth the salva-tion of the race of man, Thine Only-Begotten SON, our GOD and LORD JESUS CHRIST, look down upon Thy servants, the Catechumens, who have bowed their necks unto Thee; and make them worthy, in due season, of the laver of regeneration, of the forgiveness of sins, of the robe of immortality; unite them to Thy Holy Catholic and Apostolic Church, and number them together with Thy elect flock. (*Aloud.*) That they also, together with us, may glorify Thy honourable and majestic Name, FATHER, SON, and HOLY GHOST, now and ever, and to ages of ages.

Choir. Amen.

The Priest unfolds the Corporal.

EXPULSION OF THE CATECHUMENS.

Deacon. Let all the Catechumens depart; ([12]) Cate-chumens depart; let all the Catechumens, depart: let not any of the Catechumens —; let all the faithful;—

Again and again in peace let us make our supplications to the LORD. *And he saith the short Ectene: while the Priest saith secretly*

The first Prayer of the Faithful, after the unfolding of the Corporal.

We yield Thee thanks, LORD GOD of Sabaoth, Who hast thought us worthy to stand even now at Thine Altar, and to fall down before Thy mercies, for our sins and the ignorances of Thy people: receive, O GOD, our supplications; make us worthy to offer to Thee supplications and prayers, and unbloody sacrifices for all Thy people; and strengthen us, whom Thou hast placed in this Thy ministry, with the strength of the HOLY GHOST, that we may without offence, and without scandal, in a pure testi-mony of our conscience, call upon Thee in every time and place: that hearing us Thou mayest be merciful to us in the multitude of Thy goodness.

Deacon. Assist, preserve, pity.

Wisdom.

Priest. Exclamation. For to Thee belongeth all glory, honour, and worship, FATHER, SON, and HOLY GHOST, now and ever, and to ages of ages.

Deacon. Again and again in peace let us make our supplications to the LORD. *And he saith the short Ectene; while the Priest saith secretly*

([12]) Literally, *pass forward*, (προέλθετε) but used quite in the sense of *depart;* and so translated in the Slavonic.

The second Prayer of the Faithful.

Again and oftentimes we fall down before Thee, and beseech Thee, O good GOD and lover of men, that Thou wouldest look upon our prayers, purify our souls and bodies from all pollution of flesh and spirit, and grant that our standing before Thy holy Altar may be irreprehensible and unblameable. Grant, O LORD, to them who pray together with us, advance in [holy] life, wisdom, and spiritual understanding: grant them at all times with fear and love to serve Thee irreprehensibly; and without condemnation to partake of Thy holy mysteries, and to be thought worthy of Thy heavenly kingdom.

Deacon. Assist, preserve, &c.

Wisdom.

Priest. Exclamation. That, being ever guarded by Thy might, we may ascribe glory to Thee, FATHER, SON, and HOLY GHOST, now and ever, and to ages of ages.

Choir. Amen.

The Choir sing the Cherubic Hymn.

Let us, who mystically represent the Cherubim, and sing the holy hymn to the quickening TRINITY, lay by at this time all worldly cares; that we may receive the King of Glory, invisibly attended by the angelic orders. Alleluia, Alleluia, Alleluia.

Prayer which the Priest saith secretly, while the Cherubic Hymn is being sung. ([13])

([13]) As the Cherubic hymn was composed only in the time of Justinian, it is clear that the prayer of that hymn must be an insertion. And accordingly, it is not to be found in the very ancient Barberini MS. of this Liturgy, to which Goar so often refers.

None is worthy among them that are bound with fleshly desires and pleasures to approach Thee, nor to draw near, nor to sacrifice unto Thee, King of Glory; for to minister to Thee is great and fearful, even to the heavenly powers themselves. Yet through Thine ineffable and measureless love, Thou didst unchangeably and immutably become man, and didst (¹⁴) take the title of our High *P*riest, and didst give to us the Hierurgy of this liturgic and un-bloody Sacrifice, as being LORD of all: for Thou only, O LORD our GOD, rulest over things in heaven and things on earth, Who sittest upon the cherubic throne, LORD of Seraphim, and King of Israel, only holy, and resting in the holies. On Thee I impor-tunately call, (¹⁵) That art only good and ready to hear, look upon me, a sinner, and Thine unworthy servant, and cleanse my soul and heart from an evil conscience; and strengthen, with the might of Thy HOLY GHOST, me that have been endued with the grace of the *P*riesthood, that I may stand by this Thy holy Altar, and sacrifice Thy holy and spotless Body and precious Blood. For Thee I approach bowing my neck, and pray of Thee, Turn not Thy face away from me, nor reject me from the number of Thy sons; but condescend that these gifts may be offered to Thee by me, a sinner and Thine unworthy servant. For Thou art He that offerest, (¹⁶)

(¹⁴) 'Εχρημάτισας. King, less correctly, " becamest." But in the new Greek, this verb means to assume a name; so Polybius, more than once.

(¹⁵) King, " I call upon Thee:" Goar, "Te deprecor." But δυσωπῶ is more than this; it is " to put a man out of counte-nance," and so "to be importunate:" and is frequently thus used by Plutarch, though not by more classical authors.

(¹⁶) *That offerest and art offered, and receivest and art dis-tributed.* One should have thought that no great difficulty could be found or made in these words. *That offerest—*

and art offered, and receivest and art distributed, CHRIST our GOD ; and to Thee we ascribe, &c.

When this prayer is finished, they also say the Cherubic Hymn. Then the Deacon, taking the censer, and putting incense on it, goes to the Priest: and after receiving a blessing from him, censes the holy Table in a circle, and all the sanctuary, and the Priest: and he saith the 51st Psalm, and other penitential Troparia, such as he will, with the Priest. And they go to the Prothesis, the Deacon preceding. And the Deacon having censed the holy things, and said to himself,

GOD be merciful to me a sinner, *saith to the Priest,* Sir, lift up.

And the Priest raising the Air, ([17]) puts it on the left shoulder of the Deacon, saying,

Lift up your hands in the sanctuary, and bless the LORD.

Then, taking the holy disk, he puts it with all care and reverence on the Deacon's head, the Deacon also holding the censer with one of his fingers. And the Priest himself taking the holy chalice in his hands, they go through the north part, preceded by tapers, and make

---

"for this He did once, when He offered up Himself,"—*and art offered,* in the Oblation of the Mystic Sacrifice,—*That receivest* that Sacrifice, *and art received* by them that present it. However, about the year 1155 a great dispute arose on the question. A Deacon of Constantinople taught that this could not be the meaning of the passage, because the sacrifice was not offered to CHRIST, but to the FATHER and the HOLY GHOST alone. A Council met at Constantinople, January 26th, 1156, under the Patriarch, Luke Chrysoberges, to decide the question: and Soterichus Panteugenus, Patriarch elect of Antioch, who had taught the new dogma, was declared unworthy of his office.

([17]) The fine veil which lies over the paten and chalice.—L.

THE GREAT ENTRANCE, ([18])

both praying for all, and saying, The LORD GOD remember us all in His kingdom, always, now and ever, and to ages of ages.

And the Deacon, going within the holy doors, stands on the right hand; and when the Priest is about to enter in, he saith to him,

The LORD GOD remember thy *P*riesthood in His kingdom.

Priest. The LORD GOD remember thy *D*iaconate in His kingdom, always, now and ever, and to ages of ages.

And the Priest sets down the chalice on the holy Table, and taking the holy disk from the head of the Deacon, he places it there also, saying,

Honourable Joseph took Thy spotless Body from the cross, and wrapped it in clean linen with spices, and with funeral rites placed it in a new tomb.

In the grave bodily, in Hades spiritually, as GOD, with the thief in paradise as in a throne, wast Thou, O CHRIST, with the FATHER and the HOLY GHOST, Who art incircumscript and fillest all things.

How life-giving, how more beautiful than paradise, and verily more splendid than any royal chamber, is Thy tomb, O CHRIST, the fountain of our resurrection.

([18]) It is the custom of those who are sick, or who stand in need of any especial blessing, to kneel in the path of the Great Entrance, in order to receive the virtue of the Holy Mysteries. The custom of adoring that which is, as yet, mere bread and wine, with anticipative adoration, has always cost the Orientals much trouble to defend it; and it has been abolished by the Roman Censors in Uniat rites. A treatise on the subject, by Gabriel of Philadelphia, was published at Venice in 1604.

Then, taking the coverings from the holy disk and the holy chalice, he places them on one part of the holy Table; and taking the Air from the Deacon's shoulder, and censing it, he covers with it the holy things, saying,

Honourable Joseph, *down to* in a new tomb.

And taking the censer from the Deacon's hands, he censeth the holy things thrice, saying,

Then shall they offer young bullocks upon Thine Altar.

And putting down the censer, and letting fall his phelonion, ([19]*) and bowing his head, he saith to the Deacon,*

Remember me, brother and fellow-minister.

Deacon. The LORD GOD remember thy *Priesthood,* in His kingdom.

Then the Deacon also himself slightly bowing his head, and holding his Orarion with the three fingers of his right hand, saith to the Priest,

Holy Sir, pray for me.

Priest. The HOLY GHOST shall come upon thee, and the power of the Highest shall overshadow thee.

Deacon. The same SPIRIT shall be fellow-minister with us, all the days of our life.

And again, Holy Sir, remember me.

Priest. The LORD GOD remember thee in His kingdom, always, now and ever, and to ages of ages.

Deacon. Amen.

And having kissed the Priest's hand, he goes out, and standing in the customary place, saith,

---

[19] The Eastern chasuble.—L.

Let us accomplish our supplications to the LORD.

Choir. Kyrie eleison.   *And so to the end of each suffrage.*

Deacon. For the precious gifts that have been proposed, let us make our supplications to the LORD.

For this holy house, and them that with faith, reverence, and the fear of GOD, enter into it, let.

That we may be delivered from all afflictions, passion, danger, and necessity, let.

Assist, preserve.

That the whole day may be perfect, holy, peaceful, without sin, let us ask from the LORD.

Choir. Grant, O LORD.   *And so at the end of every suffrage.*

Deacon. The angel of peace, faithful guide, guardian of our souls and bodies, let.

Pardon and remission of our sins and our transgressions, let.

Things that are good and profitable for our souls, and peace to the world, let.

That we may accomplish the remainder of our lives in peace and penitence, let.

Christian ends of our lives, without torment, without shame, peaceful, and a good defence at the fearful tribunal, let us ask from CHRIST.

Commemorating the all-holy.

As this Ectene ([20]) *is being said, the Priest saith secretly the Prayer of Oblation, after the Divine Gifts are placed on the holy Table.*

LORD, GOD Almighty, Only Holy, Who receivest the sacrifice of praise from them that call upon Thee with their whole heart, receive also the sup-

---

([20]) It is not worth while to notice the verbal differences of this Ectene. In no part of the Liturgy do MSS. and editions so much vary. But the variations are quite non-essential.

plication of us sinners, and cause it to approach to Thy holy Altar, and enable us to present gifts to Thee, and spiritual sacrifices for our sins, and for the errors of the people: and cause us to find grace in Thy sight, that this our sacrifice may be acceptable unto Thee, and that the good SPIRIT of Thy grace may tabernacle upon us, and upon these gifts presented unto Thee, and upon all Thy people.

Priest. (*Exclamation.*) Through the mercies of Thine Only-Begotten SON, with Whom Thou art to be blessed, and with the all-holy, and good, and quickening SPIRIT, now and ever, and to ages of ages.

Peace to all.

Deacon. Let us love one another, that we may with one mind confess.

Choir. FATHER, SON, and HOLY GHOST, the Consubstantial, and Undivided TRINITY.

And the Priest, having thrice adored, kisses the Holy
Gifts, as they lie veiled, saying secretly thrice.

I will love Thee, O LORD, my strength; the LORD is my stony rock and my defence.

If there be two or more Priests, each kisses the Holy Things, and then each other on the shoulder, saying,

CHRIST is among us.

He is and will be.

In like manner also the Deacon adores thrice where he stands, and kisses his Orarion on its cross, and thus exclaims,

The doors! the doors! ([21]) Let us attend in wisdom.

([21]) The meaning of this sentence is very obscure. Some authors, as Cabasilas, explain it mystically, as an injunction to close the doors of the mind against worldly business and thoughts; others, much more naturally, take it as an injunction to the Clerks, not to allow heathens, &c., to be present at the Divine Mysteries.

People. I believe in one God, &c.

Deacon. Stand we well : stand we with fear : let us attend to offer the holy Oblation in peace.

Choir. The mercy of peace, the sacrifice of praise.

And the Deacon adores, and comes to the holy Bema; and taking the fan, fans the Oblation reverently.

And the Priest taking the Air from the Holy Gifts, lays it on one side, saying,

The grace of our LORD JESUS CHRIST, and the love of GOD the FATHER, and the fellowship of the HOLY GHOST, be with you all.

Choir. And with thy spirit.

Priest. Lift we up our hearts.

Choir. We lift them up unto the LORD.

Priest. Let us give thanks unto the LORD.

Choir. It is meet and right to worship the FATHER, the SON, and the HOLY GHOST, the consubstantial and undivided TRINITY.

Priest. It is meet and right to hymn Thee, to bless Thee, to praise Thee, to give thanks to Thee, to worship Thee, in every part of Thy dominion. For Thou art GOD, ineffable, inconceivable, invisible, incomprehensible, the same from everlasting to everlasting; Thou and Thine Only-Begotten SON, and the HOLY GHOST. For Thou broughtest us forth to being from nothing, and when we had fallen didst raise us up again, and gavest not over until Thou hadst done every thing that Thou mightest bring us to heaven, and bestow on us Thy kingdom to come. For all these things we give thanks to Thee, and to Thine Only-Begotten SON, and Thy HOLY GHOST, for Thy benefits which we know, and which we know not, manifest and concealed, which Thou hast bestowed upon us. We give Thee thanks also for this ministry which Thou hast vouchsafed to receive

at our hands : although there stand by Thee
thousands of Archangels, and ten thousands of
Angels, the Cherubim, and the Seraphim that have
six wings, and are full of eyes, and soar aloft on
their wings, singing, vociferating, shouting, and
saying the triumphal hymn :

Choir. Holy, Holy, Holy, Lord of Sabaoth;
heaven and earth are full of Thy glory. Hosanna
in the highest: blessed is He that cometh in the
Name of the Lord : Hosanna in the highest.

*Then the Deacon, taking the asterisk from the holy
disk, signs it with the sign of the cross, and having
saluted it, replaces it.*

Priest. We also with these blessed powers, Lord
and Lover of men, cry and say, Holy art Thou and
All-Holy, Thou and Thy Only-Begotten Son, and
Thine Holy Ghost. Holy art Thou and All-Holy,
and great is the majesty of Thy glory :
Who didst so love Thy world, as to give Thine
Only-Begotten Son, that whoso believeth in Him
might not perish, but might have everlasting life :
Who having come, and having fulfilled for us all
the dispensation, in the night wherein He was
betrayed, or rather surrendered Himself for the life
of the world, took bread in His holy and pure and
spotless hands, and gave thanks, and blessed, and
hallowed, and brake, and gave to His holy *Disciples*
and Apostles, saying, (*aloud,*) Take, eat: this is
My Body which is broken for you for the remission
of sins.

Choir. Amen.

Priest, (*in a low voice,*) Likewise after supper He
took the cup, saying, (*aloud,*) Drink ye all of this :
This is My Blood of the New Testament, which is
shed for you and for many for the remission of sins.

I

Choir. Amen.

Priest, (*in a low voice,*) We therefore remembering this salutary precept, and all that happened on our behalf, the Cross, the Tomb, the Resurrection on the third day, the Ascension into heaven, the Session on the right hand, the second and glorious coming again, (*aloud,*) in ([22]) behalf of all, and for all, we offer Thee Thine own of Thine own.

Choir. Thee we hymn, Thee we praise : to Thee we give thanks, LORD, and pray to Thee, our GOD.

Priest, (*in a low voice,*) Moreover we offer unto Thee this reasonable and unbloody sacrifice : and beseech Thee and pray and supplicate ; send down Thy HOLY GHOST upon us, and on these proposed gifts.

The Deacon lays down the veil, and goes nearer to the Priest, and they both adore thrice before the holy Table, praying secretly, saying,

GOD be merciful to me a sinner.

Then

LORD, Who didst send down Thy HOLY GHOST the third hour on the Apostles, take Him not from us, O good GOD, but renew Him in us who pray to Thee :

Then

Make me a clean heart, O GOD, and renew a right spirit within me. Cast me not away from Thy presence.

Glory.

Blessed art Thou, CHRIST our GOD, Who didst fill the fishermen with all manner of wisdom, sending down upon them the HOLY GHOST : and by them

---

([22]) κατὰ πάντα is better rendered by *in relation to all*, or *in behalf of all*, than by the usual version, *in all.*

hast brought the whole world into Thy net, O Lover
of men : glory be to Thee.

Both now.

When the Highest came down and confounded the
tongues, He divided the nations; when He distributed the tongues of fire, He called all to unity, and
with one voice we praise the HOLY GHOST.

*Then the Deacon bowing his head, and pointing
with his Orarion to the Holy Bread, saith in a low
voice,*

Sir, bless the holy bread.

*The Priest standeth up, and thrice maketh the sign of
the Cross on the Holy Gifts, saying,*

And make this bread the precious Body of Thy
CHRIST.

Deacon. Amen.   Sir, bless the holy cup.

Priest. And that which is in this cup, the precious
Blood of Thy CHRIST.

Deacon. Amen.   *And pointing with his Orarion
both the Holy Things,*

Sir, bless.

Priest. Changing them by Thy HOLY GHOST.

Deacon. Amen, Amen, Amen.

*Then the Deacon bows his head to the Priest, and
saith,*

Holy Sir, remember me a sinner.

*Then he stands in his former place, and taking the fan,
fans the Oblation as before.*

Priest. So that they may be to those that participate, for purification of soul, forgiveness of sins,
communion of the HOLY GHOST, fulfilment of the
kingdom of heaven, boldness towards Thee, and not
to judgment nor to condemnation.

And further we offer to Thee this reasonable service on behalf of those who have departed in the faith, our ancestors, Fathers, Patriarchs, Prophets, Apostles, Preachers, Evangelists, Martyrs, Confessors, Virgins, and every just spirit made perfect in the faith.

The Deacon censes the holy Table in a circle, and commemorates such of the living and dead as he will.

Priest, (*aloud.*) Especially the most holy, undefiled, excellently laudable, glorious Lady, the Mother of God and Ever-Virgin Mary.

Choir. In Thee, O full of grace, (*as in the Liturgy of S. James.*)

The Deacon reads the diptychs of the departed.

Priest. The holy John the Prophet, Forerunner, and Baptist, the holy, glorious, and all celebrated Apostles, Saint N. (*the Saint of the day*), whose memory we also celebrate, and all Thy Saints, through whose prayers look down upon us, O God. And remember all those that are departed in the hope of the resurrection to eternal life, and give them rest where the light of Thy countenance shines upon them. Furthermore we beseech Thee, remember, O Lord, every orthodox bishopric of those that rightly divide the word of truth, the presbytery, the diaconate in Christ, and for every hierarchical order. Furthermore we offer to Thee this reasonable service for the whole world: for the Holy Catholic and Apostolic Church, and for them that live in chastity and holiness of life. For our most faithful kings, beloved of Christ, all their court and army. Grant to them, Lord, a peaceful reign, that we, in their peace, may lead a quiet and peaceable life in all godliness and honesty. (*Aloud.*) Chiefly,

O LORD, remember our Archbishop N., whom preserve to Thy holy Churches in peace, in safety, in honour, in health, in length of days, and rightly dividing the word of Thy truth.

The Deacon, by the holy doors, saith,

N. the Patriarch, Metropolitan, or Bishop, (*as the case may be.*)

Then he commemorates the diptychs of the living.

Priest, (*secretly.*) Remember, LORD, the city in which we dwell, and every city and region, and the faithful that inhabit it. Remember, LORD, them that voyage, and travel, that are sick, that are labouring, that are in prison, and their safety. Remember, LORD, them that bear fruit, and do good deeds in Thy holy Churches, and that remember the poor. And send forth on us all the riches of Thy compassion, (*aloud,*) and grant us with one mouth and one heart to glorify and celebrate Thy glorious and majestic Name, FATHER, SON, and HOLY GHOST, now and ever, and to ages of ages. And the mercies of the great GOD and our SAVIOUR JESUS CHRIST shall be with all of us.

The Deacon taking his time from the Priest, and standing in the accustomed place, saith,

Commemorating all Saints, again and again in peace let us make our supplications to the LORD.

Choir. LORD, have mercy. (*And so at the end of each petition.*)

Deacon. For the venerable gifts now offered before Him and hallowed.

That our merciful GOD, the Lover of mankind, Who hath received them unto His holy and heavenly and spiritual Altar, for the savour of a sweet spiritual scent, may in return send down on us His *D*ivine grace, and the gift of the HOLY GHOST.

That we may be preserved from all affliction, wrath, &c.

The Deacon continues the Ectene down to Christian ends of life.

The Priest meanwhile saith secretly,

To Thee, O LORD and Lover of men, we commend in pledge all our life and our hope, and beseech and pray, and supplicate : make us worthy to partake of Thy heavenly and terrible mysteries of this holy and spiritual Table, with a pure conscience, for the remission of sins, forgiveness of transgressions, participation of the HOLY GHOST, inheritance of the kingdom of heaven, boldness of access to Thee : not to judgment nor to condemnation.

Deacon. Having prayed for the oneness of the faith, and the participation of the HOLY GHOST, let us commend ourselves and each other and all our life to CHRIST our GOD.

Priest, (*aloud.*) And make us worthy, O LORD, with boldness and without condemnation to dare to call upon Thee, our GOD and FATHER which art in heaven, and to say,

People. Our FATHER.

Priest. For Thine is the kingdom.

Priest. Peace to all.

Deacon. Let us bow our heads to the LORD.

Priest. We render thanks unto Thee, O King invisible, Who hast framed all things by Thy measureless power, and in the multitude of Thy mercy hast brought all things into being from non-existence. Look down, O LORD, from heaven, upon them that have bowed their heads unto Thee, for they bowed them not to flesh and blood, but to

Thee, the fearful God. Bestow, therefore, O Lord, on all of us an equal benefit from these offerings, according to the need of each : sail with them that sail, journey with them that journey, heal the sick, Thou Who art the Physician of our souls and bodies.

(*Aloud.*) Through the grace, and mercy, and love to men, of Thine Only-Begotten Son, with Whom, together with the most Holy, and good, and life-giving Spirit, Thou art blessed, now and ever, and to ages of ages. Amen.

Hear us, O Lord Jesus Christ our God, out of Thy holy dwelling-place, and from the throne of the glory of Thy kingdom, and come and sanctify us, Thou That sittest above with the Father, and art here invisibly present with us : and by Thy mighty hand make us worthy to partake of Thy spotless Body and precious Blood, and by us all Thy people.

The Priest and the Deacons adore in the place where they stand, saying secretly thrice,

God be merciful to me a sinner.

And when the Deacon sees the Priest stretching forth his hands, and touching the holy Bread, to make the holy elevation, he exclaims,

Let us attend.

And the Priest, elevating the holy Bread, exclaims,

Holy things for holy persons.

Choir. One Holy, one Lord, Jesus Christ, to the glory of God the Father.

And the Choir sing the Koinonicon: ([23]) e.g. on the festivals of Apostles.

([23]) This is a stichos, deriving its name, of course, from the Communion which it precedes; and is equivalent, though not exactly answering in place, to the Mozarabic Communion.

Their sound is gone out into all lands : and their words into the ends of the world.

The Deacon then girds his Orarion crosswise, and goes into the holy Bema, and standing on the right hand, (the Priest grasping the holy Bread,) saith,

Sir, break the holy Bread.

And the Priest, dividing It into four parts with car and reverence, saith,

The LAME of GOD is broken and distributed; He That is broken and not divided in sunder; ever eaten and never consumed, but sanctifying the communicants.

And the Deacon, pointing with his Orarion to the holy Cup, saith,

Sir, fill the holy Cup.

And the Priest taking the upper portion, (that is, the IHC,) *makes with It a Cross above the holy Cup, saying,* The fulness of the cup, of faith, of the HOLY GHOST: *and thus puts It into the holy Cup.*

Deacon. Amen.

And taking the warm water, he saith to the Priest,

Sir, bless the warm water. ([24])

And the Priest blesseth, saying,

([24]) This very strange rite, the pouring warm water into the chalice after consecration, occasioned the greatest astonishment among the Latins at the Council of Florence. Dorotheus, Bishop of Mitylene, is said to have given the Pope ample satisfaction by his explanation, which, however, is unfortunately lost. But S. Germanus tells us: "As Blood and warm Water flowed both of them from the side of CHRIST, thus hot water, poured into the chalice at the time of consecration, gives a full type of the mystery to those who draw that holy liquid from the chalice, as from the life-giving side of our LORD."

Blessed is the fervour of Thy Saints, always, now and ever, and to ages of ages. Amen.

And the Deacon pours forth a sufficiency into the holy Cup, in the form of a Cross, saying,

The fervour of faith, full of the HOLY GHOST. Amen. (*Thrice.*)

Then, setting down the warm water, he stands a little way off. And the Priest, taking a particle of the holy Bread, saith,

([25]) The blessed and most holy Body of our LORD and GOD and SAVIOUR JESUS CHRIST, is communicated to me, N., Priest, for the remission of my sins, and for everlasting life.

I believe, LORD, and confess.

Of Thy Mystic Supper to-day.

Let not, O LORD, the communion of Thy holy mysteries be to my judgment or condemnation, but to the healing of my soul and body.

And thus he partakes of that which is in his hands with fear and all caution. Then he saith,

Deacon, approach.

And the Deacon approaches, and reverently makes an obeisance, asking forgiveness. And the Priest, taking the holy Bread, gives it to the Deacon; and the Deacon, kissing the hand that gives it, saith,

Sir, make me partaker of the precious and holy Body of our LORD and GOD and SAVIOUR JESUS CHRIST.

Priest. N. the holy Deacon is made partaker of

([25]) The MSS. and printed editions vary excessively in the whole Communion both of the Priest and the people: so that it would be hard to find two copies exactly alike.

the precious and holy and spotless Body of our Lord and God and Saviour Jesus Christ, for the remission of his sins, and for eternal life.

And the Deacon going behind the holy Table, boweth his head and prayeth, and so doth the Priest.

Then the Priest standing up, takes the holy Chalice with its covering in both hands, and drinks three times, saying, I, N., Priest, partake of the pure and holy Blood of our Lord and God and Saviour Jesus Christ, for the remission of my sins, and for eternal life.

And then he wipes the holy Cup and his own lips with the covering he has in his hands, and saith,

Behold, this hath touched my lips, and shall take away my transgressions, and purge my sins.

Then he calls the Deacon, saying, Deacon, approach. *The Deacon comes, and adores once, saying,*

Behold, I approach the Immortal King.
I believe, Lord, and confess.
Priest. N. the Deacon and servant of God is made partaker of the precious and holy Blood of our Lord and God and Saviour Jesus Christ, for the remission of sins, and for eternal life.

And when the Deacon hath communicated, the Priest saith,

Behold, this hath touched thy lips.

Then the Deacon, taking the holy disk, and holding it over the holy Chalice, wipes it thoroughly with the holy sponge; and with care and reverence covers it with the veil. In like manner he covers the disk with the asterisk, and that with its veil.

The Priest saith the prayer of Thanksgiving.

We yield Thee thanks, O Lord and Lover of men,

Benefactor of our souls, that Thou hast this day thought us worthy of Thy heavenly and immortal mysteries. Rightly divide our path, confirm us all in Thy fear, guard our life, make safe our goings: through the prayers and supplications of the glorious Mother of GOD and Ever-Virgin Mary, and all Thy Saints.

(²⁶) *And thus they open the doors of the holy Bema; and the Deacon, having made one adoration, takes the Chalice with reverence, and goes to the door, and raising the holy Chalice, shews it to the people, saying,* Approach with the fear of GOD, faith and love.

They who are to communicate draw near with all reverence, and hold their arms crossed on their breast; and the Priest, as he distributes the mysteries to each, saith,

N. the servant of GOD is made partaker of the pure and holy Body and Blood of our LORD and GOD and SAVIOUR JESUS CHRIST, for the remission of his sins, and life everlasting.

Then the Priest blesseth the people, saying aloud,

O GOD, save Thy people, and bless Thine heritage.

(²⁶) From the Communion to the end of the office, all the Liturgies, except that of S. Chrysostom and the Armenian, where we have the rubrics in full, become almost inextricably confused; but most of all that of S. James. Three different stages have, however, to be distinguished: 1. The return of the Priest to the Altar; 2. His going thence to the prothesis, which in some of the Liturgies precedes, in others follows, the dismissal; 3. His return to the Altar, the gift of the antidoron, and the disrobing, which in the Constantinopolitan family is done before the dismissal: to which S. James adds, 4. The prayer said as he final'y goes to the sacristy.

The Deacon and the Priest return to the holy Table, and the Priest censeth thrice: saying secretly,

Be Thou exalted, LORD, above the heavens: and Thy glory above all the earth.

Then, taking the holy disk, he puts it upon the head of the Deacon, and the Deacon taking it with reverence, and looking out towards the door, goes in silence to the prothesis, and puts it down: and the Priest having made obeisance, takes the holy Chalice, and turns towards the doors, saying secretly,

Blessed be our GOD: (*then aloud,*) always, now and ever, and to ages of ages.

And the Deacon having come out, and standing in the accustomed place, saith,

Standing upright, and having partaken of the divine, holy, spotless, immortal, heavenly, life-giving, and terrible mysteries of CHRIST, let us worthily give thanks to the LORD.

Assist, preserve.

That we may pass this whole day.

Exclamation. For Thou art our sanctification, and to Thee we ascribe glory, FATHER, SON, and HOLY GHOST, now and ever, and to ages of ages.

Choir. Amen.

Priest. Let us go on in peace.

Deacon. Let us make our supplications to the LORD.

Prayer behind the ambon, ([27]*) said aloud by the Priest without the bema.*

LORD, Who blessest them that bless Thee, and sanctifiest them that put their trust in Thee, save

---

([27]) This means behind the ambon as respects the bema: that is, before it as regards the people.

Thy people, and bless Thine inheritance: guard
with care the fulness of Thy Church: hallow those
that love the beauty of Thine house.   Glorify them
in return by Thy divine might, and forsake not
them that put their trust in Thee; give Thy peace
to Thy world, to Thy Churches, to our *Priests* and
Kings: to the army, and to all Thy people; because
every good gift and every perfect gift is from above,
and cometh down from Thee, the Father of lights:
and to Thee we ascribe.

*This being ended, the Priest goes through the holy
doors, and departs into the prothesis, and saith this
Prayer.*

Thou, O CHRIST our God, Who art Thyself the
fulness of the Law and of the *Prophets*, Who didst
accomplish all the dispensation of Thy Father, fill
our hearts with joy and gladness always, now and
ever, and to ages of ages.   Amen.

· *Deacon.* Let us make our supplication to the
LORD.

Priest. The blessing of the LORD upon you. *Then,*
Glory to Thee, our GOD : Glory to Thee.

People. Glory.   Both now.

*Then the Deacon, also going through the north part,
gathers together the Holy Things, with fear and all
safety : so that not the very smallest particle should fall
out, or be left: and he washes his hands in the accustomed place.   And the Priest goes forth, and gives the
antidoron* ([28]) *to the people.   Then he goes into the holy*

([28]) The Antidoron is the bread which has been offered for
the service of the Altar, but which has not been required for
consecration : it in some respects resembles the *pain béni* of
most of the French rites.   It is not so very unusual a thing in
Russia that those monks who practise the most regular asceticism, should take no other food during Lent, except the
Antidoron.

bema, and puts off his priestly vestments, saying, Nunc dimittis, *the* Trisagion, *and the other things. Then he saith the dismissory prayer of S. Chrysostom.*

The grace of Thy lips, shining forth like a torch, illuminated the world, enriched the universe with the treasures of liberality, and manifested to us the height of humility: but do thou, our instructor by thy words, Father John Chrysostom, intercede to the WORD, CHRIST our GOD, that our souls may be saved.

LORD, have mercy, (*twelve times.*)

Glory. Both now.

Thee, the more honourable than the Cherubim.

And he makes the dismission: and having adored, and given thanks to God for all things, ([29]) *he departs.*

([29]) This expression is taken from the favourite exclamation of S. John Chrysostom—the last words which he spoke—"Glory be to GOD for all things."

THE DIVINE LITURGY

OF OUR FATHER AMONG THE SAINTS,

Basil the Great.

Prayer for the Catechumens before the Holy Oblation, which the Priest utters secretly.

O LORD our GOD, Who dwellest in the highest, and lookest upon all Thy works; look upon Thy servants the Catechumens, who have bowed down their necks before Thee, and grant them the easy yoke: make them worthy members of Thy holy Church, and fit them for the laver of regeneration, the forgiveness of sins, and the garment of incorruption, unto the knowledge of Thee, our Very GOD.

Exclamation.

That they with us may glorify, etc., *as in Liturgy of S. Chrysostom.*

First Prayer of the Faithful after the Corporal is unfolded, which the Priest utters secretly.

Thou, O LORD, hast disclosed to us the great mystery of salvation; Thou hast counted us, Thy humble and unworthy servants, worthy to be ministers of Thy holy Altar, do Thou make us, by the power of the HOLY GHOST, fit for this office, that standing uncondemned before Thy holy glory, we may present unto Thee the sacrifice of praise. For Thou art He that workest all things in all men; grant, O LORD, that our sacrifice may be acceptable and well-pleasing in Thy sight, for our own sins, and for the ignorances of Thy people.

When the Priest has said the prayer, the Deacon recites the petition for Peace, if appointed, outside the holy Bema.

Again and again. Assist, preserve. Making mention of the all-holy, immaculate.

Deacon.—Wisdom.

The Priest (aloud).—For thee befits all glory, honour, and adoration, the FATHER, the SON, and the HOLY GHOST, now and ever, and to all ages of ages. Amen.

Second Prayer of the Faithful, which the Priest utters secretly.

O GOD, Who lookest in pity and compassion on our lowliness, Who hast set us, Thy lowly and sinful and unworthy servants, before Thy holy glory, to minister at Thy holy Altar, do Thou strengthen us by the might of Thy HOLY SPIRIT for this office, and give us a word in the opening of our mouth, to invoke the grace of Thy HOLY SPIRIT upon the gifts about to be set before Thee.

Prayer of the Offertory, after the deposition of the divine Gifts upon the Holy Table, which the Priest utters secretly.

O LORD our GOD, Who hast created us, and brought us into this life, Who hast shewn us ways unto salvation, Who hast graciously bestowed on us the revelation of heavenly mysteries; Thou art He Who hath appointed us unto this office, in the power of Thy HOLY SPIRIT. Vouchsafe then, O LORD, that we may be ministers of Thy New Testament, celebrants of Thy holy Mysteries: receive us, according to the multitude of Thy mercy, drawing near to Thy holy Altar, that we may be worthy to offer Thee this reasonable and unbloody sacrifice, for our own sins, and for the ignorances of the people : receiving which at Thy holy and spiritual altar, for a sweet-smelling savour, send down on us in return the grace of Thy HOLY SPIRIT. Regard us, O GOD, and look upon this our service, and accept it, as Thou didst accept the gifts of Abel, the sacrifices of Noah, the whole burnt-offerings of Abraham, the priestly ministrations of Moses and Aaron, the peace-offerings of Samuel, as Thou didst accept this true service from Thy holy Apostles, so accept these Gifts in Thy goodness, O LORD, from the hands of us sinners, that, counted worthy to minister blamelessly at Thy holy Altar, we may find the reward of faithful and wise stewards, in the dreadful day of Thy just retribution.

The Priest aloud.

The grace of our LORD JESUS CHRIST, and the love of GOD the FATHER, and the fellowship of the HOLY GHOST, be with you all.

Choir. And with thy spirit.

Priest. Let us lift up our hearts.

Choir. We lift them up unto the LORD.

Priest. Let us give thanks unto the LORD.

Choir. It is meet and right to worship the FATHER, SON, and HOLY GHOST, consubstantial and undivided Trinity.

The Priest, bending down, prays secretly.

JEHOVAH, MASTER, LORD, GOD, FATHER ALMIGHTY, adored : it is truly meet, and right, and befitting the majesty of Thy holiness, to praise Thee, hymn Thee, bless Thee, worship Thee, give thanks to Thee, glorify Thee, the one only GOD, and to offer Thee this our reasonable service in a contrite heart

K

and a spirit of lowliness : for Thou art He Who hath
vouchsafed unto us the knowledge of Thy truth.
And who is sufficient to express Thy noble acts, or
make all Thy praises to be heard, or to tell of all
Thy wondrous works at every time ?   Master of all
things, Lord of heaven and earth, and of every
creature visible and invisible, Who sittest upon the
throne of glory, and beholdest the abysses, unbeginning, invisible, incomprehensible, uncircumscript,
unchangeable FATHER of our LORD JESUS CHRIST the
great GOD and Saviour of our hope, Who is the image
of Thy goodness, seal of equal type, manifesting in
Himself Thee the FATHER, Living Word, Very
GOD before the worlds, Wisdom, Life, Sanctification,
Power, Very Light, by Whom the HOLY GHOST was
disclosed, the Spirit of truth, the grace of adoption,
the earnest of future inheritance, the first-fruits of
eternal blessings, the quickening might, the fount of
sanctification, by Whom every reasonable and
spiritual creature empowered serveth Thee and
sends up to Thee the everlasting doxology, for all
things are Thy servants.   For the angels, archangels, thrones, principalities, powers, dominations,
virtues, and many-eyed cherubim praise Thee, and
the seraphim stand around Thee, the one having
six wings, and the other having six wings, and with
two cover their faces and with two their feet, with
two they do fly, and shout one to the other with unceasing mouths, with unsilenced doxologies,

The Priest, aloud.

Singing, crying, shouting, and saying the triumphal
hymn :
Choir. Holy, holy, holy, LORD GOD of Hosts,
Heaven and earth are full of Thy glory.   Hosanna

in the highest. Blessed is He that cometh in the Name of the LORD. Hosanna in the highest.

Then the Deacon does the same as is set down in the Liturgy of Chrysostom, and the Priest prays secretly :

With the blessed *Powers*, O loving Master, we sinners also cry and say, Holy art Thou, of a truth, and All-holy, and there is no measure for the majesty of Thy holiness, and Thou art sacred in all Thy works, because in righteousness of true judgment Thou hast done all things unto us ; for having formed man, taking clay from the earth, and honouring him, O GOD, with Thine own image, Thou didst place him in the *Paradise* of pleasure, promising him immortality of life and enjoyment of eternal blessings in the keeping of Thy commandments, but when he disobeyed Thee the Very GOD, his Creator, and was led away by the guile of the serpent, and died in his own transgressions, Thou didst drive him forth in Thy righteous judgment, O GOD, from *Paradise* into this world, and madest him return to the earth whence he was taken, providing for him the salvation which is of regeneration, which is in Him Thine Anointed. For Thou didst not turn away utterly from Thy creature which Thou madest, O Good One, nor didst forget the work of Thy hands, but didst visit it in many ways through the bowels of Thy mercy. Thou didst send out prophets ; Thou wroughtest mighty things through Thy Saints who pleased Thee in each generation. Thou spakest unto us by the mouth of Thy servants the *Prophets*, foretelling us the future salvation ; Thou gavest the Law for an help ; Thou appointedst Angels as guardians. And when the fulness of the times was come, Thou spakest unto us in Thy SON Himself, by Whom Thou madest

K 2

the worlds. Who being the brightness of Thy glory, and the express image of Thy Person, and upholding all things by the word of His power, thought it not robbery to be equal to Thee, His GOD and FATHER, but being GOD before the worlds, was seen upon earth, and mingled with men, and incarnate of a holy Virgin, emptied Himself, taking the form of a servant, made like to the body of our humility, that He might make us like unto the image of His glory. For whereas sin entered into the world by man, and death by sin, Thine Only-Begotten Son, Who is in the bosom of Thee, GOD and FATHER, born of a woman, the holy Mother of GOD and ever-Virgin Mary, born under the Law, was pleased to condemn sin in His Flesh ; that they who died in Adam might be made alive in Him Thy CHRIST, and dwelling as a citizen in this world, giving us statutes of salvation, and withdrawing us from the error of idolatry, He brought us unto the knowledge of Thee, Very GOD and FATHER, having acquired us for Himself a peculiar people, a royal priesthood, a holy nation, and having cleansed us in water, and hallowed us with the HOLY GHOST, He gave Himself a ransom unto death, wherein we were held, sold under sin, and passing by the Cross into Hades, that He might fill all things with Himself, He loosed the pains of death, and arising the third day, and having made with His flesh a way for the resurrection of the dead, because it was not possible that the Prince of Life should be overcome of corruption, He became the first-fruits of them that slept, the first-born from the dead, that He might have the pre-eminence in all things over all men, and ascending to the Heavens, he sat down on the right hand of Thy Majesty in the highest. And He shall come again to reward every man according to his works, and

He hath left us as a memorial of His saving *Passion* these things, which we have presented according to His commandments ; for when He was about to go to His voluntary, and famous, and quickening death, in the night when He gave up Himself for the life of the world, taking bread into His holy and spotless hands, having shewn it to Thee, His GOD and FATHER, having given thanks, blessed, hallowed, broken it,

The Priest, lifting the holy Paten with his right hand, shews it, saying aloud,

He gave it to His holy *Disciples* and Apostles, saying : Take, eat : this is My Body which is broken for you, for the remission of sins.

The Choir chants. Amen.

Then the Priest and the Deacon do exactly as in the Liturgy of Chrysostom.

The Priest, secretly.

Likewise taking the Chalice of the fruit of the vine, having mingled, given thanks, blessed, hallowed it,

And lifting the holy Chalice in like manner reverently with his right hand, he shews it, saying aloud,

He gave it to His holy *Disciples* and Apostles, saying, *Drink* ye all of it, for this is My Blood of the New Testament, which is shed for you and for many, for the remission of sins.

The Choir chants. Amen.

The Priest, bowing his head, prays secretly :

Do this in remembrance of Me. For as often as ye shall eat this Bread, and drink this Cup, ye declare My *Death*, and confess My Resurrection. Therefore, we also, O Master, remembering this saving *Passion*, the quickening Cross, the three days' Burial, the Resurrection from the dead, the Ascension to the heavens, the Session on Thy Right Hand, GOD and FATHER, and His glorious and terrible second Coming,

The Priest, aloud.

Offer Thee Thine own of Thine own, according to all, and through all. (¹)

The Choir chants. We hymn Thee, we bless Thee, we give thanks to Thee, O LORD, and beseech Thee, our GOD.

The Priest bowing his head, prays secretly.

Therefore, All-holy Master, we also, Thy sinful and unworthy servants, who have been counted worthy to minister at Thy holy Altar, not through our own righteousness, (for we have done no good thing upon the earth) but through Thy mercies and compassions, which Thou hast richly poured upon us, have courage to draw near to Thy holy Altar, and presenting the antitypes of the holy Body and Blood of Thy CHRIST, we beseech Thee, and invoke Thee, Holy of Holies, through the good-will of Thy

---

(¹) Κατὰ πάντα, καὶ διὰ πάντα. This is obscure, but from the immediate sequence of the hymn of the Choir, I think the words belong to it, rather than to the words of oblation, and that we may supply χρόνον to the first πάντα, and χώρια to the second. The whole will then run thus: *Priest.* At all times and in all places. *Choir.* We hymn Thee, &c. L.

(²) This word is not peculiar to S. Basil. It is found in this same sense, applied to the visible species of Bread and Wine, in S. Macarius, Hom. xxviii., S. Greg. Nazianz. Orat. xi., Germanus, Theor. Eccles.; Theodoret, Dialog. ii., and in the Apostolical Constitutions, v. 13. S. John Damascene and Mark of Ephesus both agree that the phrase is used only *before* consecration, just as Westerns similarly use the word *elements*, but not afterwards. But this is hardly borne out by

bounty, that Thy HOLY GHOST may come upon us, and on these Gifts lying before Thee, and bless, and hallow, and shew. (³)

The Deacon lays aside the fan which he was holding, or the veil, and comes nearer to the Priest, and both adore thrice before the holy Table, praying moreover to themselves.

GOD be merciful to me a sinner. *They say it secretly thrice.*

Then,

O LORD, Who at the third hour didst send down Thine All-holy SPIRIT on the Apostles, take Him not, O good One, away from us.

Versicle. Make me a clean heart, O GOD, and renew a right spirit within me. Glory, &c.

---

the language of the Fathers generally, as for example, Tertullian and S. Augustine, who use the term *figura* of the consecrated species. The true explanation seems to be that the visible Body and Blood of CHRIST is called the τύπος, or seal, bearing the Image of GOD, and the consecrated species the ἀντίτυπον, impressed by the power of that seal, brought upon them by the HOLY GHOST, and yet not locally nor numerically commensurate (as S. Thomas Aquinas points out) with CHRIST's visible human form, though mystically identical with it.—L.

(³) ἀναδεῖξαι. The Latin copies add here directly, " this Bread to be the precious Body of our LORD and GOD and SAVIOUR JESUS CHRIST, and that which is in this Chalice the very Blood of our LORD GOD and SAVIOUR JESUS CHRIST, which was shed for the life of the world." And as Mark of Ephesus actually cites these words in Greek as found in S. Basil, it seems that they have either dropped out here through the carelessness of copyists, or, as is more probable, that the passages which precede them are later interpolations. The verb ἀναδεικνύω does not merely mean *to shew*, but *to make or constitute* something, giving it a character which it had not before, and is so used more than once by the LXX.—L.

Blessed art Thou, CHRIST our GOD, &c., (*as in S. Chrysostom*, p. 96.)

Now and ever, &c. When the Highest, descending, &c.

Then the Deacon, bowing his head, points to the holy Bread with his stole, and says secretly,

Sir, bless the holy Bread.

And the Priest, standing up, signs the holy Gifts, saying secretly,

This bread to be the precious Body Itself of our LORD, and GOD, and Saviour JESUS CHRIST.

Deacon. Amen. *And then again,* Sir, bless the holy Chalice.

And the Priest, blessing, says,

And this Chalice, the Precious Blood Itself of our LORD, and GOD, and SAVIOUR JESUS CHRIST.

Deacon. Amen.

Priest. Which was shed for the life of the world.

Deacon. Amen. *And again, pointing with his stole to both the Holy Things, he says,*

Sir, bless both.

And the Priest, blessing both the Holy Things with his hand, says,

Changing them by Thy HOLY SPIRIT.

Deacon. Amen, Amen, Amen.

And the Deacon, bowing his head to the Priest, and saying, Remember, O Holy Master, me a sinner, *shifts to his former position, taking up the fan again, as before.*

Priest. That Thou wouldest unite all of us, who are partakers of the One Bread, and of the Chalice, to one another unto the fellowship of one HOLY

Spirit, and not cause any of us to partake of the holy Body and Blood of Thy Christ unto judgment or condemnation, but that we may find mercy and grace with all Thy Saints, who have pleased Thee from [the beginning of] the world, Forefathers, Fathers, Patriarchs, Prophets, Apostles, Heralds, Evangelists, Martyrs, Confessors, Teachers, and every just spirit, perfected in faith. (*Aloud.*) Especially of our all-holy, immaculate, supereminently blessed, glorious Lady, the Mother of God, and ever-Virgin Mary.

The Choir chants. The whole creation [*as in Liturgy of S. James,* p. 54.] *But if it be Maundy Thursday, they chant, to the second oblique tone,* (⁴)

O Son of God, receive me to-day as a guest at Thy mystic Supper, for I will not disclose Thy mystery to Thy foes. I will not give Thee a kiss, like Judas, but like the thief. I confess to Thee. Remember me, O Lord, in Thy Kingdom.

If it be Holy Saturday, they sing the troparion to the first oblique tone. (⁵)

Let all mortal flesh be silent, &c., (*as in Liturgy of S. James,* p. 38.)

The Deacon censes the Holy Table round about, and commemorates the Diptychs of both the living and the sleeping, whomsoever he will.

The Priest prays secretly. [*Commemorating*] Saint John, Forerunner and Baptist, the holy and all-celebrated Apostles, Saint N. whose memorial we observe, and all Thy Saints, through whose intercession look upon us, O God. And remember all

---

(⁴) The Fourth Gregorian Tone of the Western Church.
(⁵ Second Gregorian Tone.

who have fallen asleep in the hope of resurrection unto life eternal.

Then the Priest commemorates whom he will, living and dead. And for the living he saith,

For salvation, visitation, remission of sins of the servant of GOD, N.

And for the dead, he saith,

For repose, and remission of the soul of Thy servant N. in a place of light, where sorrow and sighing are put away. Give him rest, O our GOD.

Then this prayer, secretly.

And give them rest, where the light of Thy countenance looketh upon them. Further we beseech Thee, O LORD, remember Thy holy Catholic and Apostolic Church, from one end of the world unto the other, and give peace unto it, which Thou hast purchased with the precious Blood of Thy CHRIST, and strengthen this holy House until the consummation of the world. Remember, O LORD, them who have offered their holy gifts unto Thee, and them for whom, and through whom, or for what ends they have offered them. Remember, O LORD, them who bring forth fruit, and do good works in Thy holy Churches, and who remember the poor. Recompense them with Thy rich and heavenly graces. Vouchsafe them things heavenly for things earthly, eternal for temporal, incorruptible for corruptible things. Remember, O LORD, those in deserts, and mountains, and dens, and caves of the earth. Remember, O LORD, them who live in virginity, and piety, and discipline, and holy conversation. Remember, O LORD, our most pious and faithful Sovereigns, whom Thou hast given the right to reign over the earth. Crown them with the shield of truth, the shield of good will, ([6]) over-shadow their head in the day of battle, strengthen their arm ; uplift their right hand, stablish their kingdom; put all barbarous nations, which desire war, under them, vouchsafe them profound and inviolate peace ; speak good things unto their heart for Thy Church and all Thy people, that we may spend during their calm time, a quiet and tranquil life in all piety and holiness. Remember, O LORD, every magistracy and authority, and our brethren in the palace, and all the army. Preserve the good in Thy goodness, and make the evil good in Thy bounty. Remember, O LORD, the people which stand around, and those who are absent for reasonable causes, and have mercy on them and us, according to the multitude of Thy mercy. Fill their stores with every good thing, keep their unions in peace and concord, rear up the infants, guide the youth, strengthen the old, comfort the timid, collect the scattered, bring back the erring, and unite them to Thy holy Catholic and Apostolic Church. Free those troubled by unclean spirits ; sail together with them that sail; journey with travellers, stand before the widows, shield the orphans, deliver the captives, heal the sick. Remember, O GOD, them that are in trials, and banishments, and all tribulation, and ne-cessity, and distress, and all them that need Thy great loving-kindness, and them which love us, and which hate us, and those who have enjoined us, unworthy as we are, to pray for them. And, O LORD our GOD, remember all Thy people, and pour out on all men Thy rich mercy, granting to all their petitions unto salvation. And them whom we, through ignorance, or forgetfulness, or the number of

([6]) Psalm v. **13.** LXX. and Vulgate.

names, have not remembered, do Thou, O GOD, remember them, Who knowest the age and the name of each one, Who knowest each from his mother's womb. For Thou, O GOD, art the Help of the helpless, the Hope of the hopeless, the Saviour of the tempest-tost, the Harbour of mariners, the Physician of the sick.   Be Thou Thyself all things to all men, Who knowest each, and his petition, his dwelling, and his need.   Deliver, O LORD, this city, and every city and country, from famine, pestilence, earthquake, inundation, fire, sword, incursion of foreigners, and from civil war. (*Aloud.*) In the first place, remember, O LORD, our Archbishop N., whom vouchsafe to Thy holy Churches in peace, safe, honoured, healthful, long-lived, and rightly dividing the word of truth.

And the Deacon, standing by the door, saith,

For the most sacred Metropolitan, *or* Bishop, N., and for him who presents these holy gifts, etc., *as far as* And of all Thy servants and handmaids.

The Choir chants. And of all Thy servants and handmaids.

Priest, (*secretly.*) Remember, O LORD, every see of the orthodox, who rightly divide the word of Thy truth.   Remember, O LORD, according to the multitude of Thy compassions and of my unworthiness; forgive me every offence voluntary and involuntary, and withdraw not the grace of Thy HOLY SPIRIT from the Gifts lying before Thee, because of my sins.   Remember, O LORD, the Presbytery, the Diaconate in CHRIST, and every priestly order, and make none of us ashamed who compass Thy holy Altar.   Visit us in Thy bounty, O LORD, be manifest unto us in Thy rich compassions, vouchsafe us temperate and wholesome weather, bestow showers on the earth for the produce of fruit, bless the crown of the year of Thy goodness, quiet the schisms of the Churches, quench the boastings of the nations, quickly destroy the uprisings of heresies, by the power of Thy HOLY SPIRIT; receiving us all into Thy kingdom, making us children of light, and children of the day. Vouchsafe us Thy peace and Thy love, O LORD our GOD, for Thou hast given us all things. (*Aloud.*) And grant us with one mouth and one heart to glorify and praise Thine all-honoured and majestic Name, of the FATHER, and of the SON, and of the HOLY GHOST, now and ever, and to ages of ages.

The Priest turns to the door, and blessing, saith aloud,

And the mercies of the great GOD and our Saviour JESUS CHRIST, shall be with us all.

And the Deacon (if he be present, otherwise, the Priest) goes forth, and standing in the usual place, saith,

Making mention of all the Saints. Again and again in peace, let us beseech the LORD.

Choir. LORD, have mercy.

And so on, as in the Liturgy of Chrysostom.

For the precious Gifts offered and hallowed.
That our loving GOD.
That we may be delivered.
Priest, (*secretly.*) O our GOD, GOD of salvation, teach us Thyself to give Thee worthy thanks for Thy benefits, which Thou hast done, and still doest amongst us. *Do* Thou, our GOD, Who acceptest these Gifts, purify us from every pollution of flesh and spirit, and teach us to maintain perfect holiness

in Thy fear, that receiving in the pure witness of our conscience the portion of Thy hallowed things, we may be united to the holy Body and Blood of Thy CHRIST, and receiving them worthily, we may have CHRIST dwelling in our hearts, and become the temple of Thy HOLY SPIRIT. Yea, O our GOD, and make none of us guilty of these awful and heavenly mysteries, nor weak in soul and body from partaking of them unworthily; but grant us unto our last breath worthily to receive the portion of Thy hallowed things, as the viaticum of life everlasting, as an acceptable plea at the terrible Judgment-seat of Thy CHRIST, that we also, with all Thy Saints, who have pleased Thee from [the beginning of] the world, may become partakers of Thine everlasting good things, which Thou hast prepared, O LORD, for them that love Thee.

Deacon.

Assist, save, have mercy, &c.

That we may pass all this day.

The angel of peace, a faithful guide.

Pardon and remission.

What are good and profitable to our souls.

That we may pass the remainder of our time.

That the ends of our life may be Christian.

Asking for the unity of the Faith, and the fellowship of the HOLY SPIRIT, let us present ourselves and one another, and all our life to CHRIST our LORD.

Priest, (*aloud.*) And count us worthy, O Master, boldly to venture, uncondemned, to call on Thee our heavenly GOD and FATHER, and to say,

People. Our FATHER, &c.

Priest. For Thine is the Kingdom, &c. *Then,* Peace to all.

Deacon. **Let** us bow down our heads unto the LORD.

Priest. **Master**, LORD, FATHER of compassions, and GOD of all consolation, bless, hallow, strengthen, stablish them who have bowed down their heads unto Thee, withdraw them from every evil deed, unite them to every good deed, and make them worthy to partake uncondemned of these Thy spotless and quickening mysteries, for the remission of sins, for the fellowship of the HOLY GHOST. (*Aloud.*) Through the grace, and compassion, and loving-kindness of Thine Only-Begotten SON, with Whom Thou art blessed, together with Thine all-holy, and good, and quickening SPIRIT, now and ever, and to ages of ages. Amen.

Priest. Advance, O LORD JESUS CHRIST, our GOD, from Thy holy dwelling-place, and from the throne of the glory of Thy kingdom, and come to hallow us, Who sittest on high with the FATHER, and art here invisibly present with us, and deign with Thy mighty Hand to give us a share in Thy spotless Body and Precious Blood, and by us to all the people. (*Aloud.*)

Deacon. Let us attend.

Priest. HOLY THINGS FOR HOLY PERSONS.

When the Communion is ended, and the holy Mysteries have been taken from the sacred Table, the Priest prays.

We give thanks to Thee, O LORD our GOD, for the reception of Thy holy, spotless, immortal, and heavenly mysteries, which Thou hast given us for the benefit and sanctification and healing of our souls and bodies. .Thyself, O Master of all things, grant that the Communion of the holy Body and Blood of Thy CHRIST may be to us unto faith that maketh not ashamed, unto love unfeigned unto fulness of wisdom, unto healing of soul and body, unto defeat of every foe, unto fulfilment of Thy commandments, unto an acceptable plea at the terrible judgment-seat of Thy CHRIST.

Deacon. Rightly partaking of the divine, holy, spotless, immortal, heavenly, and quickening mysteries.

Assist, preserve, have mercy, &c.

Priest, (*aloud.*) For Thou art our sanctification, and unto Thee we ascribe the glory, FATHER, SON, and HOLY GHOST, now and ever, and to ages of ages. Amen.

Priest. Let us go forth in peace.

Deacon. Let us beseech the LORD

Prayer behind the Ambon, pronounced by the Priest.

O LORD, Who blessest them that bless Thee, and hallowest them that trust in Thee, save Thy people and bless Thine inheritance; guard the fulness of Thy Church, hallow them that love the beauty of Thine house; give them a glorious reward through Thy divine power, and leave us not, who hope in Thee. Grant peace unto Thy world, to Thy Churches, to the Priests, to our sovereigns, to the army, and to all Thy people, because every good gift, and every perfect gift is from above, coming down from Thee, the FATHER of lights; and to Thee we ascribe the glory, and thanksgiving, and adoration, FATHER, SON, and HOLY GHOST, now and ever, and to ages of ages.

Prayer while the Holy Things are put away.

The Mystery of Thy dispensation, O CHRIST our GOD, is accomplished and perfected, so far as lies in our power. For we have the memorial of Thy death, we have seen the figure of Thy resurrection, we have been filled with Thine unending life. We have enjoyed Thine inexhaustible pleasure, of which vouchsafe to count us all worthy in the world to come. Through the grace of Thine unbeginning FATHER, and Thy holy, and good, and quickening SPIRIT, now and ever, and to ages of ages. Amen.

THE LITURGY

𝔐alabar.

The Priest advances with the Deacon to the Altar.

Priest. Glory to God in the highest.

Deacon. Amen.

Priest. Glory to God in the highest.

Deacon. Amen.

Priest and Deacon. And on earth peace, and a good hope to men. Our FATHER, Which art in heaven, hallowed be Thy Name: Holy, Holy, Holy: Our FATHER, Which art in heaven, heaven and earth are full of the majesty of Thy glory, and Angels and men exclaim to Thee, Holy, Holy, Holy. Our FATHER, Which art in heaven, hallowed be Thy Name: Thy kingdom come: Thy will be done in earth as it is in heaven: Give us this day the bread of our necessity: And forgive us our sins, as we also forgive our debtors: And lead us not into temptation, but deliver us from evil: for Thine is the kingdom, and the power and the glory, for ever and ever. Amen.

Priest. Strengthen, O LORD GOD, our infirmity by Thy mercy, that we may minister in Thy holy Sacraments, given for the salvation and renewal of our nature, through the love of Thy most dearly beloved SON, O LORD of all things, FATHER, SON, and HOLY GHOST.

Deacon. Amen.

Priest. Adored and glorified, honoured and exalted, landed and blessed in heaven and in earth, be the glorious Name of Thy most resplendent TRINITY, at all times, O LORD of all things, FATHER, SON, and HOLY GHOST.

Deacon. Amen.

The Priest and Deacon say alternately Psalms **15**, **150**, and **117**.

Priest. Glory be to the FATHER, and to the SON, and to the HOLY GHOST, from ages to ages. Amen and Amen.

Deacon. Set me, O LORD, with pure thoughts before Thy altar.

Priest. LORD, who shall dwell in Thy tabernacle, and who shall rest upon Thy holy hill? How glorious and lovely is Thy sanctuary, GOD, the Sanctifier of all things.

Deacon. Peace be with us.

Priest. Before the exceeding glorious throne of Thy Majesty, my LORD, and the lofty and supreme seat of Thy domination, and the Altar of expiation, which Thy will hath fixed in the place of the habitation of Thy glory, we Thy people, and the sheep of Thy pasture, with the thousands of Seraphim that praise Thee, and the ten thousands of Angels and Archangels that minister to Thee, bend our knees before Thee, and ever adore and glorify FATHER, SON, and HOLY GHOST, to ages of ages.

To the Name of Thy ever-glorious TRINITY, great, formidable, holy, laudable and incomprehensible; also to Thy mercy which Thou hast manifested towards our race, we are bound to return continual thanks, and to attribute laud and adoration; O LORD of all things, FATHER, SON, and HOLY GHOST.

R. Amen.

Priest. Thee, the LORD of all things, we praise:

Thee, JESUS CHRIST, we glorify; because Thou art
the raiser up of our bodies, and the most holy
Saviour of our souls; I have washed my hands in
innocency, O LORD, and have compassed Thine
altar.

Deacon. Thee, the LORD of all things. (*As the
Priest, who then repeats it again.*)

Deacon. Peace be with us all.

Priest. Thou art truly my LORD, and the raiser up
of our bodies, and the good Saviour of our souls,
and the constant Keeper of our life : and it is meet
that we should laud and glorify Thee at all times,
FATHER, SON, and HOLY GHOST.

Deacon. Amen.

Priest. LORD, our GOD, when the most sweet odour
of Thy goodness and love shall breathe upon us,
and when our souls shall have been enlightened
with the splendour of Thy truth, then we shall
meet Thy most beloved SON Who shall be revealed
from heaven, and in Thy Church, already honoured
with the crown, shall praise Thee incessantly, for
Thou art the LORD and Creator of all things, FATHER,
SON, and HOLY GHOST.

Deacon. Amen. Bring your voices, and praise, O
all ye people, the Living GOD.

Priest. Holy GOD, Holy and Mighty, Holy and
Immortal, have mercy upon us. Glory be to the
FATHER, and to the SON, and to the HOLY GHOST.

Deacon. Holy GOD, Holy and Mighty, Holy and
Immortal, have mercy upon us.

Priest. From everlasting to everlasting. Amen
and Amen.

Deacon. Holy GOD, &c.

Priest, turning to the people. Let us all stand in
order, and with joy and gladness let us seek and
say,

People. O our Lord, have mercy upon us. (*And so at the end of every petition.* (¹)

Deacon. Father of mercies and God of all Consolation, we beseech Thee.

Our Saviour, the *D*ispenser of our salvation, and the Captain of all things, we, &c.

For the peace and unity and well-being of the whole world, and of all Churches :

For the healthfulness of the air, the richness of year and its provisions, and the beauty of the whole world :

For our holy Fathers, our *P*atriarch, the universal *P*astor of the whole Catholic Church ; and our Bishop, that they may enjoy good health :

The merciful God Who governeth all things by His love :

Him That is rich in mercy and Whose loving-kindness is shed abroad :

Him That is good in His Essence, and the Giver of all gifts :

Him that is glorious in heaven, and exceeding laudable upon earth :

The Immortal Nature That inhabits that most glorious light, we beseech :

Save us all, O Christ, our Lord and God, by Thy grace, and multiply in us peace and love, and have mercy upon us.

Let us pray and beseech the Lord, the God of all, that He may hear the voice of our prayers, and listen to our supplications, and have mercy upon us.

Let us pray also for the holy Catholic Church, which is spread over the whole orb of the world,

---

(¹) This manifestly answers to the first Ectene in the preceding Liturgies, although the form differs considerably.

that the peace which is from GOD may remain in it
till the consummation of all things :

Let us pray also for the holy Fathers, our Bishops,
that without blemish and complaint they may
remain all the days of their life in the government
of their Churches : but chiefly we are bound to pray
for the safety of the Lord Patriarch, the *Pastor* of
the whole Church, and the Lord Bishop of this Me-
tropolis : let us pray that the LORD may keep them
and preserve them at the head of their flocks, that
they may feed and govern and prepare for the LORD
a perfect people, zealous of all good works.

Let us pray also for the *Presbyters* and *Deacons*
who are occupied in the ministry of the truth ;
that with a good heart and a pure conscience they
may accomplish their ministry before GOD.

Let us pray also for every holy and sober congregation of the sons of the holy Catholic Church, that
they may accomplish the most excellent course of
sanctity, and may receive the hope and promise of
the LORD in the land of the Living.

Let us commemorate the most blessed Virgin
Mary, the Mother (²) of CHRIST and our Saviour.

Let us pray that the HOLY GHOST, Who dwelt in
her, may sanctify us by His grace, and accomplish
His will in us, and sign His truth in us, all the
days of our life.

Let us venerate the memory of *Prophets*, Apostles,
Martyrs, and Confessors : let us pray that by their
prayers and the passions which they endured, GOD
may give to us with them a good hope and salva-

(²) *Mother of* CHRIST.   Notice here the Nestorian heresy—
Mother of CHRIST, instead of Mother of GOD.   This is one of
the few expressions which was rightly altered at the Synod of
Diamper.

tion; and that we may be made worthy of their blessed commemoration, and their living and true promises in the kingdom of heaven. Let us commemorate also our fathers and the doctors of truth, S. Nestorius, (⁸) S. Diodorus, S. Theodore, S. Ephraim, S. Abraham, S. Narcissus, and all *Doctors* and *Presbyters*, followers after truth. Let us pray that by their prayers, the pure truth and the sincere doctrine which they taught may be preserved in the holy Church till the consummation of the world.

Let us remember also our fathers and our brethren who have departed out of this world in the orthodox faith; let us pray, I say, to the LORD that He may absolve them, and may forgive them their offences, and may vouchsafe that they, with all just and righteous men who have obeyed the *Divine* will, may rejoice for ever and ever.

Also for this province and city, and for them that dwell therein, especially for this congregation; let us pray that the LORD by His grace may turn away from us sword, captivity, rapine, earthquake, famine, pestilence, and other things which are injurious to the soul and the body.

For those also that have departed from the true faith, and are held in captivity by the net of Satan: let us pray that the LORD GOD may convert their hearts, and that they may verily acknowledge GOD the true FATHER, and His SON, JESUS CHRIST, our LORD.

Let us pray also for the sick: and especially for them who are vexed with cruel diseases, and are tried by most evil spirits: we pray that the LORD our GOD may send to them His holy Angel of love

(⁸) The arch-heretic.

and salvation, and may visit and heal and help
them, through the greatness of His grace and
mercy.

Also for the poor, orphans, widows, and afflicted;
and them that suffer persecution: let us pray
that the Lord may govern them by His grace,
and nourish and console them by His pity, and by
His loving-kindness set them free from them that do
violence to them.

Pray and beseech the love of the God of all, that
we may be to Him a kingdom, a priesthood, and a
holy people. Cry to the Lord, the mighty God,
with all your heart, and all your soul, for God is a
tender Father, and merciful and clement, and
willeth not that His handywork should perish, but
rather should be converted and live. But above
all things it is fit and meet that we should pray to,
laud and adore, glory and adore, glory and honour,
and exalt the One God, the Father, the Lord of all,
most worthy of adoration, Who by Christ hath
made to us a good hope and salvation for our souls,
that He may accomplish His grace and love in us
even to the end.

*While the Deacon saith these things, the Priest,
standing in the middle of the Altar, taketh the Paten;
and the Deacon giving incense, and holding the Thurible
with both hands, he censeth it in the form of a Cross,
saying,*

Lord, our God, cause this paten to have a sweet-
smelling savour, after the pattern of Aaron, the
most illustrious Priest in the tabernacle of testi-
mony, Thou That art the Creator and the Lord of
the roots and spices that breathe a sweet odour, in
the Name of the Father, and of the Son, and of
the Holy Ghost. Amen.

Then he censeth the Veil of the Chalice, and saith:

LORD, our GOD, cause this veil to have a sweet savour, after the fashion of the mantle wherewith Elias, the prophet of truth, clothed himself; in the Name.

Then he censeth the Chalice, and saith:

LORD, our GOD, cause this chalice to send forth a sweet smell, after the fashion of Aaron the Priest in the tabernacle of witness, Thou Who art the Creator of roots and spices that breathe forth a sweet odour, in the Name.

Then he poureth wine into the Chalice, and saith:

Let the precious Blood of our LORD JESUS CHRIST be mingled in the chalice. (⁴)

He poureth in water, and saith;

One of the soldiers came, and with a spear pierced the side of our LORD JESUS CHRIST, and forthwith came thereout Blood and Water, and he that saw it bare record, and his record is true.

Again pouring in wine, he saith:

Let water be mingled with wine and wine with water, in the Name of the FATHER, and of the SON, and of the HOLY GHOST. (⁵) *Then he saith:* Expecting I expected the LORD, the Body of CHRIST, and

(⁴) This anticipative calling that which is simple wine, "the Blood of CHRIST," is on a par with the anticipative adoration of the Holy Mysteries at the Great Entrance, common through all the Eastern Church.

(⁵) Here follows, in the modern edition, a long rubric, of the insertion of which no notice is given, but which is evidently taken from the Roman Missal.

His precious Blood on the holy Altar. Let us all offer it with fear and honour, and with the Angels let us exclaim, Holy, Holy, Holy, is our LORD GOD.

Deacon. The poor shall eat and be satisfied with the Body of CHRIST and His precious Blood upon the holy Altar: let us all offer it with fear and honour, and with Angels let us exclaim, Holy, Holy, Holy, is our LORD GOD.

Let us pray.   *Peace* be with us.

Priest (*secretly*). Let glory be offered and immo- lated to Thy ever-glorious TRINITY, for ages of ages: and may CHRIST Who was offered as an oblation for our salvation, and has commanded us that we should sacrifice in memory of His *Passion, Death,* Sepul- ture, and Resurrection, receive this sacrifice from our hands, through His grace and His love, for ever and ever.

He puts the Holy Gifts on the Altar.

Let these exceeding glorious, holy, and life-giving mysteries be constituted and ordained upon the holy Altar of CHRIST, until the glorious Advent from heaven of the Same, to Whom is laud, glory, and adoration now and at all times, and to ages of ages.

(*Aloud.*) Glory be to the FATHER, and to the SON, and to the HOLY GHOST. Be there a commemoration upon the holy Altar of the Virgin Mary, the Mother of CHRIST.

Deacon. From everlasting to everlasting.   Amen and Amen. Apostles of the very SON, friends of the Only-Begotten, pray ye that there may be peace in the creation.

Priest. Let all the people say Amen and Amen. Be Thy commemoration, Apostle Thomas, our holy father, upon the holy Altar, together with the just who have conquered, and the martyrs who have received the crown.

Deacon. The Mighty GOD is with us, our FATHER is with us, our Angel, and our Helper, the GOD of Jacob.

Priest. The little ones, with the elders, behold all the faithful who have fallen on sleep in a good hope, who have paid the debt of humanity. By Thy exceeding glorious resurrection, Thou shalt raise them up to Thy glory. (⁶)

Deacon. Pour forth before him your hearts in prayer, fasting and penitence. They have made propitiation to CHRIST, the FATHER, and His SPIRIT.

The Priest saith, while he covereth the Oblations,

Thou coverest Thyself with light as with a garment, and stretchest out the heavens like a curtain, now and ever, and to ages of ages.

While the Priest washeth his hands the Deacon saith:

By the prayer and supplication of the Angels of peace and of love, we ask,

People. From Thee, O LORD.

Deacon. Night and day, and all the days of our life, we ask for eternal peace to Thy Church, and a life without sins.

People. From Thee, O LORD.

Deacon. Remission of sins, and that which may be profitable to our life, and may appease His *Divinity*, we ask,

---

(⁶) If we compare these versicles and responses with the " GOD is with us," in the Great Apodeipnon of the Constantinopolitan rite, (which we know to be, at the very latest, of the beginning of the fourth century,) we may conclude them in like manner to be of the most remote antiquity.

People. From Thee, O LORD.

Deacon. The mercies of the LORD, and His benignity, ever and at all times we ask,

People. From Thee, O LORD.

Deacon. Ourselves and our souls let us commend
to the FATHER, the SON, and the HOLY GHOST.

People. To Thee, O LORD GOD.

Priest. We pray and beseech Thee, LORD GOD, the
Mighty, perfect in us Thy grace, and by our hands
pour forth Thy gifts and love, and the tender mercy
of Thy *Di*vinity ; and let them be for the propitiation
of the debts of Thy people, and for the remission of
all the sins of the sheep of Thy pasture, which, by
grace and Thy love, Thou hast chosen to Thyself :
of all, O LORD, FATHER, SON, and HOLY GHOST.

Deacon. Amen. Bow down your heads for the
imposition of hands, and receive the blessing.

Priest (secretly). LORD, Mighty GOD, Thine is the
holy Catholic Church, purchased by the wonderful
*Passion of Thy CHRIST : on the sheep of Thy flock,
by the grace of the HOLY GHOST, Who is equal to
Thee in most glorious *Deity, the orders of true priesthood are conferred. Thou, my LORD, by Thy
clemency, hast vouchsafed to the exiguity of the
nature of our misery, that we men should become
glorious members of that mighty body which is the
Catholic Church, and by Thy ministry may confer
on believing souls, spiritual helps. Do Thou therefore, my LORD, accomplish in us Thy grace, and
pour forth by our hands, Thy gifts : let also Thy love
be upon us, and the piety of Thy *Deity upon this
people which Thou hast chosen to Thyself. (*Aloud.*)
Grant also, my LORD, through Thy mercy, that we
all, in all the days of our life, may equally please
Thy *Deity by the best works of righteousness, which
render us acceptable to the glorious will of Thy

Majesty; and that in this manner we may be made worthy of the assistance of Thy grace, that we may ever offer to Thee hymns, honour, laud, and adoration, LORD of all, FATHER, SON, and HOLY GHOST.

[EXPULSION OF THE CATECHUMENS.]

Deacon, Amen. He that hath not received baptism let him depart.

Choir. Amen.

Deacon. He that hath not received the seal of life, let him depart.

Choir. Amen.

Deacon. He that hath not received it, let him depart.

Priest. Go, auditors, (⁷) and see the doors. Let us pray: peace be with us. Illuminate, O LORD our GOD, the motions of our thoughts, that we may listen to and understand the most sweet voice of Thy precepts, life-conferring and divine. Grant to us also by Thy grace and Thy loves, that from them we may gather advantage, that is to say, love, hope, and salvation, as may be expedient to soul and to body, and that we may ever sing praise to Thee, without cessation, at all times, LORD of all things, FATHER, SON, and HOLY GHOST.

Deacon. Amen.

Priest. Thee, the most wise Governor and marvellous preserver of Thy servants, and great treasury whence every good thing and all help proceedeth from Thy mercy: we beseech Thee, turn Thee, O my LORD, and be propitious to us, and have mercy upon

---

(⁷) He is addressing of course that class of Catechumens who are called Auditors or *Audientes.*

us always, as Thou art accustomed, LORD of all, FATHER, SON, and HOLY GHOST.

Deacon. Keep silence. Paul the Apostle : the Epistle to the . . . . . my brethren : Sir, bless.

Priest. CHRIST bless thee. ([8])

[*The Epistle is read.*]

Choir. Glory to CHRIST the LORD.

Priest, ([9]) *before the middle of the Altar, bowing:* Thee, the splendour of the glory of the FATHER Himself, and the Image of the Substance of Him That begat Thee, Who didst appear in the body of our humanity, and didst illuminate our soul by the light of Thy life-giving Gospel, Thee, I say, we laud and adore and glorify at all times, LORD of all, FATHER, SON, and HOLY GHOST.

Make me wise, O LORD, with Thy holy wisdom, and grant to me that, without intermission and without spot, I may minister to Thee by the keeping of Thy Commandments, life-conferring and divine, LORD of all, FATHER, SON, and HOLY GHOST.

Deacon. There is silence. Be silent.

Priest. Peace be with us.

Choir. With thee and with thy spirit.

Deacon. The holy Gospel of our LORD JESUS CHRIST, the preaching of . . . . .

Choir. Glory to CHRIST the LORD.

Deacon. Sir, bless.

Priest. CHRIST bless thee.

([8]) The respective speeches of the Priest and Deacon are curiously counterchanged in the printed copies. The actual Liturgy given is that for a departed Priest: the Epistle is 2 Cor. v. 1—12 ; the Gospel, S. John vi. 24—25.

([9]) Here again I follow Le Brun : Raulin gives this prayer to the Deacon.

[*The Gospel is read.*

Choir. Glory to CHRIST the LORD.

The Nicene Creed is recited as at page **12.**

Deacon. Let us pray. *Peace be with us.* Pray,
bearing in memory our fathers, the Catholics, (¹⁰)
and all *P*resbyters and *D*eacons, youths and virgins,
and all the faithful who have departed from the
living and are dead in the true faith. And all our
fathers and brethren, and sons and daughters: also
faithful kings beloved of CHRIST, and all *P*rophets,
Apostles, and Martyrs: let us pray, I say, that, in
the resurrection from the dead they may be rewarded
by GOD with the crown, with a good hope, and the
inheritance of the life of the kingdom of heaven:
furthermore, that this oblation may be confidently
received, that by the (¹¹) Word of GOD and the HOLY
GHOST it may be consecrated, that it may be to us
for help and salvation and eternal life in the kingdom
of heaven, through the grace of CHRIST.

In the meanwhile the Priest saith secretly : Glory
be to Thee, Finder of them that were lost : glory
be to Thee, Collector of them that are dispersed,
and Bringer-back of them that are afar off : glory to
Thee Who convertest the erring to the knowledge
of the truth. Glory to Thee, my LORD, Who hast

(¹⁰) The original petition referred of course to the Catholic
of Babylon or Mosul, the spiritual head of the Church of
Malabar. But it was left by the Roman Censors, as it stood,
they intending to receive it in the sense of "our Catholic
Fathers."

(¹¹) The reference is 1 Timothy iv. 5, as alluding to the
Words of institution, and prayer for the Descent of the HOLY
GHOST, as both necessary, according to the teaching of the
Eastern Church, to a valid Eucharist.

called wretched me by Thy mercy and grace to approach to Thee, and hast made me, as it were, an
illustrious member in the mighty body of the Holy
Church, that I may offer to Thee this one, holy, and
acceptable Sacrifice, which is the memorial of the
Passion and Death, Burial and Resurrection of our
LORD and Saviour JESUS CHRIST, through Whom it
pleased Thee to forgive the sins of all men.

*The Priest censeth those who are on the right of the
Altar, and saith to them :*

Bless, my lords, and pray for me, my fathers, and
my brethren, and my masters, that this oblation
may be consecrated by my hands.

They reply with the Deacon :

May CHRIST hear thy prayers and receive thy
oblation, and cause thy priesthood to shine before
Him ; and may He be well-pleased with this sacrifice
which thou offerest for thyself, for us, and for all the
world, from the least to the greatest, through Thy
grace and love for ever and ever. Amen.

The Priest adores, bowing before the Altar.

Yea, O LORD our GOD, look not upon the multitude, nor let Thy domination be angry at the weight
of my sins; but by Thy ineffable grace consecrate
this great sacrifice, and bestow it in virtue and
power, that it may abolish our many sins : and when
at the latter day Thou appearest in the human
body which Thou didst assume of our race, we may
find before Thee grace and love, and may be made
worthy to praise Thee with the multitude of angels.

Rising, he saith:

We confess and praise, LORD our GOD, the riches of Thy grace shed abroad over us ; for when we were sinners and weak, Thou nevertheless, through the multitude of Thy mercy, didst make us worthy of the dispensation of the holy sacrament of the Body and Blood of CHRIST : we beseech therefore Thy help, the Strength of our souls, that with perfect love and true faith, we may administer Thy gift which we have, and may offer to Thee hymns, honour, laud and adoration, now and for ever.

Deacon. Amen.

Priest. Peace be with all.

Deacon. With thee and with thy spirit.

Priest. Give the peace to each other.

And for *Patriarchs*, Bishops, *Presbyters* and Deacons, and for those who having accomplished this life, have departed out of this congregation of the Church ; and for the peace of the world and the crown of the year, that it may be blessed and filled with Thy mercy : and for all Thy servants, and for us all, that this oblation be accepted for ever and ever.

Deacon. ([12]) Let us confess, and let us all of us beseech the LORD with the voice of choral melody ; stand rightly and attend to these things which are done in the tremendous mysteries which are consecrated : the *Priest* is praying that by his intercession peace may be multiplied in you : cast your eyes down to the ground, and vigilantly take care to raise your mind to heaven ; seek and petition at this time, and let no one venture to speak ; and he

---

([12]) The following speech is not in the books attributed to the Deacon, but clearly belongs to him, and is followed by a prayer which is " said in the meanwhile " by the Priest.

M

that prayeth, let him pray mentally, while he remaineth in silence and fear.   *Peace be with us.*

In the meanwhile the Priest saith :

LORD, Mighty GOD, strengthen my weakness by
Thy mercy, and make me worthy of the assistance
of Thy grace, that I may offer to Thee an oblation
for the benefit of all men, and to the praise of Thy
exceeding glorious TRINITY, FATHER, SON, and HOLY
GHOST, for ever.

*He unveils the mysteries and blesses incense, and puts
it in the censer and saith :*

[BEGINNING THE ANAPHORA.]

The grace of our LORD JESUS CHRIST, and the
love of GOD the FATHER, and the communion of
the HOLY GHOST, be with us all, now and for ever.
Deacon. Amen.
Priest. Lift up your hearts.
Choir. To Thee, GOD of Abraham, Isaac, and
Israel, the exceeding glorious King. ([13])

([13]) This sentence is precisely the same as that in the
Liturgy of the Apostles, which is the Nestorian norm. In the
Liturgies of Nestorius and Theodore the Interpreter, themselves apparently of the fifth century, it is very much amplified,
as thus in the former:
Priest. Up in the sublime heights, in the feaful and glorious
region, where the Cherubin cease not to agitate their wings,
and there is no end to the hymns and the sweet sounds of the
sanctification of the Seraphim, there be your minds.
Choir. They are lifted up to Thee; GOD of Abraham, Isaac,
and Israel, King of Glory.
Hence I gather the extreme antiquity of the Malabar
Anaphora, clearly a much earlier form.

Priest. The oblation is offered to the LORD, the GOD of all.

Choir. It is meet and right. *Peace be with us.*

Priest. LORD, Mighty GOD, give us boldness before Thee, that we may confidently perform this quickening and holy ministry with consciences pure, and free from all malice, simulation, and guilt, and bitterness, and sow in us, my LORD, charity and mutual unity of soul; and guard Thy holy Catholic Church here and everywhere, from everything noxious, from all fault and perturbation, by Thy grace and love for ever.

Choir. Bless, my LORD.

Priest. By the mouth of all be it glorified, by the tongue of all be it praised, by all creatures be it worshipped and exalted, the adorable and exceeding glorious Name of the most illustrious TRINITY, FATHER, SON, and HOLY GHOST, Who created the world and all that dwell therein by His goodness, and hath saved the sons of men by his loving-kindness, and hath shown great mercy to mortals. Thy Majesty, my LORD, is adored and venerated by thousand thousands of heavenly beings, and ten thousand times ten thousand of holy Angels; and the hosts of the Spirits of fire glorify Thy Name. And with holy Cherubim and Seraphim, they offer adoration to Thy greatness, they cry, they glorify without intermission, and say one to another :

Choir. Holy, Holy, Holy, LORD, mighty GOD : heaven and earth are full of His songs : Hosanna in the highest : Hosanna to the Son of *David* : blessed is He That cometh and shall come in the Name of the LORD : Hosanna in the highest.

Priest. Holy, Holy, Holy, LORD, mighty GOD : full are the heavens and the earth of His songs, [1.] and of the essence of His substance, and the splendour

M 2

of His exceeding glorious beauty, so that —— Do I
not fill heaven and earth, saith the LORD ? Holy
art Thou, GOD, the FATHER of Truth, from Whom
all paternity in heaven and in earth is named : holy
also is Thine Only-Begotten SON, our LORD JESUS
CHRIST, by Whom all things were made : holy also
is the SPIRIT, the cause of all truth, by Whom all
are sanctified. Woe is me, woe is me; for I am
astonished; because I am a man of polluted lips,
and I dwell in the midst of a people of polluted
lips, and mine eyes have seen the King, the LORD
of Hosts. How terrible is this place to-day, in
which face to face the LORD is seen ! And now, O
LORD, let Thy mercy be upon us, and purify our
filth, and sanctify our lips, and commingle the voices
of our imbecility with the praises of Seraphim and
Archangels, who sing glory to Thy love: for cor-
poreal men Thou hast associated with spirits. With
these celestial hosts then, we also, Thy miserable
servants, weak and useless, praise Thee, my LORD,
because Thou hast shewn great mercy to us, for
which we cannot return equal thanks. For Thou
didst take upon Thyself our humanity, that Thou
mightest quicken us with Thy divinity ; Thou didst
exalt our humanity, and set up our fall, and forgive
our sins, and justify us by wiping out our offences,
and didst illuminate our understandings, and didst
prove, O LORD our GOD, our enemies to be guilty,
and because of the love of Thy grace shed abroad
over us, didst bestow the victory on the weak
exiguity of our nature. For all helps, therefore,
and mercies bestowed on us, let us offer to Thee a
song, laud and honour, and adoration, now and
ever, and to ages of ages.

Deacon. Amen. Pray in your hearts. Peace be
with us.

He kisseth the Altar thrice, and saith: Glory to Thy Holy Name, and adoration to Thy *D*ivinity, [7.] at all times, LORD JESU CHRIST, Living Bread, giving life, Who didst descend from heaven, and quickenest the whole world, and they that eat this Bread shall never die, and they that receive it in truth are freed and sanctified by it, and are cleansed and live for ever.

Our LORD JESUS CHRIST ([14]) in the same night wherein He was betrayed, took the holy bread into His pure and loving hands, and lifted up His eyes to heaven, and gave thanks to GOD the FATHER, the Creator of all things, and blessed and brake, and gave to His *D*isciples and said,—Take and eat of this bread all of you : for this is My Body. In like manner after He had supped, He took the Chalice into His pure hands, and gave thanks, and blessed, and gave to His *D*isciples, saying, Take and drink ye all of this Chalice : for as often as ye

---

([14]) I have ventured to make a considerable alteration in the order of the above prayers. As we have the Malabar Liturgy from the Portuguese revisers, the sequence of the Collects is that which is given by bracketed numerals in the margin. Here the Invocation of the HOLY GHOST, contrary to the use of every other Oriental Liturgy, preceded the words of Institution. This, in itself, would be a sufficient proof that an alteration had been made ; though very carelessly, if not *malâ fide*, no notice is given of it. But fortunately the Nestorian Liturgy of Theodore the Interpreter bears a sufficient resemblance to this to shew what was the original order : I have therefore arranged the prayers according to that. The Liturgy of All Apostles, the Nestorian norm, bears as would be natural, a closer resemblance still to the Malabar; but as All Apostles, from whatever cause, has not the words of Institution at all, it is not so useful in shewing how the Malabar was arranged. Renaudot has a note on the Malabar, (vol. ii. p. 599. edit. Leslie), but he manifestly refers to a very different edition of it from that which we are employing.

eat this Bread, and drink this Cup, ye shew forth
My remembrance: for this is the Chalice of My
Blood, of the New Testament, which for you and
for many shall be poured forth for the remission of
sins: this shall be My pledge even to the consummation of all things.

Glory to Thee, my LORD: glory to Thee, my LORD:
glory to Thee my LORD, for Thine ineffable gift.

The Priest signs the Oblations, and saith:

[2.] LORD GOD of Hosts, hear the voice of my cry,
and listen, my LORD, and give ear to my groans
and my sighs, and receive the prayers of me, a
sinner: for in this hour in which the Sacrifice is offered
to Thy FATHER, I beseech Thy grace to have mercy
upon all creatures; to forgive the offenders, to
bring back the wanderers, to console the afflicted,
to give peace to the disturbed, to heal the infirm, to
hear them that are troubled in spirit, and to impart
tranquillity to them; to accomplish the almsdeeds
of them that work righteousness, and for Thy holy
Name's sake to be propitious ever to me, a sinner,
through Thy grace.

[3.] Thanks be to Thee, LORD GOD of Hosts: let this
oblation be received for the whole Catholic
Church, and for priests and princes; for the poor
also that are oppressed in sorrow and misery, and for
the faithful departed, and for all them who desire the
prayer of my weakness, and for my sins. Yea, O
LORD, my GOD, visit Thy people, and my un-
happiness, according to Thy love, and the multitude
of Thy mercy, and not according to my sins and
iniquities: but grant that we may be made worthy
of the remission of our sins by the Holy Body which
we shall in faith receive, through grace which is
from Thee. Amen.

Prostrating himself, he continues: Thou, my LORD, according to Thy exceeding love, receive this best and acceptable commemoration of the fathers who are just and upright, and please Thee,—the remembrance of the Body and Blood of Thy CHRIST, which we shall offer to Thee upon the pure and holy altar, as Thou hast taught us, and give peace to us and tranquillity all the days of our life. Yea, O LORD, give us peace, that all the inhabitants of the earth may know that Thou art GOD, the only FATHER of truth. Thou didst send Thy most beloved Son, and He the LORD our GOD came and taught us, all the holiness and purity of *Prophets* and *Apostles, Martyrs* and *Confessors, Bishops* and *Doctors, Priests* and *Deacons,* and all the sons of the holy Catholic Church, who have been sealed with holy baptism. We, therefore, my LORD, Thy weak and unprofitable servants, who are gathered together in Thy Name, and at this time stand before Thee, and by holy tradition have received a pattern from Thee, with exultation and joy, glorify, exalt and venerate this memorial, and sacrifice this Mystery, great, terrible, holy and divine, of the *Passion* and *Death, Burial* and Resurrection of our LORD and Saviour JESUS CHRIST.

[4.]

And the Priest stretcheth forth, purely, his hands to heaven and consecrateth the Body and Blood of Christ.

[9.]

Send then, my LORD, Thy Holy SPIRIT, and let Him rest upon this oblation of Thy servants and sanctify it, that it may be to us, my LORD, for the payment of our debts and the remission of our sins, and the great hope of resurrection from the dead, and a new life in the heavenly kingdom, with all who have pleased Thee. Moreover, for all Thy

[4.]
continued.

admirable dispensation carried on towards us, we praise and glorify Thee without ceasing in the Church, which hath been redeemed by the Blood of Thy Son, and with open mouth and unveiled countenance, we will offer unto Thee a song and honour laud and adoration, to Thy living, holy, and quickening Name, now and ever and to ages of ages. Amen.

*The Priest saith P*salm li. 1—13 ; *and P*salm cxxiii.

[5.] 1—3. *Then :* Stretch forth Thy hand, and let· Thy right hand save me, O LORD ; let Thy love remain over me for ever, and despise not the works of Thy hands.

[6.] *He riseth and saith :* CHRIST, the peace of things that are on high, and the great rest of those that are below, stablish, O LORD, in Thy peace and rest, the four regions of the world, but principally Thy holy Catholic Church, and destroy wars and battles from the ends of the earth, and disperse the people that delight in war, and pacify by the mercy of Thy Divinity, the Priesthood, and the kingdom, that we may have a secure habitation with all sobriety and piety, and forgive the debts and sins of them that have departed this life, through Thy mercy and love for ever.

The Priest blesses Incense, and puts it in the thurible,
saying :

Let us offer a hymn to Thy most glorious TRINITY, at all times and for ever. O LORD our GOD, cause the savour of our souls to be pleasant to Thee, through the sweet savour of the mercy of Thy love, and cleanse us by it from the defilements of sin.

He censeth the Oblations therewith, and saith thrice :

The LORD our GOD give us access by the clemency

of His mercy to these sacraments, most glorious, holy, quickening, and divine. For in truth we are not worthy.

Deacon. I am the Living Bread Which came down from heaven: I am the Bread Which descended from on high, said the SAVIOUR in a Mystery to [8.] His *Disciples*: whosoever approacheth in love, and receiveth Me, shall live in me for ever, and shall by heritage acquire the kingdom.

Choir. The ministers, who do His will, Cherubim and Seraphim, and Archangels, stand with fear and trembling before the Altar, and behold the *Priest*, when he breaks and divides the Body of CHRIST for the propitiation of sin.

Deacon. Open to me the gates of righteousness, O Thou Merciful One, Whose door is open to penitents, and Who invitest sinners to draw near to Thee ; open to us, my LORD, the gate of Thy loves, that we may enter in, and sing praise to Thee day and night.

Choir. Set, O LORD, a watch before my mouth. Glory be to the FATHER, SON, and HOLY GHOST.

Deacon. O Merciful One, have pity on us, and show mercy to us ; and despise us not in the time of affliction, for night and day we hope in Thee : [10.] and they that trust in Thee shall not be confounded.

Choir. Let all the people say, Amen and Amen. Isaiah kissed the fire in the kindled coal, and his lips were not burnt, but his iniquity was pardoned : mortals in this very bread receive fire, and it guards their bodies and burns out their sins.

Deacon. From everlasting to everlasting: the Altar is fire in fire: fire surrounds it: let *Priests* beware of the terrible and tremendous fire, lest they fall into it, and be burnt for ever.

The Priest breaks the Host, and saith :

We draw near, my LORD, in the faith of Thy
Name to these Holy Mysteries, and in Thy love
we break, and in Thy pity we sign the Body and
Blood of our SAVIOUR JESUS CHRIST, in the Name
of the FATHER, and of the SON, and of the HOLY
GHOST.

*The Priest layeth that part of the Oblation which
he holdeth in his left hand, on the paten: he dips the
other in the Blood, up to the midst.*

Let the Precious Blood be signed with the Holy
Body of our LORD JESUS CHRIST, in the Name of
the FATHER, and of the SON, and of the .HOLY
GHOST.

(15) *The Priest marks with his right thumb nail
that part of the Oblation which hath been dipped in
the Blood.*

Let the Holy Body be signed with the Blood of
Propitiation of our LORD JESUS CHRIST, in the Name
of the FATHER, and of the SON, and of the Holy
GHOST.

Then joining the two together, he says :

These predestinated Mysteries, exceeding glorious,
holy, and quickening, and divine, are consecrated,
perfected, completed, and united together in the
venerable and illustrious Name of the glorious
TRINITY ; that they may be to us, O LORD, for the

---

(15) This rubric was altered by the Portuguese censors ; for
which Le Brun sharply rebukes them ; and it is not very easy
to make out from the rubrics that remain, what the original
direction was.

propitiation of our sins, and a great hope of resurrection from the dead; and the renewal of life in
the kingdom of heaven.

Glory to Thee, my LORD, because Thou didst create
me by Thy grace: glory to Thee, my LORD, because
Thou didst call me by Thy mercy: glory to Thee,
my LORD, because Thou hast made me the mediator
of Thy gifts; and for all the dispensation which
Thou hast carried out towards my weakness, let
praise, laud, honour and adoration ascend to Thee,
now, and to ages of ages.

The grace of our LORD JESUS CHRIST, and the love
of GOD the FATHER, and the communion of the
HOLY GHOST be with us all, now and ever, and to
ages of ages.

Deacon. Let us all with fear and reverence approach
the mystery of the Body and precious Blood of our
SAVIOUR: and with pure heart and true faith let us
call to memory His *Passion* and Resurrection, and
understand it plainly: for our sakes the Only-
Begotten took on Himself a mortal body, and
spiritual reason and immortal soul: and in His precepts, which confer life, and in His holy law, has
brought us back from error to the acknowledgement
of the truth: and after all the dispensations which
He wrought for us, He offered the first-fruits of our
nature as a sacrifice on the Cross, and bestowed on
us this Holy Sacrament, by means of which we
might remember all the grace which He manifested
to us. Let us then with overflowing charity, and
humble will, receive the gift of eternal life, and with
pure prayer, and earnest grief for our sins, be made
partakers of the Holy Mysteries of the Church, and
be, by the hope of penitence, converted from our
iniquities, and grieve for our transgressions: let us
furthermore ask for love and mercy, and let us call

on GOD the LORD of all, and let us forgive the debts
of our fellow servants.

People. LORD, have mercy on the sins and iniquities of Thy servants.   [*And so on at the end of each
clause.*]

> *Deacon.* Let us cleanse our consciences from
>   division and contention ;
> Let our souls be thoroughly perfect, both from
>   all hatred and malice to others.
> Let us receive, sanctity, and be inflamed by the
>   HOLY GHOST.
> Let us receive the fellowship of the *D*ivine
>   Mysteries in unanimity of mind and mutua
>   peace.
> And may it be, O LORD, to us for the resurrec-
>   tion of our bodies, and the salvation of our
>   souls, and the life that is to ages of ages.
>   Amen.

Meanwhile the Priest saith: Blessed art Thou, LORD
GOD of our fathers, and highly exalted and excellently laudable is Thy Name for ever : in that Thou
hast not dealt with us after our sins, neither rewarded us according to our iniquities, but according
to the multitude of Thy love hast delivered us from
the power of darkness, and hast called us to the
kingdom of Thy most dearly beloved SON our LORD
JESUS CHRIST, by Whom Thou hast made bare, and
hast brought to nought, the power of darkness, and
hast bestowed on us life incorruptible. And now,
O LORD, Thou Who hast vouchsafed that I should
stand before this Thy pure and holy Altar, to offer
unto Thee this loving and holy sacrifice, make us
also worthy, by Thy love, that in all pureness and
holiness we may receive the Gift : and that it may
not be unto us for judgment or vengeance, but for
love and piety and the remission of sins, and resurrec-

tion from the dead, and eternal life : so that we may all be the fullest witnesses of Thy glory, and the habitation of a holy shrine : that after we have been incorporated into the Body and Blood of Thy CHRIST with all Thy Saints, we may shine with light, in His ever-glorious and lofty revelation : for to Thee and to Thine with the HOLY GHOST, is glory and honour and laud and adoration, now and ever, and to ages of ages.

Blot out, O LORD, the sins and transgressions of Thy servants, and sanctify our life by the songs of the HOLY GHOST, to the end that we, with all Thy Saints, may offer to Thy most High *Divinity* the fruits of glory and praise ; and make us worthy, O LORD, to stand in Thy *Presence* ever with pure heart and open countenance ; and that with the confidence which by Thy love is conferred on us, we may all of us together invoke Thee, and thus say :

Our FATHER.

Priest. Yea, O LORD, ([16]) GOD of Hosts, O our most glorious GOD, and our merciful FATHER, we earnestly ask, beseech and implore the clemency of Thy goodness : lead us not, my LORD, into temptation, but save and deliver us from the evil one, and from his host; for Thine is the kingdom and the strength, the glory and the power, the empire and the might, in heaven and in earth, now and to ages of ages.

Deacon. Amen.

Priest. Peace be with you.

Deacon. And with thee and with thy spirit.

([16]) The *Embolismus* : as in S. Mark, p. 25; S. James, p. 57 ; S. Basil, p. 143.

Priest. That which is holy befits the holy, my LORD, to be received.

Deacon. One holy FATHER, one holy SON, one HOLY GHOST. Glory be to the FATHER, and to the SON, and to the HOLY GHOST, to ages of ages. Amen.

The Deacon goes to the Altar: the Priest takes his right hand and puts it into the Paten.

Deacon. The glory of our LORD.

Priest. Be with them and with us, in the heavenly kingdom: glory be to the Living GOD.

Deacon. Glorify the Living GOD.

People. Glory to Him and to Thy Church: His love and His pity. Amen.

Priest. LORD, my GOD, I am not worthy, nor is it indeed meet that I should receive Thy Body and the Blood of propitiation, nor that I should touch them; but let Thy words sanctify my soul, and heal my body, in the Name of the FATHER, and of the SON, and of the HOLY GHOST.

And he receives the Body of our LORD. In the meantime the Deacon sings:

Let this oblation be received above in the heavenly places, together with that which Abel, Noah, and Abraham offered to the heavenly kingdom.

Priest. Let the gift of the grace of our Saviour Himself, JESUS CHRIST, be accomplished through love in all of us.

Deacon. To ages of ages. Amen.

The Priest receives the Chalice, and then saith:

The Blood of the propitiation of our LORD JESUS CHRIST nourish my soul and body in this life, and in the life to come.

Deacon. My brethren, receive the Body of the Son Himself, saith the Church, and drink His Blood.

And while the people communicate, the Deacon saith :

Strengthen, O LORD, the hands which are stretched out to receive the Holy Thing : vouchsafe that they may daily bring forth fruit to Thy Divinity; that they may be worthy of all things which they have sung to Thy praise within Thy sanctuary, and may ever laud Thee.([17]) Grant, moreover, My LORD, that the ears which have heard the voice of Thy songs, may never hear the voice of clamour and dispute. Grant also that the eyes which have seen Thy great love, may also behold Thy Blessed hope ; ([18]) that the tongues which have sung the *Sanctus* may speak the truth. Grant that the feet which have walked in the church may walk in the region of light : that the bodies which have tasted Thy living Body may be restored in newness of life. On this congregation also, which adores Thy Divinity, let Thy aids be multiplied, and let Thy great love remain with us; and by Thee may we abound in the manifestation of Thy glory, and open a door to the prayers of all of us. We all then, who have drawn near by the gift of the grace of the HOLY GHOST, and to whom it has been vouchsafed to become fellow participators in the reception of these mysteries, most excellent,

---

([17]) This seems to be the sense of a very obscure expression.

([18]) Notice this remarkable prayer, which has no parallel that I am aware of in any Eastern rite : there is nothing like it in the kindred Nestorian Liturgies, nor in the mongrel Nestorian service of John of Bassora. It appears to me of the most remote antiquity.

holy, divine, and quickening, let us all praise and exult in GOD, the Giver of them.

Priest. Glory be to Him for His unspeakable gift. It is meet, just, and right, O LORD, that at all times, and days, and hours, we should laud, adore, and glorify the terrible Name of Thy Majesty ; since by Thy grace and Thy love, my LORD, Thou hast vouchsafed to the weak nature of the mortal sons of men, to hallow Thy Name with blessed spirits, and hast given us to be partakers of the gift of Thy mysteries, and to be delighted with the sweetness of Thy words which give life and are divine, and always to offer praise to Thy Divinity, FATHER, SON, and HOLY GHOST. ([19])

Then all say, Our FATHER.

The Priest turneth to the people, and blesseth them, saying,

He Who blesseth us with all benediction in hea-ven, by the Son of humanity, ([20]) and hath invited to His kingdom and eternal sweetness :

And Who hath given His promise to the apos-tolic congregation, and also in verity hath signed His word, that there should be no doubt in it :

Ye shall say, Verily, verily, I say, and in verity I sign My words : every one that eateth My quicken-ing Body, and drinketh my Blood of the salutary Chalice,

I forgive him all his debts, and I blot out all his sins, and I call him to the kingdom ; and let it

---

([19]) Then follows, in the original, a thanksgiving alter-native with the above.

([20]) This singular substitution for the Son of Man was altered by the Diamperese censors into His Son.

deliver you from affliction, and save you from scandals.

He bless ([21]) the seeds of your fields, He bless the fruits of your trees, and He multiply and bless your substance, and of His love give you long life.

O GOD, the LORD of men, bless this congregation, and give strength to the weak, for behold, he beginneth from the beginning.

By the living sign of CHRIST, may the glorious throne of the Oriental Catholics be blessed, that righteousness may rise and shine in it.

Let the father full of splendour, the Bishop who is pastor and lord of the whole flock, full of sobriety, be guarded from evil.

Bless the holy presbyters, clerks and ministers : let them be set free from dangers and devils, and very evil men.

To the ancient of days, to old men, illustrious through age, may the LORD give them a good end, and call them to the kingdom.

Young men, fair in stature and possessed of strength, may He cause them to increase in splendour, and fill them with purity.

The frail nature of women, virgins also and the wedded, may they be kept from fall, from snares and scandals.

The LORD that sitteth in heaven, give us a quiet peace, a good and sweet peace, that we may rejoice day and night.

He give you peaceful times, that we may ever rejoice and not be turbulent and unquiet, but loving each other through charity.

And since ye are assembled together this day, in

([21]) This verb of course is to be connected with the first clause of the benediction.

the solemnity of this oblation may the Cross of the Celestial King guard you.

The LORD receive your oblation and your sacrifice, and your prayers, and may His SPIRIT rest upon your alms, and may your petitions enter into His Presence.

May he that is illustrious in the congregation of the Saints, the religious Hormisdas, ([22]) the holiness of holinesses, keep you from plague and devils and very evil men.

May he pray also for this crowd, the poor, the miserable, for they are disciples of this Saint, that thus they may be free from calamity.

Furthermore may they who have modestly laboured and served with simplicity in this world, be guarded in righteousness from ill.

And they who are strangers among us, and are far off from their homes, may the King of ages of ages cause them to return in peace.

Let this feast be holy upon you, O humble people, and may the LORD be your establisher and counsellor to good things.

Now and ever, and at all times and occasions, by nights also and days, and even to ages of ages.([23])

([22]) Hormisdas, a celebrated ascetic in Malabar, bears the same relation to the Church of India that S. Antony does to Egypt, S. Sabbas to Palestine, or Tekla-Haimanoth to Ethiopia.

([23]) In the original there follow three alternative benedictions. That translated above, I take to be for lesser festivals. The others are—1, For the highest feasts : 2, For ferial days : 3, For masses of the dead—which last I imagine to be Roman.

THE OFFICE OF THE PROTHESIS.

THE ORDER OF THE HOLY PROTHESIS, AS PER-
FORMED IN THE GREAT CHURCH, AND THE HOLY
MOUNTAIN.

The Priest and Deacon go to the prothesis, (¹) *and wash
their hands,* (²) *saying,* (³)

I will wash my hands in innocency, O LORD,
and so will I go to Thine Altar, *to the end of the
Psalm.*

*Then they make three adorations before the prothesis,
and each saith,*

GOD be merciful to me a sinner, and have pity
upon me.

(¹) *i.e.* into the chapel of Πρόθεσις: the name, being the
same for both it and the credence, may create confusion.

(²) In most churches, there is a lavatory for this purpose
near to the credence.

(³) The antiquity of this rite in the Eastern Church is
shewn by S. Cyril, (Catech. Myst. 5.) "Ye have seen the
Deacon giving water to the Priest to wash his hands, and to
the Presbyters, who surrounded the Altar of GOD. Did he
give it them to the end that the filth of the body might be
purged away? I trow not: for we use not to enter the Church
polluted with filth. But that cleansing of the hands is a
symbol, that we must be made clean from all our sins and
iniquities." And of old the custom was, that all who intended
to be communicants should wash their hands. S. Maximus:
"All men who propose to communicate first wash their hands."

Thou hast redeemed us from the curse of the law, by Thy precious Blood, being nailed to the Cross, and wounded with the lance, and didst pour forth streams of immortality to men: glory be to Thee, our SAVIOUR.

Deacon. Sir, give the blessing.

Priest. Blessed be our GOD always, now and ever, and to ages of ages. Amen.

Then the Priest takes in his left hand the Oblations ([4]) and in his right the holy spear.

In remembrance of our LORD and GOD and SAVI- OUR JESUS CHRIST. (*This he saith thrice.*)

He then thrusts the spear into the right ([5]) side of the ([6]) seal, and saith, as he cuts,

---

([4]) Five small loaves, of the form indicated in the text, are provided in the prothesis. They are round, symbolically representing, under the shape of a piece of money, the price of our redemption, (Durandus, 4, 41 ;) but each has a square projection rising from it, usually called the Holy Lamb, but sometimes simply the Holy Bread. This, in the Greek Church, is stamped with the words, IC XC NIKA. JESUS CHRIST conquers.

([5]) That is, of the Holy Lamb, which he is now going to divide from the rest of the Oblation.

([6]) The seal (σφραγίς) is, properly speaking, the Cross

He was led as a sheep to the slaughter.

Into the left, saying,

And as a blameless lamb dumb before His shearers, so He opened not His mouth.

Into the upper part, saying,

In His humiliation His judgment was taken away.

Into the lower, saying,

And who shall declare His generation ?

The Deacon, looking devoutly on this rite, saith, at each incision,

Let us make our supplications to the LORD: *holding his orarion in his hand.*(7)

After these things, (8) he saith,

Sir, take up.

---

impressed on the Holy Lamb, and is so to be taken here ; but is sometimes used for the thing thus sealed, namely, the Holy Lamb itself, as in what follows.

(7) The posture, which continually occurs in the Liturgy, can scarcely be understood except from actual sight. The Deacon is now, like S. John the Baptist, preaching the Lamb of GOD ; or, according to the before-named system of S. Germanus, he represents the Angel saluting the Blessed Virgin at her Annunciation, τὸν ἄγγελον μιμεῖται τὸ χαῖρε τῇ Παρθένῳ προσφθεγγόμενον. In the same way, the separation of the Lamb from the Oblation sets forth, so to speak, the separation of our LORD from His Mother at His birth : ἡ προσφορὰ .. εἰς τύπον τῆς ἀειπαρθένου λαμβάνεται· τὸ Κυριακον Σῶμα, ὡς ἐκ τινὸς κοιλίας .. τοῦ ὅλου ἄρτου, φημὶ, διατέμνεται.

(8) The Holy Lamb being now entirely separated from the Oblation.

And the Priest, thrusting the holy spear obliquely into the right side of the Oblation, raises up the holy Bread, ([9]) saying,

For His life is taken away from the earth; [always, now and ever, and to ages of ages.]

And layeth it, cross downwards, ([10]) in the holy disk.

The Deacon saith, Sir, sacrifice.

The Priest saith, while he cuts it crosswise,

The Lamb of God is sacrificed, Which taketh away the sin of the world, for the life and salvation of the world.

Then he turns it cross upwards, ([11]) and the Deacon saith, Sir, stab.

And the Priest, piercing the right side ([12]) with the holy spear, saith,

One of the soldiers with a spear pierced His side, and forthwith came thereout Blood and Water: and he that saw it bare record, and his record is true.

The Deacon then pours into the holy chalice wine and water, first saying to the Priest,

Sir, bless the Holy Union. *And the Priest blesses them.*

([9]) That is, the Lamb.

([10]) This is evidently done for convenience, that the softer part of the bread may be cut by the holy spear: but mystically represents the helplessness of a lamb expiring under the deathblow.

([11]) This is explained of Christ's bearing His Cross. ὁ γὰρ σταυρός, says an anonymous writer quoted by Goar, οὐκ ἔμπροσθεν, ἀλλ' ὄπισθεν τοῦ σώματος τοῦ Κυρίου ἐτέθη· τὰ δὲ ὑποκάτω—ι.e. of the Lamb—τὰ ἔμπροσθεν τούτου ἀναμφιβόλως δηλοῖ.

([12]) This shews that the Greek Church had the same tradition as the Latin, that our Lord's Wound was on His right side.

Then the Priest, taking the second ([13]) *Oblation, saith,*

In honour and memory of the most excellent and glorious Lady, the Mother of GOD and Ever-Virgin Mary, by whose intercessions receive, O LORD, this Sacrifice to Thy heavenly altar.

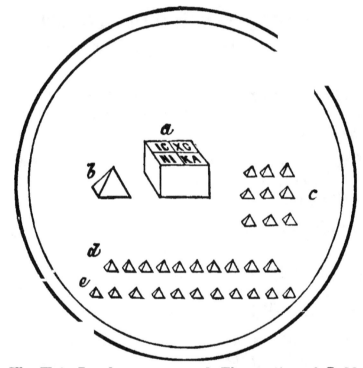

a The Holy Lamb   *b* The portion of S. Mary.
c The nine portions of Prophets, Apostles, Martyrs, &c.
d Portions for the living.   *e* Portions for the dead.

([13]) According to the present use of the Eastern Church, five Oblations are originally set on the prothesis, probably in commemoration of the miracle of the five loaves. Anciently, indeed, the number of Oblations varied with the number of offerers. But, though five be the usual number, and invariable in the Russian Church, yet often in Greece one Oblation only is offered; the *portions* being taken from the same loaf from which the Holy Lamb has been previously cut. And this not only in small places, but even in the Patriarchal Church.

And taking a portion, (^{14}) *he places it on the right side of the holy Bread near its middle part, saying,*

At Thy right hand did stand the Queen in a vesture of gold, wrought about with divers colours.

Then, taking the third Oblation, he saith,

Of the honourable and glorious Forerunner, Prophet, and Baptist John.

And taking one portion, he places it on the left side of the holy Bread, making a beginning of the first row: then he saith:

Of the holy and glorious Prophets, Moses and Aaron, Elijah, Elisha, David and Jesse, the Three Holy Children, and all holy Prophets.

And he places the second portion orderly under the first. Then he saith :.

Of the holy and glorious and all celebrated Apostles, Peter and Paul, the Twelve, and the Seventy, and all holy Apostles.(^{15})

And thus he places the third portion below the second, finishing the row. Then he saith :

Of our holy Fathers, and œcumenical great

(^{14}) This portion, μέρις, is called the Virgin's; and hence, perhaps, arose the error by which the Greeks were accused of pretending to consecrate it into the body of S. Mary. The portions are pyramidal pieces of bread, cut out of the Oblation with the holy spear.

(^{15}) The Eastern Church commemorates in the Menæa the Seventy, and others who were immediately connected with our LORD as Apostles: hence the necessity for the addition. Saints, next in her estimation, she denominates ἰσαπόστολοι, the equals of the Apostles.

Doctors and Hierarchs, Basil the Great, Gregory the Theologian, and John Chrysostom, Athanasius and Cyril, Nicolas of Myra, and all holy Hierarchs.

And taking the fourth portion, he places it near the first, beginning a second row. Then he saith again,

Of the holy Proto-martyr and Archdeacon Stephen, the great and holy Martyrs *D*emetrius, George, Theodore, and all holy Martyrs, both men and women.

And taking the fifth portion, he lays it under the first of the second row. Then he saith :

Of our holy Fathers, filled with G*OD*, Antony, Euthymius, Sabbas, Onuphrius, and Athanasius of Mount Athos, and all holy ascetics, men and women.

And thus, taking the sixth portion, he places it below the second portion, to the accomplishment of the second row. After this he saith :

Of the wonderworking and unmercenary Saints, Cosmas and *D*amian, Cyrus and John, Panteleëmon and Hermolaus, and of all unmercenary Saints.

Then taking the seventh portion, he puts it at the top, beginning the third row.

Of the holy and just parents of G*OD*, Joachim and Anna, of N. (*the Saint of the day*,) and all Saints, through whose intercessions G*OD* look upon us.

*And taking the eighth portion, he places it in order **a** little below the first (of the third row.)*

Yet further he saith :

Of our holy Father, John Chrysostom, Archbishop of Constantinople, (*if his Liturgy be said that
day ; but if S. Basil's, he commemorates him.*)

*And thus, taking the ninth portion, he finishes with
it the third row.   Then taking the fourth Oblation, he
saith :*

Remember, O LORD and Lover of men, all Orthodox Sees, our Bishop N., the venerable *P*resbytery,
the *D*iaconate in CHRIST, and every hierarchical
rank, the Hegumen N., our brothers and fellow-
ministers, *P*riests and *D*eacons, and all our brothers,
whom Thou hast called to Thy Communion, through
Thy mercy, O good LORD.

*And taking a portion, he places it below the holy
Bread.   Then he commemorates also those living whose
names he has, ([16]) and thus taking their portions, places
them below the holy Bread.   Then taking the fifth
Oblation, he saith :*

For the memory and forgiveness of sins of the
blessed founders of this holy habitation.

([16]) "Before they go to the prothesis to begin the Liturgy,"
says Dr. Covel, "all good people who are disposed to have
their absent friends, dead or living, commemorated, go to
them that celebrate, and get their names set down, there being
two catalogues, one for the living, one for the dead, for which
they deposit some aspers, or richer presents, in silver or gold,
as they are able or disposed ; this being a great part of a
common Priest's maintenance, especially in country villages.
And as the Priest reads over these catalogues, at every name
there written, there is a scrape made upon the crust to rub off
some mites as their particular portions." This custom much
resembles that which is referred to by S. Innocent I., in his
Epistle to Decentius : "The Oblations are first to be commended to GOD, and then their names, whose are the Oblations, to be recited, that they may be named in the mysteries."
And S. Jerome (Homil. in Ezech., cap. 6 and 18,) rebukes
the pride which some offerers took in hearing their names thus
recited.

He then commemorates the Bishop that ordained him, and such other of the dead as he pleases; and lastly, saith thus:

And of all our Orthodox fathers and brethren, who have departed in the hope of the resurrection and in Thy communion to eternal life, O LORD and Lover of men. (*And he takes a portion.*)

Then the Deacon, himself also taking a Seal and the holy spear, commemorates ([17]) those of the living whom he pleases; and lastly saith thus:

Remember also, O LORD, my unworthiness, and forgive me every sin, voluntary and involuntary.

Then, in like manner, he takes another Seal, and commemorates whom he will of the departed: and puts the portions below the holy Bread, in the same way as the Priest. Then he takes the sponge, ([18]) and gathers together the portions in the dish under the holy Bread, so that they are safe, and that nothing can fall off. Then the Deacon, taking the censer, and incense in it, saith to the Priest:

Sir, bless the incense. **Let** us make our supplications to the LORD.

The Priest saith the prayer of Incense.

We offer to Thee incense, O CHRIST our GOD, for a savour of a spiritual perfume: receive it unto Thy

([17]) This is an innovation. S. Symeon of Thessalonica distinctly condemns it. "The Deacons must not offer portions; for they have not the grace of offering to GOD." (οὐ δεῖ διακόνους μερίδας προσφέρειν ... ἐπεὶ καὶ τὸ χάρισμα τοῦ προσφέρειν τῷ Θεῷ οὐκ ἔχουσι.

([18]) The Greeks use a "holy sponge," in place of the *purificatorium* of the Latins. It is generally called Σπόγγος, but here μοῦσα, the more modern term for the same thing.

heavenly altar, and send down in its stead the grace of Thy most HOLY SPIRIT.

Deacon. Let us make our supplications to the LORD. *The Priest censes the Asterisk, ([19]) and places it over the holy Bread, saying :*

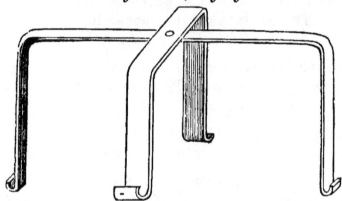

And the star came, and stood over where the young Child was.

Deacon. Let us make our supplications to the LORD. *And the Priest taking the first veil, ([20]) covers with it the holy Bread with the disk, saying :*

([19]) The asterisk is as shown in the text; it folds and unfolds for the purpose of being more conveniently put away. Its *use* is to prevent the veil of the disk from disarranging the order of the *portions ;* its mystical *meaning*, as the versicle shews, is the star which led the Wise Men to the Infant SAVIOUR. S. Germanus, who usually finds a reference to the Nativity where the context of the office refers to the Death of our Saviour, here finds a reference to the latter where the Liturgy intends the former, and explains the asterisk of our LORD's bier and its coverings.

([20]) This veil is called the διϭκοκάλυμμα. The second veil has no distinctive name, but the third is called 'Aὴρ or νεφέλη. It is called *air*, because, as the air surrounds the earth, so does this surround the holy gifts; and *cloud*, because it is written, " There came a cloud and overshadowed them." This name, *air*, has found its way into our own Church, through Bishop Andrewes and the divines of his time, who (especially Wren) were well versed in the Eastern Liturgies.

The LORD hath reigned; He hath put on glorious apparel: the LORD hath put on His apparel, and girded Himself with strength.

Deacon. Let us make our supplications to the LORD. Sir, cover. (κάλυψον.)

And the Priest, censing the second veil, covers with it the holy chalice, saying:

Thy glory, O CHRIST, hath filled the heavens, and the earth is full of Thy praise.

Deacon. Let us make our supplications to the LORD. Sir, shelter. (σκέπασον.) ([21].)

The Priest censing the covering which is called the Air, *and covering both chalice and disk with it, saith:*

Shelter us with the covering of Thy wings, chase away from us every enemy and foe; give peace in our time; LORD, have mercy upon us, and on Thy world, and save our souls, for Thou art good, and the lover of men.

Then the Priest, taking the censer, censes the prothesis, saying thrice:

Blessed be our GOD, who is thus well pleased: glory be to Thee.

The Deacon saith at each time:

Always, now and ever, and to ages of ages. Amen.

([21]) The difference of the two expressions used for the covering with the first and with the second veil will shew the propriety of the exclamations by the Priest that follow each.

Then they both adore reverently, three times.   Then the Deacon, taking the censer, saith :

At the oblation of the Holy Gifts, let us make our supplications to the LORD.

The Priest saith the Prayer of Prothesis : ([22])

O GOD, our GOD, Who didst send forth the Heavenly Bread, the nourishment of the whole world, our LORD and GOD, JESUS CHRIST, as a Saviour and Redeemer and Benefactor, blessing and hallowing us; Thyself bless this Oblation, and receive it to Thy heavenly altar : remember, of Thy goodness and love to men, them that offered it, and them for whom they offered it ; and keep us without condemnation in the celebration of Thy holy mysteries.   For blessed and hallowed is Thy holy and glorious Name, FATHER, SON, and HOLY GHOST, now and ever, and to ages of ages. Amen.

And after this he there makes the Dismission, saying thus :

Glory be to Thee, CHRIST, our GOD and Hope : glory be to Thee.
Deacon. Glory.   Both now.   LORD have mercy. Sir, give the blessing.

And the Priest gives the Dismission, saying :

{ *if it be Sunday,* CHRIST, that arose from the dead, }
{ *if not*   CHRIST, our true GOD,   }
through the intercessions of His spotless Mother, and our holy Father, John Chrysostom, Archbishop

---

([22]) This prayer is word for word from the Liturgy of S. James, where it is said by the Priest when the Oblations are brought from the Prothesis to the altar, *i.e.* at the Great Entrance.

of Constantinople, (*or, if it be the Liturgy of S.
Basil, of* S. Basil the Great, of Cæsarea in Cappadocia,) and All Saints, have mercy upon us, and
save us; for Thou art good and the lover of
men.

Deacon. Amen.

*After the Dismission, the Deacon censes the holy
prothesis; then he goes and censes the holy Table all
round in the form of a Cross, saying secretly:*

In the tomb bodily, in Hades spiritually, in
Paradise with the thief, while Thou wast, O Christ,
with the Father and the Holy Ghost on the throne,
as God filling all things and incircumscript. *Then
he saith the fifty-first Psalm. In the meantime he
censes the Sanctuary and all the Church, and comes
again to the holy Altar, and again censes the holy Table
and the Priest; then he puts down the censer in its
place, and comes close to the Priest; and they stand in
front of the holy Table, and make three reverences;
praying secretly, and saying:*

O Heavenly King, the Paraclete, the Spirit of
truth, Who art every where present, and fillest all
things, the Treasure of good things, and Giver of
life, come and tabernacle in us, and cleanse us from
all stain, and save our souls, O good God.

Glory to God in the highest, and on earth peace,
good-will towards men. *Twice.*

O Lord, open Thou my lips, and my mouth shall
shew forth Thy praise.

*Then the Priest kisses the Holy Gospel, and the
Deacon the holy Table. Then the Deacon, bowing his
head to the Priest, and holding his orarion with the
three fingers of his right hand, saith:*

It is time to sacrifice (²⁸) to the LORD.   Holy Sir, give the blessing.

The Priest, signing him with the Cross, saith :

Blessed be our GOD always, now and ever, and to ages of ages.   Amen.

Deacon. Holy Sir, pray for me.

Priest. The LORD make straight **thy** goings to every good work.

Deacon. Holy Sir, remember me.

Priest. The LORD our GOD remember thee in His kingdom, always, now and ever, and to ages of ages.

Deacon. Amen. *Then he makes a reverence, and goes out, and standing in the accustomed place, over against the holy doors, makes three reverences, saying to himself:* O LORD, open Thou my lips, and my mouth shall shew Thy praise. *After this, he begins,* Sir, give the blessing.

Priest. Blessed be the kingdom, &c.

[*The Liturgy will be found at page* 92.]

(²⁸) Ποιεῖν. King translates "to perform;" and Goar, doubtfully, "faciendi." The word often, in late Greek, signifies to sacrifice. So the LXX. Isaiah xix. 21; 1 Kings xi. 33; Levit. ix. 7. So in S. Luke ii. 27, "τοῦ ποιῆσαι αὐτοὺς κατὰ τὸ εἰθισμένον τοῦ νόμου"—ought to be translated— "that they might offer a sacrifice according to the custom of the law." So *facere* is often used in Latin, Virg. iii. 77, "Cum *faciam* vitula pro frugibus." And the similar word ῥέζειν, as every one knows, constantly means the same thing.

APPENDIX I.

THE FORMULÆ OF INSTITUTION

As they occur in every extant Liturgy.

[ALPHABETICALLY ARRANGED.]

1. ALL APOSTLES. I.

[Ethiopic: Monophysite.]

In the same night in which He was betrayed, He took bread into His hands, holy, blessed, and immaculate, He looked up to heaven, to Thee, His FATHER, He gave thanks, He blessed, He sanctified, and gave to His disciples, saying: Take, eat ye all of this : THIS BREAD IS MY BODY, WHICH IS BROKEN FOR YOU FOR THE REMISSION OF SINS. Amen.

People. Amen. Amen. Amen. We believe and are certain. We praise Thee, O LORD, our GOD : this is truly, and we thus believe, Thy Body.

Priest. In like manner the cup of thanksgiving He blessed and sanctified, and said to them : Take, drink ye all of it : THIS IS THE CHALICE OF MY BLOOD WHICH SHALL BE SHED FOR YOU, FOR THE REDEMPTION OF MANY.

People. Amen. This is verily Thy Blood : we believe.

[The first formula has been made the subject of great rejoicing by Protestants : while by some Liturgical writers it has been considered invalid.   But the extremely strong language employed in the response of the people, ought to set the Ethiopic canon above suspicion.   I do not mean to defend its compilers from the charge of presumption in altering our LORD's own most sacred words : I would only urge with most Catholic writers, that they are perfectly orthodox.   When the Priest says, holding the paten in his hand,—*This bread*, that which is in the paten is bread, and no more : were he to terminate then, the bread would be only so far sanctified as being an oblation to GOD, but true bread still.]

* 2. ALL APOSTLES. II. (*Ethiopic*.) ([1])

In that night in which they betrayed Him, He took bread.

People. We believe that this is He, truly we believe.

Priest. In His holy and blessed hands, which are without stain ; He looked up to heaven unto Thee, unto His Father, gave thanks, blessed, and brake, and gave unto them, to His own, His disciples, and said to them : Take, eat, THIS BREAD IS MY BODY, WHICH IS BROKEN FOR YOU FOR THE REMISSION OF SINS.

People. Amen. Amen. Amen. We believe and are sure ; we praise Thee, our LORD and our GOD, this is He, truly we believe.

Priest. Likewise the cup too He blessed, consecrated, and sanctified, and gave it to them, His own, His disciples, and said to them : Take, drink, THIS CUP IS MY BLOOD WHICH IS POURED OUT FOR YOU FOR THE REMISSION OF SINS.

People. Amen. Amen. Amen.

Priest. And when ye do this, make commemoration of Me.

([1]) Brit. Mus., Orient. 545, fol. 47 *a*.

3. AMBROSIAN.

Who, on the day before He suffered for the salvation of us and of all, taking bread, He lifted His eyes to heaven to Thee, GOD, His Father Almighty; giving thanks to Thee, He blessed, He brake, and gave to His disciples, saying to them: Take and eat ye all of it; FOR THIS IS MY BODY.

In the like manner, after they had supped, taking the chalice, He lifted up His eyes to heaven, to Thee, GOD, His Father Almighty: also giving thanks to Thee, He blessed, and gave to His disciples, saying to them: Take, and drink ye all of it; FOR THIS IS THE CHALICE OF MY BLOOD, OF THE NEW AND ETERNAL TESTAMENT, THE MYSTERY OF FAITH, WHICH FOR YOU AND FOR MANY SHALL BE POURED FORTH FOR THE REMISSION OF SINS. Commanding also, and saying to them, These things as oft as ye shall do, ye shall do them in memorial of Me: ye shall preach My Death: ye shall announce My Resurrection: ye shall hope for My Advent, till again I shall come to you from heaven.

4. APOSTLES (*Nestorian*).

[*In this Liturgy the Words of Institution are wanting.*]

5. APOSTLES (*Syro-Jacobite*). (²)

Who, when for us He was made man, without mutation, He came to the Cross; and before His quickening *Passion*, He took bread into His holy hands, He blessed, He sanctified, He brake, and ate, and gave to His disciples, saying: Take and eat of it: FOR THIS IS MY BODY, WHICH FOR YOU AND FOR

(²) Brit. Mus., Add. 14,493; 14,496; 14,693; 17,128.

o 2

MANY IS BROKEN AND GIVEN FOR THE REMISSION OF SINS
AND LIFE ETERNAL.

People. Amen.

Priest. In like manner the chalice also, after they
had supped, He mingled with wine and water, He
blessed, He sanctified, and when He had tasted it,
He gave it to His disciples, saying: Take, drink ye
all of it: FOR THIS IS THE NEW TESTAMENT IN MY
BLOOD, WHICH FOR YOU AND FOR MANY IS POURED FORTH
FOR THE EXPIATION OF SINS AND LIFE ETERNAL.

People. Amen.

Priest. As often as ye shall eat this bread and
drink this chalice, ye shall make memory of Me till I
shall come.

People. Amen.

6.   ARMENIAN.

He instituted this great mystery of faith and religion when He was about to give Himself up to death
for the life of the world.

People. We believe.

Priest. Taking bread into His Hands, holy, divine,
most spotless, and venerable, He blessed, He gave
to His elect, holy, and fellow-disciples, saying,

Deacon. Sir, bless.

Priest. THIS IS MY BODY, WHICH FOR YOU AND FOR
MANY IS GIVEN FOR REMISSION AND PARDON OF SINS.

People. Amen.

Priest. In like manner He took the chalice, He
blessed, He gave thanks, He drank, and gave it to
His elect, holy, and fellow-disciples, saying,

Deacon. Sir, bless.

Priest. THIS IS MY BLOOD OF THE NEW TESTAMENT,
WHICH FOR YOU AND FOR MANY IS SHED FOR THE RE-
MISSION AND PARDON OF SINS.

People. O Heavenly FATHER, Who didst give up

APPENDIX I. **197**

Thy Son to death, as the *Debtor* of our debts, we beseech Thee for the sake of His Blood, which hath been shed, to have mercy upon Thy rational flock.

Deacon. Sir, give the blessing.

Priest. And Thine Only-Begotten Son, the Lover of men, commanded us to do this in remembrance of Him.

* 7. S. Athanasius (*Ethiopic*). ([8])

Thou didst take up bread before them, didst give thanks, bless, and break, and give unto them, saying: Take, eat; THIS BREAD IS MY BODY, from which there is no being separated. And in like manner the cup too Thou didst mingle (with) water and wine, didst give thanks, bless, and consecrate, and say: Take, drink: THIS CUP IS MY BLOOD, from which there is no being divided. As often as ye eat this Bread and drink this Cup, set forth My *Death* and My Resurrection, and confess My Ascension to heaven and My coming again with glory, whilst ye await.

8. S. Basil (*Orthodox*).

[*See* page 127.]

9. S. Basil (*Copto-Jacobite*).

He instituted this great mystery of piety and religion when He had determined to give Himself up to death for the life of the world.

People. We believe that it is in truth so.

Priest. He took bread into His hands, holy, pure, immaculate, blessed and life-giving, and looked up to heaven to Thee, O God, His Father, and the Lord of all.

People. Amen.

([8]) Brit. Mus., Orient. 545, fol. 86 *b* ; Add. 16,202.

Priest, (*raising his eyes.*) And gave thanks. *Amen.* And blessed it. *Amen.* And sanctified it. *Amen.* And brake it, and gave it to His holy Apostles and disciples, saying : Take, eat ye all of this : FOR THIS IS MY BODY, WHICH FOR YOU IS BROKEN, AND FOR MANY IS GIVEN FOR THE REMISSION OF SINS : do this in remembrance of Me. *Amen.*

Priest. Likewise also the cup after supper, He mingled with wine and water. *Amen.* He gave thanks. *Amen.* He blessed. *Amen.* He sanctified it. *Amen.* He tasted, and gave it to His disciples and holy Apostles, saying : Take, drink ye all of it: FOR THIS IS MY BLOOD OF THE NEW TESTAMENT, WHICH IS SHED FOR YOU AND FOR MANY FOR THE REMISSION OF SINS : do this in remembrance of Me.

People. Amen. It is so.

Priest. As often as ye shall eat of this Bread and drink this Chalice, ye shall set forth My Death and confess my Resurrection, and remember Me until I come.

10. S. BASIL (*Syro-Jacobite.*)

For when He was about to go forth to His voluntary and salutary Cross, in the night in which He was betrayed for the life and redemption of the world, He took bread in His holy, immaculate, pure, and spotless hands, He gave thanks, He blessed, He sanctified, He brake, and gave to His disciples and His holy Apostles, saying : Take, eat of this : FOR THIS IS MY BODY, WHICH FOR YOU AND FOR MANY IS BROKEN AND DIVIDED FOR THE EXPIATION OF TRANSGRESSIONS, AND THE REMISSION OF SINS, AND FOR LIFE ETERNAL.

People. Amen.

Priest. In like manner also the Chalice of wine from the vine, after they had supped, He took, He mingled with water, He gave thanks, He blessed, He sanctified and tasted and divided to His disciples and holy Apostles, saying : Take, drink ye all of it : THIS IS THAT MY BLOOD OF THE NEW TESTAMENT, WHICH FOR YOU AND FOR MANY IS POURED FORTH AND SPRINKLED, FOR THE EXPIATION OF TRANSGRESSIONS, AND REMISSION OF SINS, AND FOR LIFE ETERNAL.

People. Amen.

Priest. For as often as ye do this, ye announce My Death, and celebrate the memory of My Burial and Resurrection, until I shall come.

People. We announce Thy Death, O LORD, and confess Thy Resurrection, and expect Thy Second Advent : let Thy mercies be upon all of us.

* 11.   S. BASIL (*Ethiopic*). ([4])

He took bread in His holy and pure hands, which are without pollution, and blessed and life-giving. He looked up to heaven unto Thee, unto His FATHER, GOD and LORD of all, Who is above all.   He gave thanks, blessed, and brake, tasted, and gave unto His own, His holy disciples and His pure Apostles, and said to them : Take, eat of it, all of you ; THIS BREAD IS MY BODY, WHICH IS BROKEN FOR YOU FOR THE REMISSION OF SIN ; AND THUS MAKE COMMEMORATION OF ME.

People. Amen.

Priest. And in like manner the cup too after they had supped, He mingled water and wine, gave thanks, blessed and consecrated, tasted, and gave to His own, His holy disciples and His pure Apostles, and said to them : Take, drink of it, all of you ; THIS CUP IS MY BLOOD, WHICH IS SHED FOR YOU FOR THE RE-

([4]) Brit. Mus., Orient. 545, fol. 113 *b*.

MISSION OF SIN ; AND THUS MAKE COMMEMORATION OF
ME.

People. Amen.

Priest. Whenever ye eat this bread and drink this
cup, set forth My *D*eath and confess My Resurrection, and make commemoration of Me until I
come.

People. We set forth Thy *D*eath.

* 12.   S. Celestine (*Syro-Jacobite*). ([5])

He Who, when He was about to give completion
to His dispensation in the flesh, on that evening,
priestly and full of mysteries, in the upper-chamber,
handed to His holy disciples the mystery of the
mystic service of His sacrifice, when He had taken
bread into His hands, holy and spotless and immaculate, and showed (it) to Thee, God the Father;
and when He had given thanks, He blessed, consecrated, brake, and gave to His disciples, the holy
Apostles, saying : Take, eat of it, all of you ; this
is My Body, which, for your sake and that of many,
is broken, and given for the remission of sins and
for everlasting life.

People. Amen.

Priest. And thus, over the cup too, when
He had given thanks, He blessed, consecrated, (and)
gave to His disciples, the holy Apostles, saying :
Take, drink of it, all of you ; for this is My Blood
of the New Testament, which for you and for many
is shed, and given for the remission of sins and for
life everlasting.

People. Amen.

Priest. For whenever ye celebrate this service,

([5]) Brit. Mus., Add. 14,493.

for the preservation of your lives, ye perform the commemoration of My Death and Resurrection until that I come.

13. S. CHRYSOSTOM.

[*See* page 92.]

* 14. S. CHRYSOSTOM (*Ethiopic*). ([6])

He took bread in His Hands, holy, and blessed, and pure, which are without stain; He looked up to heaven unto Thee, unto His FATHER, GOD and LORD of all, Who is above all. He gave thanks, blessed, and brake, and gave unto His disciples, and said to them: THIS IS MY BODY, THE FOOD OF RIGHTEOUSNESS, WHEREOF VERILY HE WHO EATS HATH EVERLASTING LIFE ; take, eat of it, all of you. And similarly the cup too He mingled (with) water and wine, gave thanks, blessed and consecrated and gave to His disciples, and said to them : THIS IS MY BLOOD, THE DRAUGHT OF LIFE, WHEREOF VERILY HE WHO DRINKS HATH EVERLASTING LIFE ; take, drink of it, all of you ; a sign it is to you and to those after you ; and thus make commemoration of Me until I come ; and whenever ye are gathered together in My Name, set forth My Death and My Resurrection and My Ascension into heaven.

15. S. CHRYSOSTOM. I. (*Syro-Jacobite*). ([7])

For in that night in which He was betrayed to death, for the life and salvation of the world, He

---

([6]) Brit. Mus., Orient. 545, fol. 76 *b* ; Add. 16,202 ; Bodleian, xvii. 5.

([7]) Brit. Mus., Add. 14,690 ; 17,128 ; 17,229.

took bread into His holy hands, He looked up to Thee, GOD and FATHER, and gave thanks, He sanctified, and brake, and gave it to His disciples the holy Apostles, saying : Take, eat of it : FOR THIS IS TRULY MY BODY, WHICH FOR YOU AND FOR MANY IS BROKEN AND GIVEN TO THE REMISSION OF SINS, AND LIFE ETERNAL.

In like manner also, taking the Chalice after they had supped, He mingled it moderately and temperately with wine and water, He gave thanks, He blessed, He sanctified, and gave it to the same His disciples, the holy Apostles, saying : Take, drink ye all of it : FOR THIS IS TRULY MY BLOOD, THE SAME WHICH FOR YOU AND FOR MANY IS POURED FORTH AND IS GIVEN FOR THE REMISSION OF SINS, AND LIFE ETERNAL : do this in remembrance of Me. For as often as ye shall eat this Bread, and drink this Chalice, ye shall set forth My Death, until I come.

People (*As in* 18.)

Notice : 1. the remarkable addition, *truly* My Body : *truly* My Blood : as some of the Nestorians hold extremely unsound doctrine on the Blessed Eucharist, this likewise may be considered a protest against that. The date of this Liturgy is only to be guessed from internal evidence : from which I should be disposed to consider it neither one of the earliest or latest :—perhaps of the 8th or 9th centuries.

2. Observe also the *temperately and moderately*, as applied to the mixed Chalice.

16. S. CHRYSOSTOM. II. (*Syro-Jacobite.*)

And in the night of His *Passion* He took bread into His holy hands, He blessed, He sanctified, He brake, and gave to His disciples, saying : Take, eat : THIS IS MY BODY, WHICH IS GIVEN FOR THE REMISSION OF SINS, AND THE NEW LIFE WHICH IS FOR EVER.

In like manner also He took the Chalice, and blessed and gave to His disciples, and said : Take,

drink ye all of it : THIS IS MY BLOOD, WHICH FOR
YOU IS POURED FORTH FOR THE EXPIATION OF TRANS-
GRESSIONS, THE REMISSION OF SINS, AND THE NEW
LIFE WHICH IS FOR EVER. And in the first place He
commanded them, saying : As often as ye shall
celebrate this Mystery of Gladness, ye shall commemorate My Death and Resurrection, until I shall
come.

People. (*As in* 18.)

17. S. CLEMENT.

[*See* page 65.]

18. S. CLEMENT (*Syro-Jacobite*).

When therefore He was prepared, of His own free
will, to taste of His Passion, to ascend the Cross
and the place of suffering, and to undergo death for
the life of the whole world, in that evening in which
He accomplished the consummation of mysteries
and marvels, He took bread into His pure and holy
hands, and giving thanks, He blessed, and sanctified,
and brake, and gave to them that were initiated in
this His Mystery, His holy Apostles, saying : Take,
and eat of it : because THIS IS MY BODY, WHICH FOR
YOU IS BROKEN AND GIVEN, FOR THE FORGIVENESS OF
ALL THE FAITHFUL, OF VERY MANY FOR WHOM IT IS
IMMOLATED AND DIVIDED, TO THE PROPITIATION OF
TRANSGRESSIONS, THE REMISSION OF SINS, AND LIFE
ETERNAL.

People. Amen.

Priest. After that mystical supper, He mingled
the Chalice of Life with wine and water, and raising
His eyes to Thee, GOD and FATHER, He gave thanks,

blessed, sanctified, and gave to the band of His elect disciples and holy Apostles, and said : Take, drink ye all of it : THIS IS MY BLOOD, WHICH CONFIRMS THE TESTAMENT OF MY *DEATH* : WHICH FOR YOU IS POURED FORTH, AND FOR MANY IS GIVEN AND DIVIDED, TO THE PROPITIATION OF TRANSGRESSIONS, THE REMISSION OF SINS, AND LIFE ETERNAL.

People. Amen.

Priest. When therefore ye shall communicate of this Bread, and shall use this Chalice of Life, ye shall make commemoration of My *Death*, and make memorial of My Resurrection, until I shall come.

People. We make memory, O LORD, of Thy *Death*, we confess Thy Resurrection, and we look for Thy Second Advent : we beseech from Thee mercy and grace : we pray for the redemption of our sins : let Thy mercies be upon us all.

* 19.   CYRIACUS OF ANTIOCH (*Syro-Jacobite*). ([8])

And when He had taken bread into His priestly hands, He looked up to heaven, gave thanks, blessed, consecrated, brake, and gave to His disciples, the holy Apostles, saying : TAKE, EAT OF IT ; THIS IS MY BODY, WHICH IS BROKEN FOR YOU AND FOR MANY, AND GIVEN FOR THE REMISSION OF SINS, AND FOR LIFE EVER-LASTING.

People. Amen.

Priest. And in like manner, over the cup also, after the mystic supper, He mingled it in moderation with both wine and water, gave thanks,

---

([8]) Brit. Mus., Add. 14,690, fol. 166 *b*.

blessed, consecrated, and gave to His disciples, the holy Apostles, saying: THIS IS MY BLOOD OF THE NEW TESTAMENT, WHICH IS SHED FOR YOU AND FOR MANY, AND GIVEN FOR THE REMISSION OF SINS, AND FOR LIFE EVERLASTING.

People. Amen.

Priest. Whensoever then ye eat this bread and drink this cup, ye proclaim My *D*eath and confess My Resurrection, until I come.

20. S. CYRIL (*Copto-Jacobite*).

For Thine Only-Begotten SON our LORD GOD, the Saviour and Universal King JESUS CHRIST, in that night in which He gave Himself up that He might suffer for our sins, before the death which by His own free will He undertook for us all.

People. We believe.

Priest. He took bread into His holy, immaculate, pure, blessed, and quickening hands, and looked up to heaven, to Thee His GOD and FATHER, and the LORD of all, and gave thanks.

People. Amen.

Priest. And blessed **it.**

People. Amen.

Priest. And sanctified it.

Priest. And brake it, and gave it His holy disciples and pure Apostles, saying: Take, eat ye all of it: FOR THIS IS MY BODY, WHICH SHALL BE BROKEN FOR YOU, AND FOR MANY SHALL BE GIVEN FOR THE REMISSION OF SINS: do this in remembrance of Me.

People. Amen.

Priest. In like manner also He mingled the Chalice after supper with wine and water, and gave thanks.

People. **Amen.**

Priest. And blessed it.

People. Amen.

Priest. And sanctified it.

People. Amen.

Priest. And tasted it, and gave it to His glorious holy disciples and Apostles, saying : Take, drink ye all of it : THIS IS MY BLOOD OF THE NEW TESTAMENT, WHICH FOR YOU IS POURED FORTH, AND FOR MANY SHALL BE GIVEN TO THE REMISSION OF SINS : do this in remembrance of Me.

People. Amen.

Priest. For as often as ye shall eat of this Bread and drink of this Chalice, announce My *D*eath, and confess My Resurrection, and keep My memory till I come.

People. We announce Thy *D*eath, O LORD, and we confess Thy Resurrection.

NOTE. S. Cyril's is one of the most valuable of the second class of Liturgies. From its singular resemblance to, and in some respects its even more singular departure from, that of S. Mark, it is *very probably* the real composition, or rather edition, of the Saint whose name it bears.

21. S. CYRIL (*Syro-Jacobite*). (⁹)

He then before His salutary *P*assion took bread into His holy hands, and blessed, and brake, and gave it into the hands of His disciples, and said : THIS IS MY BODY, WHICH IS BROKEN FOR YOU AND PREPARES YOU AND MANY OF THE FAITHFUL TO LIFE ETERNAL.

People. Amen.

Priest. He also mingled with wine and water the Chalice of Life, and blessed it, sanctified it, and

---

(⁹) Brit. Mus., Add. 14,493 ; 14,495 ; 14,690 ; 14,691 ; 17,128.

gave it to the band of His disciples, and said: T<small>HIS</small> IS M<small>Y</small> B<small>LOOD</small>, WHICH SEALS THE TESTAMENT OF M<small>Y</small> *D*<small>EATH</small>, AND PREPARES YOU AND MANY OF THE FAITHFUL TO ETERNAL LIFE.

People. Amen.

Priest. And when He had made them partakers of holiness, and of the benefit of remission of sins, and of His Blood, He first commanded them and enjoined, When ye shall communicate of this Bread and this Chalice, be mindful of, and celebrate the memory of My *D*eath, and make its commemoration until I shall come.

People. (*as in* 18.)

* 22.   S. C<small>YRIL</small> (*Ethiopic*). ([10])

In that night in which they betrayed Him, He took bread in His Hands holy and blessed, which are without stain; He looked up to Heaven to Thee, to His F<small>ATHER</small>; gave thanks, blessed, and brake, and said: Take, eat; THIS BREAD IS M<small>Y</small> B<small>ODY</small>, WHICH IS BROKEN FOR YOU, AND IS GIVEN FOR THE RE-DEMPTION OF THE WHOLE WORLD THROUGH THE REMISSION OF SIN. And again, after they had supped, He took the cup, gave thanks, blessed and consecrated, and said to His disciples: Take, drink; THIS CUP IS M<small>Y</small> B<small>LOOD</small> OF THE N<small>EW</small> T<small>ESTAMENT</small>, WHICH IS SHED FOR YOU, FOR THE REDEMPTION OF THE WHOLE WORLD THROUGH THE REMISSION OF SIN.

23.   S. *D*<small>IONYSIUS</small> OF A<small>THENS</small> (*Syro-Jacobite*). ([11])

And at the end and consummation of His dispen-sation, for our sakes, and before His salutary Cross,

---

([10]) Brit. Mus., Orient. 545, fol. 124 *b*.
([11]) Brit. Mus., Add. 14,690, fol. 56 *b*.

He took bread into His pure and holy hands, and looked to Thee, His God and Father, and, giving thanks, blessed, sanctified, brake, and gave to His disciples, the holy Apostles, saying, Take and eat of it : and believe ([12]) that THIS IS MY BODY : THE VERY SAME WHICH FOR YOU IS BROKEN AND GIVEN FOR THE EXPIATION OF TRANSGRESSIONS, THE REMISSION OF SINS, AND LIFE ETERNAL.

People. Amen.

Priest. In the same manner also over the Chalice, which He mingled with wine and water, He gave thanks, He blessed, He sanctified, and gave the same to His disciples and holy Apostles, saying: Take, drink ye all of it : and believe ([12]) that THIS IS MY BLOOD OF THE NEW TESTAMENT, WHICH FOR YOU AND FOR MANY IS POURED FORTH AND GIVEN FOR THE EXPIATION OF TRANSGRESSIONS, THE REMISSION OF SINS, AND LIFE ETERNAL.

People. Amen.

Priest. And He gave to the whole company and congregation of the faithful, through the same holy Apostles, this precept, saying, Do this in remembrance of Me : as often as ye shall eat this Bread and drink that which is mingled in this Chalice, and shall celebrate this feast, ye shall commemorate My *Death* until I shall come.

People. (*As in* 18.)

([12]) This most presumptuous and unlawful alteration does not render the formula invalid, since it leaves the vital portion, *This is My Body, This is My Blood,* untouched. The disposition, however, to interfere with the plain words of our LORD, here manifested, led, as we shall presently see, to consequences more serious on some of the Syro-Jacobite Liturgies.

* **24.** Dionysius Bar-Salibi (*Syro-Jacobite*). ([13])

And when He had prepared Himself for the saving Passion, the bread which He took, He blessed, brake, and named it His holy Body for life everlasting to those who receive it. And the cup, which He mingled with wine and with water, He blessed, and consecrated, and perfected it (into) His precious Blood for life everlasting to those who receive it. And when He had delivered this to His holy Apostles, He commanded them, saying, Thus do for My commemoration until I come. ([14])

25. [S.] Dioscorus. I. (*Ethiopic*).

In that night in which they betrayed Him, He took bread into His hands, holy, pure, and immaculate; He looked up to Heaven, there, where His Father is, He gave thanks, He blessed and brake, and gave to His holy disciples and pure Apostles, and said to them: Take, eat: this bread is My Body, which is broken for you for the remission of sins.

In like manner also He mingled wine and water, He gave thanks, He blessed, sanctified, and gave to His holy disciples and His pure Apostles, and said to them: Take, drink; this cup is My Blood, which for you is poured forth for the remission of sins.

[This is translated from the very rare edition of Wansleb. I suppose that the responses of the people are supplied from the Ethiopic norm, whence the expression, *this bread*, is borrowed.

([13]) Brit. Mus., Add. 14,691, fol. 104 *a*.
([14]) An invalid formula.

P

* 26.   [S.] DIOSCORUS. II. (*Ethiopic*). (¹⁵)

In that night in which they betrayed Him, He took bread in His holy and blessed hands, which are without stain, He looked up to Heaven, to Thee, to His Father, gave thanks, blessed, and brake, and gave to His own, His disciples, to His disciples the holy, and to His Apostles the pure, and said to them: Take, eat; THIS BREAD IS MY FLESH, WHICH IS BROKEN FOR YOU FOR THE REMISSION OF SIN. And again, after they had supped, He mixed water and wine, gave thanks, blessed and consecrated, and handed to His disciples, to His disciples the holy, and to His Apostles the pure, and said to them: Take, drink; THIS CUP IS MY BLOOD, WHICH IS SHED FOR YOU FOR THE REDEMPTION OF MANY.

* 27.   DIOSCORUS OF ALEXANDRIA (*Syro-Jacobite*). (¹⁶)

He Who, when He wished, in His dispensation as Saviour, before His life-giving passion, after He had feasted with His disciples on the Mosaic lamb, took the bread of life in His hands, pure and stainless and with blessings; blessed it, and consecrated it, and handed to the Apostolic band, saying: Take, eat; VERILY THIS IS MY BODY, WHICH FOR THE SAKE OF THE LIFE OF THE WORLD IS BROKEN AND DIVIDED FOR THE REMISSION OF SINS AND FOR LIFE EVERLASTING.

People. Amen.

Priest. Similarly also, over the cup of life, when He had mingled it with wine and water moderately, and with His holiness, He blessed, and consecrated, and perfected, and handed it to His holy Apostles, saying: Take, drink of it, all of you; for in truth.

(¹⁵) Brit. Mus., Orient. 545, fol. 105 *b.*
(¹⁶) Brit. Mus., Add. 14,690, fol. 153.

THIS IS MY BLOOD, WHICH FOR THE SAKE OF THE LIFE OF THE WORLD IS SHED, AND DIVIDED FOR THE REMISSION OF SINS AND FOR LIFE EVERLASTING.

People. Amen.

28.   [S.] DIOSCORUS OF CARDU (*Syro-Jacobite*).

But in that night in which He was prepared to suffer for the life of creatures, He gave to us the pledge of life, and prepared for us the mystery of His holy Body and Blood: He took bread, after He had accomplished the Mosaic *Pascha*, and laid it upon His holy hands, in the sight of the band and fellowship of His disciples, gave thanks to Thee, GOD the FATHER, blessed, sanctified, brake it, and gave to the band of His twelve after He Himself had communicated, and said: Take, eat of it; THIS IS MY BODY, WHICH FOR THE LIFE OF THE WORLD IS BROKEN AND GIVEN FOR THE EXPIATION OF TRANSGRESSIONS, AND THE REMISSION OF SINS.

People. Amen.

Priest. In like manner, after they had supped, He took the Chalice of Life, mingled it temperately with wine and water, gave thanks, blessed, sanctified it, and gave it also to the same band of holy Apostles, saying: Take, drink ye all of it: THIS IS MY BLOOD OF THE NEW TESTAMENT, WHICH FOR YOU IS POURED FORTH, AND PREPARETH YOU, AND MANY THAT BELIEVE, FOR ETERNAL LIFE.

People. Amen.

Priest. And when ye shall celebrate this quickening and holy Mystery believe and be certain that ye eat of My Body and live; and drink of My Blood, to the expiation of transgressions, and the remission of sins.   And when ye perform all these things, remember and commemorate My *Death*, Sepulture, and Resurrection, until I come.

* 28.   ELEAZAR OF BABYLON ([17]), *otherwise called*
      LAZARUS BAR SABTA. (*Syro-Jacobite*). ([18])

And when He wished to aid His creatures by
means of His divine gifts, and destroyed the power
of death by His death—and this before His salutary
Passion—He took bread into His pure and holy
hands, and looked up to heaven, and shewed (it) unto
Thee, GOD the FATHER. When He had given thanks,
He blessed, consecrated, and brake, and gave to His
disciples, the holy Apostles, and said: Take, eat of
it; THIS IS MY BODY, WHICH IS BROKEN FOR YOU AND
ON ACCOUNT OF MANY, AND GIVEN FOR THE EXPIATION
OF OFFENCES AND THE REMISSION OF SINS, AND FOR LIFE
EVERLASTING.

People. Amen.

Priest. In like manner, too, after they had supped,
when He had mingled with wine and water, and
given thanks, He consecrated, blessed, and gave to
His disciples, the holy Apostles, and said: Take,
drink of it, all of you; THIS IS MY BLOOD OF THE
NEW TESTAMENT, WHICH IS SHED FOR YOU AND FOR
MANY, AND GIVEN FOR THE EXPIATION OF OFFENCES AND
THE REMISSION OF SINS, AND FOR LIFE EVERLASTING.
This do for a remembrance of My *Death*, because,
whenever ye eat this bread and drink the mixture
which is in this cup, ye are accomplishing the
memorial of My *Death* and Resurrection until I
come.

([17]) [This writer is identical with Philoxenus of Bagdad,
cited below by Dr. Neale; but the Anaphora there given is
not identical with this one.—L.]

([18]) Brit. Mus., Add. 14,690, fol. 144 *b.*

* 30. S. EPIPHANIUS (*Ethiopic*). ([19])

In that night, the evening of Thursday to the dawning of Friday, when He had sat down in the house of Lazarus His friend, He took unleavened wheaten bread, of that which they had brought to Him for supper, gave thanks, blessed, and brake, and gave to His own, His disciples, and said to them: Take, eat; THIS BREAD IS THE COMMUNION OF MY BODY, WHICH IS BROKEN FOR YOU. And again, He mingled the cup, wine with water, gave thanks, blessed, and consecrated, and gave to His own, His disciples, and said to them: Take, drink; THIS CUP IS MY BLOOD, WHICH IS SHED FOR YOU. And let this rite be to you for the commemoration of My *Death* and My Resurrection.

[Observe the express mention of unleavened bread, peculiar to this Liturgy.]

31. S. EUSTATHIUS (*Syro-Jacobite*). ([20])

Who, when by His own free will, He went, as it were, a substitute for us sinners to death, took bread into His holy hands, He blessed, sanctified, brake, and gave to His holy disciples, and said: Take, eat of it: THIS IS MY BODY, WHICH PREPARETH YOU, AND ALL THE FAITHFUL THAT RECEIVE IT, FOR LIFE ETERNAL.

People. Amen.

Priest. In like manner the Chalice which He had mingled of wine and water, He blessed, He sanctified, and gave to the same His holy disciples, and said: Take, drink of it; THIS IS MY BLOOD, WHICH PREPARETH YOU, AND ALL THE FAITHFUL THAT RECEIVE IT, TO LIFE ETERNAL.

People. Amen.

([19]) Brit. Mus., Orient. 545, fol. 91 *b*. Bodleian, xvii.
([20]) Brit. Mus., Add. 14,498; 14,691; 14,693; 14,737; 14,738.

Priest. Moreover, when ye shall celebrate this mystery, keep the memory of My *Death*, until I shall come.

People. (*As in* 18.)

32. S. GREGORY (*Copto-Jacobite*).

Priest. For in the night in which Thou didst will to be given up, by Thine own will and power,

People. We believe.

Priest. Thou takest bread into Thy holy, pure, spotless, blessed, and quickening hands, Thou didst look up to Thine own FATHER, our GOD, and the GOD of all, and Thou didst give thanks, Thou didst bless it, Thou didst hallow it, Thou didst break it, Thou didst distribute it to Thy glorious holy disciples, and say to Thy pure Apostles, Take, eat, THIS IS MY BODY, WHICH IS BROKEN FOR YOU AND SHALL BE GIVEN FOR MANY FOR THE REMISSION OF SINS : do this in remembrance of Me.

In like manner after they had eaten, Thou didst take the Chalice, and didst mingle it of the fruit of the vine and of water, Thou didst give thanks and bless it, and hallow it, and distribute it to Thy glorious holy disciples, saying to Thy pure Apostles, *D*rink ye all of it : THIS IS MY BLOOD OF THE NEW TESTAMENT, WHICH FOR YOU IS POURED FORTH AND IS GIVEN FOR MANY FOR THE REMISSION OF SINS : do this in remembrance of Me. For as often as ye eat this Bread and drink this Cup, ye shall set forth My Death, and confess My Resurrection, and make memorial of Me, until I come.

People. Amen. Amen. Amen. We announce Thy death, O LORD, and set forth Thy resurrection.

* **33. S. GREGORY OF ALEXANDRIA** (*Ethiopic*). ([21])

He took bread in His hands, who was pierced and who created our father Adam; pure is He, without sin, and clear is He, without fraud; He gave thanks, blessed, and brake, and gave to His own, His disciples, and said to them : THIS IS MY BODY, THE FOOD OF RIGHTEOUSNESS, WHEREOF VERILY HE WHO EATS SHALL LIVE FOR EVER AND EVER. And again, He looked upon this cup, the water of life with wine; gave thanks, blessed and consecrated, and handed it to His own, His disciples, and said to them : THIS IS MY BLOOD, THE DRAUGHT OF LIFE, WHEREOF VERILY HE WHO DRINKS HATH EVERLASTING LIFE. Take, drink of it, all of you; let it be to you for life and for salvation.

* **34. S. GREGORY OF ARMENIA** (*Ethiopic*). ([22])

Mingle, O Lord, our humanity with Thy Divinity, Thy greatness with our humility, and our humility with Thy greatness, that we may offer this offering which Thou didst give to Thy disciples, saying : Take, eat; THIS BREAD IS MY BODY WHICH IS BROKEN FOR YOU, AND IS GIVEN THAT SIN MAY BE REMITTED AND FOR EVERLASTING LIFE.
People. Amen.
Priest. And similarly, over the cup too, Thou didst speak to them, saying: Take, drink; THIS CUP IS MY BLOOD, WHICH IS POURED OUT FOR YOU, AND IS GIVEN THAT SIN MAY BE REMITTED AND FOR EVER-LASTING LIFE.
People. Amen.
Priest. And thus make commemoration of Me,

([21]) Brit. Mus., Orient. 545, fol. 101 *b*.
([22]) Brit. Mus., Orient. 545, fol. 120 *b*.

Thou didst say to them, whenever ye eat this bread and drink this cup, whilst ye set forth My death and whilst ye rise with My resurrection and believe (in it). And make commemoration of Me with glory and praise and thanksgiving and honour.

* 35. GREGORY BAR-HEBRÆUS [ABU'LFARAJ] (*Syro-Jacobite*). ([23])

Priest. When then He had made ready to receive voluntary death for us sinners, He Who is without sin, He took bread in His holy hands, and when He had given thanks, He blessed, consecrated, and brake, and gave to His holy disciples, and said : Take, eat of it ; THIS IS MY BODY, WHICH FOR YOU AND FOR MANY IS BROKEN, AND GIVEN FOR THE REMISSION OF SINS AND FOR EVERLASTING LIFE.

People. Amen.

Priest. Similarly too as to the cup, when He had given thanks, He blessed, consecrated, and gave to His holy disciples, and said: Take, drink of it, all of you ; THIS IS MY BLOOD, WHICH FOR YOU AND FOR MANY IS SHED, AND GIVEN FOR THE REMISSION OF SINS AND FOR LIFE EVERLASTING.

People. Amen.

Priest. This do in commemoration of Me, (and) when ye communicate, remember (Me) until I come.

* 36. GREGORY BAR-HEBRÆUS. II. (*Syro-Jacobite*).

Who, when He had voluntarily fulfilled His whole dispensation, and had come to His voluntary, quickening, but unmerited *Passion*, gave us a great

---

([23]) Brit. Mus., Add. 14,693, fol. 104.

type and hope of life, to wit, bread which was made His holy Body, He took it with His holy Hands before the eyes of the band of His devout disciples, and looking with uplifted eyes to heaven and gazing on Thee, GOD and FATHER, He gave thanks to Thee, blessed, hallowed, brake, and when He had eaten, He gave it to His holy disciples, and said: Take, eat of it; THIS IS MY BODY WHICH IS BROKEN AND DIVIDED FOR YOU AND FOR MANY BELIEVING IN ME, FOR THE EXPIATION OF TRANSGRESSIONS AND THE REMISSION OF SINS, AND FOR NEW LIFE FOR EVERMORE.

People. Amen.

Priest. And the wine, which became His atoning Blood, after that mystic supper, when He had moderately mingled it with water, He gave thanks, blessed, hallowed, and gave to the band of the holy Apostles, and said: Take, drink ye all of it; THIS IS MY BLOOD WHICH IS SHED AND GIVEN FOR YOU AND FOR MANY BELIEVING IN ME, FOR THE EXPIATION OF TRANSGRESSIONS, THE REMISSION OF SINS, AND NEW LIFE FOR EVERMORE.

People. Amen.

Priest. And when He had delivered the Sacrament to the company of His Apostles, He enjoined them, and commanded them, saying, "Celebrate this Sacrament evermore, because, when ye shall eat this bread, and drink what is mingled in this cup, ye shall make commemoration of My *Death* and Resurrection until I come."

* 37. S. GREGORY NAZIANZEN (*Syro-Jacobite*). [24]

And when He had voluntarily made preparation for the saving *Passion*, on the last night of the

---

[24] Brit. Mus., Add. 14,690, fol. 70 *a*.

conclusion of his dispensation on our behalf, He took bread in His holy hands and shewed it unto Thee, GOD the FATHER, gave thanks, blessed, consecrated, brake, and distributed to His disciples the Apostles, saying: Take, eat of it; for THIS IS MY BODY, WHICH ON YOUR ACCOUNT, AND ON BEHALF OF MANY, IS BROKEN, AND GIVEN FOR THE REMISSION OF SINS AND FOR LIFE EVERLASTING.

People. Amen.

Priest. And so regarding the Cup also, He gave thanks, after He and His disciples had rejoiced over the mystic table, with the offspring of the vine and with water He mixed it moderately, and blessed, and consecrated, and gave to His same disciples the Apostles, saying: Take, drink of it, all of you; THIS IS MY BLOOD OF THE NEW COVENANT, WHICH ON YOUR BEHALF, AND FOR MANY, IS SHED, AND GIVEN FOR THE REMISSION OF SINS AND FOR LIFE EVERLASTING.

People. Amen.

Priest. Ye then, be ye so celebrating the memory of My Death, for when ye eat this Bread, and drink this Cup, ye make commemoration of Me and proclaim My Death until I come.

38. HOLY DOCTORS (*Syro-Jacobite*).

[*This is merely a cento from the Liturgies held in most esteem by the Syro-Jacobites. The Institution, from the beginning down to* This is My Blood of the New Testament, *is from the Syriac S. James; posterior to that, from the Syro-Jacobite S. Cyril.*]

89. S. IGNATIUS OF ANTIOCH (*Syro-Jacobite*). (²⁵)

Who accomplished the whole salutary dispensa-

(²²) Brit. Mus., Add. 14,690; 14,691; 17,128; 17,229.

tion for us, and by His holy *Passion* demonstrated the verity of His advent in the Flesh.([26]) For in the night of the *Pascha* in which He was betrayed for the life and salvation of the world, He took bread into His holy hands, He sanctified it, and brake, and gave to His disciples the holy Apostles, saying, Take, eat of it: THIS IS MY BODY, WHICH PREPARETH YOU AND MANY FOR THE REMISSION OF SINS AND ETERNAL LIFE.

People. Amen.

Priest. In like manner also, when He had mingled the Chalice of Life with wine and water, He sanctified it, and gave it to His holy disciples, saying, Take, drink ye all of it: THIS IS MY BLOOD, WHICH FOR THE LIFE OF THE WORLD GIVE I, AND WHICH PREPARETH YOU AND MANY FOR THE REMISSION OF SINS AND LIFE ETERNAL.

People. Amen.

Priest. Do this in remembrance of Me: for as often as ye shall eat this bread and drink this chalice, ye shall commemorate My *Death*, and confess My Resurrection until I come.

People. (*As in* 13.)

40.   IGNATIUS BAR WAHB (*or* VAHIB) (*Syro-Jacobite*).

Priest. Who, when He had willed to taste the cup of death, that He might comfort and confirm us mortals against death appointed for us by the law of nature, and to descend into the abyss of them that are buried, that they might not be deprived of His quickening visitation ; in that night which was

---

([26]) This expression, clearly directed against the Phantasiasts and other heretics of a similar character, shew the comparative lateness of this Liturgy.

of the beginning and of the end, ([27]) He took perfect
bread ([28]) into His hands full of benedictions, out of
which His holy Body was composed in the Virgin,
who knew not the nuptial couch, before His
friends : giving thanks, He blessed, He sanctified,
and brake it, and divided it into parts, and gave it
to His twelve companions, and said : Take, eat :
THIS IS MY FLESH, WHICH FOR YOU, AND FOR MANY
LIKE YOU, IS BROKEN, SANCTIFIED, AND GIVEN FOR THE
ABOLITION OF SINS AND LIFE ETERNAL.

People. Amen.

Priest. In like manner, having raised His eyes to
heaven, signifying that His Will was one with that
of His FATHER and His HOLY SPIRIT, as if to confirm
the verity of His voluntary *Death*, for the salvation
of His image which lay in corruption, He took also
the Chalice of Life, which He had mingled with
wine of grape and natural water, according to due
measure, after they had feasted on the Sacraments,
and gave thanks, blessed, sanctified, and in like
manner reached it forth to His friends, and said,
Take and drink each from the hand of the other :
FOR THIS IS MY LIVING BLOOD WHICH IS POURED FORTH
FOR THE HUMAN RACE THAT BELIEVE IN ME, FOR THE
ABOLITION OF FOLLIES AND LIFE ETERNAL.

People. Amen.

Priest. And when He had Himself accomplished
this in His person, He enjoined them in His commandments, and said, As often as, being in union

---

([27]) That is, the beginning of the New and the termination
of the Old Passover.

([28]) That is, leavened bread ; a clear proof that this Liturgy
is not older than the time of Photius. Ignatius Bar Vahib
filled the Jacobite throne of Antioch from his election in
1293 till his death in 1332. Assemani. Bib. Orient.
iii. 464.

among yourselves, ye are joined together by these
things, keep the memory of My voluntary *Death*,
make commemoration of My salutary Resurrection,
and expect my Advent until My coming again.

People. (*As in* 18.)

41. S. James (*Orthodox*).
[*See* page 30.]

42. S. James (*Syro-Jacobite*).

[*This is the same as the last, with one or two verbal
differences not worth notice.*]

43. S. James (*the shorter ; Syro-Jacobite*).

[*Abbreviated by Gregory, Catholic of the East,* in
the year 1591.]

Priest. And when He was prepared to undergo
voluntary *Death* for us sinners, He Who had done
no sin, He took bread into His holy hands, and
gave thanks, blessed, sanctified, and brake, and
gave to His holy Apostles and said : Take, eat of it :
THIS IS MY BODY, WHICH FOR YOU AND FOR MANY IS
BROKEN AND GIVEN FOR THE REMISSION OF SINS AND LIFE
ETERNAL.

People. Amen.

Priest. In like manner also He took the chalice
and gave thanks, blessed, sanctified, and gave to
the same His holy Apostles, saying, Take, drink ye
all of it : THIS IS MY BLOOD, WHICH FOR YOU AND FOR
MANY IS POURED FORTH AND GIVEN FOR THE REMISSION
OF SINS AND LIFE ETERNAL.

People. Amen.

Priest. Do this in remembrance of Me : when ye

shall communicate in this mystery, commemorate My *D*eath and My Resurrection until I come.

People. (*As in* 18.)

44. JAMES BARADÆUS. ([29]) (*Syro-Jacobite.*)

Priest. Who, when He had accomplished all His salutary dispensation, above the condition of human nature, Himself, GOD the WORD Incarnate for our sakes : in that night in which it was to be that He should suffer voluntarily, He took common bread into His holy hands, and giving thanks, He blessed, He sanctified and brake, and gave to His Apostolic band, and said to them : THIS IS MY BODY; TAKE, AND EAT OF IT, BECAUSE WITHOUT ANY DOUBT IT IS BROKEN FOR THE LIFE OF THE WORLD, AND SHALL BE TO YOU, AND TO ALL THAT BELIEVE IN ME, FOR THE PRO-PITIATION OF OFFENCES, THE REMISSION OF SINS, AND ETERNAL LIFE.

People. Amen.

Priest. And after they had supped, He took the chalice mingled with wine and water into His pure hands, and giving thanks, He blessed, He sanctified, and gave to His disciples, and said to them : THIS IS MY BLOOD OF THE NEW TESTAMENT ; TAKE, DRINK YE ALL OF IT ; FOR WITHOUT DOUBT IT IS POURED FORTH FOR THE LIFE OF THE WORLD, AND SHALL BE TO YOU AND OF ALL THAT SHALL BELIEVE IN ME, FOR THE PROPITIA-TION OF OFFENCES, THE REMISSION OF SINS, AND ETERNAL LIFE.

People. Amen.

([29]) The celebrated heretic from whom the sect of the Mono-physites derive the more usual name of Jacobites. He flourished in the sixth century; but the Liturgy which goes under his name is of far later date.

Priest. As often therefore as ye shall eat this bread and drink this cup, ye shall commemorate My *Death* and Resurrection until I come.

People. (*As in* 18.)

45.   JAMES OF EDESSA (*Syro-Jacobite.*) ([80])

Priest. When therefore He was eating that legal Lamb, which was the type of the Heavenly Lamb, with His holy disciples, and willed to deliver us from corporal sacrifices of lambs, of bulls, and of kids, and to raise us to more worthy sacrifices, celestial and divine mysteries,—in that evening, in which He was about to give Himself up to be a Sacrifice for us, He took bread into His holy hands, free from all stain, and raising His eyes to heaven, to His FATHER, He gave thanks, He blessed, He brake, He ate, and gave to His disciples, saying: Take, eat of it: THIS IS MY BODY, WHICH FOR THE LIFE OF CREATURES IS BROKEN AND DIVIDED FOR THE REMISSION OF SINS AND LIFE ETERNAL.

People. Amen.

Priest. In like manner He temperately mingled the cup with wine and water, He gave thanks over it, after He had supped with His disciples in the mystical table, He blessed, He sanctified, and reached forth to His holy Apostles, and said: THIS IS MY BLOOD, WHICH I POUR FORTH FOR THE LIFE OF THE WORLD, AND WHICH PREPARETH, FOR THEM THAT BELIEVE IN ME, ETERNAL LIFE.

People. Amen.

Priest. This do as often as ye shall eat this Body

([80]) Brit. Mus., Add. 14,691, fol. 74 *a.*

and drink this Chalice : keep memory of My Death
till I shall come.

People. (*As in* 18.)

*46. JAMES OF SERUG *or* BATNÆ (*Ethiopic*). ([31])

Thou didst take bread in Thy holy hands, that
Thou mightest give it to Thy holy disciples. Thou
Who didst then bless, Who art with glory, bless
now this bread. Thou Who didst then break, Who
art with blessing, break now this bread. And
again, Thou didst mix the cup of wine with water,
that Thou mightest give it to the pure Apostles.
Thou who didst consecrate then, consecrate now
this cup. Thou Who didst hand then, hand now
this cup. Thou Who didst unite then, unite now
this bread to this cup. Let it be Thy Flesh and
Thy Blood. ([32])

47. JAMES OF SERUG (*Syro-Jacobite*). ([33])

Priest. And when He was prepared to suffer, He
left us a commemoration of Himself. For in that
evening in which were accomplished all the mysteries of the type, and the miracles, in that night
in which He was betrayed for the life and salvation
of the world, taking bread into His holy hands, He
looked up to Thee, GOD the FATHER, He gave
thanks, He blessed, He brake, and gave to the
assembly of His disciples, and said to them, Take,
eat of it : THIS IS MY BODY, WHICH FOR YOU AND FOR

([31]) Brit. Mus., Orient. 545, fol. 108 *b* ; Add. 16,202 ;
Bodleian, xvii. 4.

([32]) This is one of the invalid forms, as there is no recitation
of the words of institution.

([33]) Brit. Mus., Add. 14,690, 14,692, 17,229.

MANY IS BROKEN AND GIVEN FOR THE REMISSION OF SINS
AND LIFE ETERNAL.

People. Amen.

Priest. In like manner, after they had supped,
He mingled also the Chalice of Life, of wine and
water, and sanctified, and gave to the assembly of
His disciples, and said to them, Take, drink ye all
of it: THIS IS THE CHALICE OF THE NEW TESTAMENT
IN MY BLOOD, WHICH FOR YOU AND FOR MANY IS POURED
FORTH AND GIVEN FOR THE REMISSION OF SINS AND LIFE
ETERNAL.

People. Amen.

Priest. As often as ye shall eat this Bread and
drink this Chalice, ye shall set forth My Death and
Resurrection till I come.

People. (*As in* 18.)

48. JOHN BAR-MAADAN (*Syro-Jacobite*).

Priest. But when He had accomplished and fulfilled in Himself the figures and shadows of the
ancient law, as the LORD of both Testaments, and
willed to take away from the eyes of the Apostolic
band the typical veil of prophecy, and to bear
witness that that true Body which of old was
obscurely, and as it were afar off, prefigured, was
now in a certain excellent manner close at hand;
in that night which destroyed the night of sin and
death; in that very night in which He was about
to celebrate this religious sacrifice as a *Priest* for
the expiation of the whole world; He took bread
into His holy hands which created the world, and
raised His calm face to the height of heaven, to
the FATHER, and giving thanks, He blessed, and
brake, and ate, and gave to the company of His
holy Apostles, and said: Take, eat of it: THIS IS

Q

MY TRUE BODY, WHICH FOR THE LIFE AND SALVATION
OF THE WHOLE HUMAN RACE IS BROKEN AND GIVEN
FOR THE EXPIATION OF TRANSGRESSIONS AND LIFE
ETERNAL.

People. Amen.

Priest. Thus also He mingled the Chalice mysti-
cally of wine and water, after He had refreshed them
at the Table of Life, He gave thanks, He blessed,
He sanctified, and gave to the band of the holy
Apostles, and said : Take, drink ye all of it : THIS
IS MY LIVING BLOOD OF THE NEW TESTAMENT, WHICH
IS POURED FORTH FOR THE SALVATION OF THE WHOLE
WORLD, AND WHICH PREPARETH THOSE THAT BELIEVE IN
ME TO LIFE ETERNAL.

People. Amen.

Priest. And again He admonished them, saying,
As often as ye are gathered together and break this
Eucharist, ye shall keep and renew the commemoration of My voluntary Death and Resurrection
and shall not suffer it to pass into oblivion until I
come.

People. (*As in* 18.)

* 49. JOHN BAR-SUSAN (*Syro-Jacobite*). [84]

And before the voluntary passion of the WORD
GOD, He took in His divine hands simple bread and
wine that (was) mingled moderately with water,
blessed, and consecrated, and brake, and handed it
to the band of the twelve, saying : Take, use (it);
and when of these ye eat and drink, believe that
they are My Body and Blood, which I give for the
salvation of the world, and they shall be to you,
and through you to the whole world, for the com-

---

[84] Brit. Mus., Add. 14,693, fol. 94 *a.*

memoration of My Burial and Resurrection, until that I come. ([85])

50. JOHN OF BASSORA (*Syro-Jacobite*). ([86])

Priest. He then, the Prince of the Revelation of our good things, on that evening of His voluntary groaning, explaining by these quickening and easily-to-be-handled Elements, this Mystery which cannot be expressed in words, He took bread into His holy hands, and as the High Priest and Apostle of our confession, rendering thanks for us, He gave thanks, He blessed, He sanctified, He brake, and gave to His disciples, saying: Take, eat of it: THIS IS MY BODY, WHICH FOR YOU AND FOR MANY IS BROKEN AND DIVIDED FOR THE EXPIATION OF TRANSGRESSIONS, AND LIFE ETERNAL.

People. Amen.

Priest. In like manner also, when He had mingled the Chalice with wine and water, He blessed, He sanctified, and divided to His disciples, saying: Take, drink ye all of it: THIS IS MY BLOOD OF THE NEW TESTAMENT, WHICH FOR YOU AND FOR MANY IS POURED FORTH AND GIVEN FOR THE REMISSION OF SINS AND ETERNAL LIFE.

People. Amen.

Priest. This, saith He, do in remembrance of Me: for I say unto you that I will be in the midst of you, and will give holiness to those rites which shall be accomplished: for he that eateth My Body, and drinketh My Blood, dwelleth in Me and I in him; and as I live through the FATHER, so also he

---

([85]) An invalid formula.   ([86]) Brit. Mus., Add. 14,525.

that eateth Me, shall live through Me. Receiving, therefore, this mystical institution, according to the disposition of Thy laws, O GOD the WORD, we have prepared Bread, and have mingled the Chalice —commemorating over them all Thy dispensation, from the first assumption of our flesh, which took place in a moment and in the twinkling of an eye, even to the *Passion*, the *Death*, the Cross, and the Resurrection worthy of GOD ; with a pure heart, and with one voice, according to that Thy divine precept, Ye shall set forth My *Death* and confess My Resurrection until Mine Advent.

People. (*As in* 18.)

* 51. S. JOHN THE EVANGELIST (*Ethiopic*). ([37])

He took bread in His holy and blessed hands, a marriage-gift for Thy spouse, and a divorce for her whom He left, the Synagogue. He gave thanks, blessed, and brake, and gave to His disciples, and said to them : THIS IS MY BODY, THE FOOD OF RIGHTEOUSNESS, WHICH VERILY HE WHO EATS SHALL NOT DIE, AND HE WHO TAKES SHALL NOT PERISH. Take, eat of it, all of you. And similarly He praised (GOD) over the Cup too, and said : THIS CUP IS MY BLOOD OF THE NEW TESTAMENT : take, drink of it, all of you. A wondrous sign it is to all those who worship Him, a bar of judgment to the crucifiers, which is written with His Blood, and sealed with His Cross, and signed with His *Death*, for everlasting life, whereby sin is forgiven. And thus make commemoration of Me when ye are gathered together.

([37]) Brit. Mus., Orient. 545, fol. 67; Add. 16,202 ; Bodleian, xvii. 1.

52. S. John the Evangelist (*Syro-Jacobite*). ([38])

Priest. And when, by His own free-will, He had come to His salutary *Passion* for our salvation, He took bread into His holy hands, before the eyes of the band of His disciples; He looked up to heaven, He gave thanks, He blessed, and sanctified, He brake, and gave to His holy Apostles, and said: Take, eat of it: THIS IS MY BODY, WHICH FOR YOU AND FOR ALL THAT BELIEVE IN ME IS BROKEN AND DIVIDED FOR THE EXPIATION OF TRANSGRESSIONS, THE REMISSION OF SINS, AND THE LIFE TO COME THAT IS FOR EVERLASTING.

People. Amen.

Priest. And after that His mystical supper, He also received the Chalice of wine and water, and gave thanks over it and blessed, sanctified, and gave to the band of His Apostles, and said to them: THIS IS THE CHALICE OF MY BLOOD OF THE NEW TESTAMENT: TAKE, DRINK YE ALL OF IT: THIS IS SHED FORTH FOR THE LIFE OF THE WORLD, FOR THE EXPIATION OF TRANSGRESSIONS, THE REMISSION OF SINS TO ALL THAT BELIEVE IN ME FOR EVER AND EVER.

People. Amen.

Priest. Thus shall ye do in remembrance of Me; for as often as ye shall eat this Sacrament, and shall drink this Blood, ye shall set forth My *Death* till I come.

People. (*As in* 18.)

[Observe in this Liturgy the remarkable transposition of the two clauses regarding the Chalice—"This is the Chalice," and "Take, drink ye all of it."]

([38]) Brit. Mus., Add. 14,690; 14,693; 14,694; 14,738, 17,229.

53.   John Maro (*Syro-Jacobite*).

[This Liturgy has not been published, nor have I been able to procure it.]

54. John the Scribe (*Syro-Jacobite*).

Priest. For our Lord Jesus Christ Himself, when it was about to be that He was to undergo a voluntary death for us sinners, Himself free from sin, He took bread into His holy and immaculate hands, and looked up to Thee, God and Father, and giving thanks, He blessed, and sanctified, and brake, and gave to His disciples who were to be initiated in His mystery, and said: Take, eat of it: This is My Body, which for you and for many is broken, and given for the expiation of transgressions, the remission of sins, and eternal life.

People. Amen.

Priest. Thus also the Chalice, which He had mingled of wine and water; giving thanks, He blessed, He sanctified, and gave to His holy disciples, and said: This is My Blood; take, and drink ye all of it; this is poured forth for the life of the world, for the expiation of transgressions, the remission of sins, and life eternal.

People. Amen.

Priest. And when ye shall accomplish this mystical ministry, according to My doctrine, for the salvation of your life, and shall eat this Bread and drink this Chalice, ye shall set forth My Death, and confess My Resurrection, until I shall come.

People. (*As in* 18.)

55. S. JULIUS (*Syro-Jacobite*). ([39])

Priest. In that last evening in which He was about to give Himself up for the life and salvation of the world, He took bread into His holy hands, and blessed, and brake, and gave to His holy disciples, and said : Take, eat of it : THIS IS MY BODY, THE VERY SAME WHICH FOR YOU AND FOR MANY IS GIVEN FOR THE EXPIATION OF TRANSGRESSIONS, THE REMISSION OF SINS, AND LIFE ETERNAL.

People. Amen.

Priest. In like manner also, He gave thanks over the Chalice, He blessed, He sanctified, and gave to His disciples, the holy Apostles, and said : Take, drink ye all of it : THIS IS MY BLOOD OF THE NEW TESTAMENT, WHICH FOR YOU AND FOR MANY IS GIVEN FOR THE EXPIATION OF TRANSGRESSIONS, AND REMISSION OF SINS, AND ETERNAL LIFE.

People. Amen.

Priest. For as often as ye shall celebrate this mystery, ye shall accomplish the commemoration of My *D*eath and Resurrection, until I shall come.

People. (*As in* **18.**)

56. S. MARK (*Orthodox*).

[*See* page 1.]

57. S. MARK (*Syro-Jacobite*). ([40])

Priest. When therefore He, for our sake, had come to His *P*assion in the flesh, by His grace, He

---

([39]) Brit. Mus., Add. 14,493 ; 14,496 ; 14,690 ; 14,694; 17,229.

([40]) Brit. Mus., Add. 14,692 ; 14,694 ; 17,229

in Whom sin was not found, took bread into His holy hands, and looked up to heaven, and gave thanks, and blessed, and sanctified, and brake, and said to His disciples: THIS IS MY BODY; TAKE, EAT, FOR THE REMISSION OF SINS OF YOURSELVES, AND OF ALL THE TRUE FAITHFUL, AND FOR ETERNAL LIFE.

People. Amen.

Priest. In like manner also, mingling the Chalice of wine and water, He blessed and sanctified, and gave to His disciples, and said: THIS IS MY BLOOD OF THE NEW TESTAMENT; TAKE, DRINK YE ALL OF IT, FOR THE REMISSION OF SINS, OF YOU AND OF ALL THE TRUE FAITHFUL, AND FOR ETERNAL LIFE.

People. Amen.

Priest. And when ye shall accomplish these My precepts, ye shall set forth My *Death* and Resurrection, until I come.

People. (*As in* 18.)

58. S. MARUTHAS (*Syro-Jacobite*). ([1])

Priest. And in that last night in which it was ordained that He should save the world, and should seal and fulfil the law, and should, at the same time, begin the New Testament, and should teach to those that were saved by Him the doctrine full of life; He took leavened bread into His pure hands, and giving thanks to the FATHER, He blessed, He sanctified, He brake and divided to His disciples, and said: Take, eat: believe and be certain, and thus preach and teach, that THIS IS MY BODY, WHICH FOR THE SALVATION OF THE WORLD, IS BROKEN, AND TO

([1]) Brit. Mus., Add. 14,694, fol. 64 *a*.

THEM THAT EAT IT AND BELIEVE IN ME, GIVETH EXPIA-
TION OF SINS, AND ETERNAL LIFE.

People. Amen.

Priest. Continuing in like manner, He took also
the wine, and when He had mingled it in just pro-
portion with water, He blessed, He sanctified, and
gave it to the same disciples, and said : Take, drink
ye all of it, and believe and be certain, and thus
preach and teach, that THIS IS MY BLOOD, WHICH
FOR THE SALVATION OF THE WORLD IS POURED FORTH,
AND TO THEM THAT DRINK IT AND BELIEVE IN ME,
GIVETH EXPIATION OF SINS AND LIFE ETERNAL.

People. Amen.

Priest. And while making them partakers of
His Body and His holy Blood, He taught them with
His holy doctrine, saying: As ye have seen Me do,
thus do and teach ye in the never-to-be-forgotten
commemoration of My dispensation, and to the
salvation of your life. Believe also My Resurrection, hope in Me, and at the same time expect My
Advent, until I come.

People. (*As in* 18.)

59. MALABAR, *originally* NESTORIAN.

[*See* page 146.]

* 60. S. MARY (*Ethiopic*). ([42])

In it [viz., in that night] JESUS CHRIST took Bread
in His holy, and blessed, and pure hands, which are
without stain, He looked up to heaven, to His
FATHER, and implored mercy of His parent, and

([42]) Brit. Mus.. Orient. 545, fol. 63 *b* ; Bodleian, xvii. 8.

commended (to Him) His disciples, that, He might guard them from all evil. He blessed, whilst it is blessed, He brake, whilst it is holy, and gave to His disciples, and said to them: Take, eat; THIS BREAD IS MY BODY, WHICH IS GIVEN FOR YOU AND FOR THE REDEMPTION OF THE WHOLE WORLD. And similarly the Cup too, after they had supped, He looked up and said: Take, drink; THIS CUP IS MY BLOOD, WHICH FOR YOU THE SPEAR SHALL SHED. And when ye do this, ye shall make commemoration of My *Death*, and commemoration of My Resurrection ye shall set forth.

61. MATTHEW THE SHEPHERD (*Syro-Jacobite*). ([43])

Priest. And when He willed to give a New Testament, by which the Old should be abolished, He took leavened bread, in which the mystery of life was concealed, and earnestly looking to Thee, FATHER, He gave thanks, He blessed, He sanctified, He brake, and gave to them that were lying at His supper, saying: Take, eat of it: THIS IS MY FLESH, WHICH FOR ALL THE FAITHFUL THAT ADHERE TO ME IS DIVIDED, THAT IT MAY BE EATEN FOR THE EXPIATION OF TRANSGRESSIONS, THE REMISSION OF SINS, AND ETERNAL LIFE.

People. Amen.

Deacon. In like manner also, He took the Chalice of Life, which He had temperately mingled with the fruit of the vine and water, and gave thanks, blessed, sanctified, and gave also to them that were initiated in His mystery, and exhorted them that all should communicate of it, and declared that in it should be salvation to them that drink it, when they use it in a pure conscience, to the expiation

---

([43]) Brit. Mus., Add. 14,693.

of transgressions, the remission of sins, and eternal life.

People. Amen.

Priest. He adjoined also an admonition and declaration, saying: As often as ye shall be partakers of the Mysteries, ye shall celebrate the memory of My *Death* and Resurrection until I come.

People. (*As in* 18.)

[Observe that, valid, though much corrupted, in the first part of the Institution, this formula is invalid in the second.]

62. MICHAEL OF ANTIOCH (*Syro-Jacobite*).

Priest. And He thus accomplished our salvation by His *Divine* dispensation, and set forth, accomplished, pointed out and taught, these Mysteries full of life. Taking bread into His holy hands, He blessed it, sanctified it, brake, and gave to His Apostles, and by their hands to the entire Holy Catholic Church, saying: THIS IS MY BODY, WHICH FOR YOU IS BROKEN, AND GIVEN FOR THE EXPIATION OF OFFENCES, THE REMISSION OF SINS, AND THE NEW LIFE THAT IS TO COME.

People. Amen.

Priest. Together also with the Bread, He took the Chalice, when He had first mingled with wine and water, He blessed it, He sanctified it, and commended it by the hands of His Apostles to His Church, saying: THIS IS MY BLOOD, WHICH FOR YOU IS GIVEN, TO THE EXPIATION OF OFFENCES, THE REMISSION OF SINS, AND THE NEW LIFE THAT IS TO COME.

People. Amen.

Priest. Ye shall perpetually make this commemoration of My *Death* and Resurrection, until I shall come.

People. (*As in* 18.)

63. MOSES BAR-CEPHAS (*Syro-Jacobite*). ([44])

Priest. And in the evening of His salutary Passion, He ate and abrogated the legal Lamb: then He took bread into His holy hands, and looked up to Thee, GOD the FATHER, giving thanks: He blessed and sanctified, and brake and gave to His holy disciples, saying: Take, eat of it: THIS IS MY BODY, WHICH FOR ALL THAT BELIEVE IN ME IS BROKEN AND DIVIDED FOR THE EXPIATION OF TRANSGRESSIONS, THE REMISSION OF SINS, AND LIFE ETERNAL.

People. Amen.

Priest. In like manner He took the Chalice, temperately mixed of wine and water, and giving thanks, He blessed and sanctified, and gave to His holy disciples, and all His Apostles, saying: Take, drink ye all of it: THIS IS MY BLOOD, WHICH FOR YOU, AND FOR THEM THAT BELIEVE IN ME, IS POURED FORTH AND GIVEN, AND WHICH PREPARETH ALL THEM THAT RECEIVE IT FOR LIFE ETERNAL.

People. Amen.

Priest. As often as ye shall thus accomplish these things, believe and be certain that ye eat My Body and drink My Blood, and keep ye memory of My Death and Sepulture and Resurrection, until I shall come.

People. (*As in* 18.)

64. MOZARABIC.

Priest. Our LORD JESUS CHRIST in the same night in which He was betrayed, took bread; and when He had given thanks, He blessed, and brake, and gave to His disciples, saying: Take, and eat: THIS IS MY BODY, WHICH SHALL BE GIVEN FOR YOU. AS

([44]) Brit. Mus., Add. 14,692.

often **as ye** shall eat, this do in remembrance of Me.

In like manner also, the Chalice, after He supped, saying : THIS IS THE CHALICE OF THE NEW TESTA-MENT IN MY BLOOD, WHICH FOR YOU AND FOR MANY SHALL BE POURED FORTH FOR THE REMISSION OF SINS : as often as ye drink, do this in remembrance of Me.   -

People. Amen.

Priest. As often as ye shall eat this Bread and drink this Chalice, ye shall set forth the *Death* of the LORD, until He come in glory from heaven.

People. Amen.

65. NARSES THE LEPER (*Nestorian*).

[*This Liturgy I cannot procure.*]

66. NESTORIUS (*Nestorian*).

Priest. For when the time had come in which He was betrayed for the life of the world, after He had supped on the *P*assover of the Mosaic law, He took bread into His holy, immaculate, and unpolluted hands : He blessed, and brake, and ate, and gave to His disciples, and said : Take, eat ye all of it : THIS IS MY BODY, WHICH FOR YOU IS BROKEN FOR THE REMISSION OF SINS.

In like manner also He mingled the Chalice of wine and water, and blessed, and drank, and gave to His disciples, and said : *D*rink ye all of it : THIS IS MY BLOOD OF THE NEW TESTAMENT, WHICH FOR MANY IS POURED FORTH FOR THE REMISSION OF SINS ; and this do ye in remembrance of Me, until I shall come. For as often as ye shall eat of this Bread, and drink of this Chalice, ye shall set forth My *D*eath, until My coming.

67. NONJURORS.

And when His hour was come to offer the pro-
pitiatory sacrifice on the Cross, when He Who had
no sin Himself, mercifully undertook to suffer death
for our sins ; in the same night that He was betrayed,
He took bread : and when He had given thanks,
He brake it, and gave it to His disciples, saying :
Take, eat : THIS IS MY BODY, WHICH IS GIVEN FOR
YOU : this do in remembrance of Me.

People. Amen.

Likewise, after supper, He took the Cup, and
when He had given thanks, He gave it to them,
saying : *D*rink ye all of this : FOR THIS IS MY BLOOD
OF THE NEW TESTAMENT WHICH IS SHED FOR YOU AND
FOR MANY FOR THE REMISSION OF SINS : do this, as oft
as ye shall drink it, in remembrance of Me.

People. Amen.

68. OUR LORD JESUS CHRIST. I. (*Ethiopic.*)

Priest. In the same night in which He was
betrayed, He took bread into His blameless hands,
full of blessings, and looking up to heaven to Thee,
His FATHER and our FATHER, He blessed, He sanctified, He brake, He ate, He gave to His disciples,
saying : Take, eat ye all of it : THIS BREAD IS MY
BODY, WHICH IS GIVEN FOR YOU AND FOR MANY FOR THE
REMISSION OF SINS.

People. Amen, Amen, Amen.   We believe and
are certain.

Priest. In like manner, He took the Chalice, He
blessed, He sanctified, He received, and said :
*D*rink ye all of it : THIS IS THE CHALICE OF MY
BLOOD, WHICH IS SHED FOR YOU AND FOR MANY.

People. Amen, Amen, Amen.

* 69. Our Lord Jesus Christ. II. (*Ethiopic.*) ([45])

In that night in which they delivered Him up, He took bread in His holy and blessed hands, which are without stain, He gave thanks, blessed, and brake, and handed to His disciples, saying: Take, eat; THIS BREAD IS MY BODY, WHICH IS BROKEN FOR YOU FOR THE REMISSION OF SINS; and when ye do this, make commemoration of Me. And similarly the Cup of wine, Thy mixing, giving thanks, blessing, and consecrating, and Thou gavest to them; verily this is Thy Blood, which was poured out for our sins. ([46])

70. S. Peter. I. (*Syro-Jacobite.*)

Priest. And when He was preparing that banquet of His Body and holy Blood, imparting it to us, and near was His salutary *Passion*, He took bread in His immaculate hands, and lifted it up, and vouchsafed to bestow on it His visible aspect and insensible benediction, and blessed it, and sanctified it, and gave it to the disciples, His Apostles, and said: Let these mysteries be the support of your journey; and whenever ye eat this in the way of food, believe and be certain that THIS IS MY BODY, WHICH FOR YOU AND FOR MANY IS BROKEN AND IS GIVEN FOR THE EXPIATION OF TRANSGRESSIONS, THE REMISSION OF SINS, AND LIFE ETERNAL.

People. Amen.

Priest. In like manner the Chalice also; after He had supped, He mingled wine and water, and blessed, and sanctified, and gave to the disciples,

---

([45]) Brit. Mus., Orient. 545, fol. 56 *b*.

([46]) The latter part of this formula is invalid, and there is **no** consecration of the Cup.

His Apostles, saying : Take, drink ye all of it ; FOR
THIS IS MY BLOOD OF THE NEW TESTAMENT, WHICH FOR
YOU AND FOR MANY IS POURED AND GIVEN FOR THE
PARDON OF TRANSGRESSIONS, THE REMISSION OF SINS, AND
ETERNAL LIFE.

People. Amen.

Priest. And that they might receive the most
sweet fruit of that divine operation, He commanded
them after this fashion : As often as ye shall be
gathered together, keep memory of Me, and eating
this offered Bread, and drinking that which is
prepared in this Cup, ye shall do it in remembrance of Me, and shall confess My death, until I
come.

71. S. PETER. II. (*Syro Jacobite.*)

Priest. Who, when He willed to taste death, and
was accomplishing the *Pascha* in the evening, He
took bread into His hands, He blessed, He sanctified
and brake, and gave to the company of the holy
Apostles, and said, Take and eat, for the remission
of sins and life eternal.

People. Amen.

Priest. In like manner, mingling the Chalice of
wine and water, He blessed, sanctified, and said to
them, Take, and drink ye all of it, for the remission
of sins and life eternal.

People. Amen.

Priest. This He commanded and admonished
them, That as often as ye shall accomplish these
mysteries, ye shall commemorate My *Death* and
Resurrection until I come.

People. (*As in* 15.)

[This is one of the liturgies which is invalid from the
omission of the words, This is My Body, This is My Blood.
It is one of the shortest of all the Syro-Jacobite offices.

and perhaps the composer ignorantly thought that the Invocation of the HOLY GHOST, which is singularly plain and expressive, might, by itself, avail for the transmutation of the Elements. He might also wish to express his dissent from the Latin practice of entirely omitting the Invocation. Some copies of this Liturgy have the words inserted by a later hand.]

72. PHILOXENUS OF BAGDAD (*Syro-Jacobite*).

Priest. But, desiring to assist the work of His hands by His gifts, and to destroy the dominion of death by His own death: He, before His salutary Passion, took bread into His pure, immaculate, and unspotted hands, and looked up to Thee, GOD the FATHER; and giving thanks, He blessed, sanctified, brake, and gave to His disciples and holy Apostles, saying: Take, eat of it: THIS IS MY BODY, THAT SAME WHICH FOR YOU IS BROKEN AND GIVEN, FOR THE EXPIATION OF TRANSGRESSIONS, THE REMISSION OF SINS, AND LIFE ETERNAL TO THEM THAT RECEIVE IT.

People. Amen.

Priest. In like manner also, after they had supped, mingling the Chalice with wine and water, and giving thanks, He blessed, He sanctified, and gave to the same His disciples and holy Apostles, saying: Take, drink ye all of it: THIS IS MY BLOOD OF THE NEW TESTAMENT, THAT SAME WHICH FOR YOU AND FOR MANY IS POURED FORTH AND GIVEN FOR THE EXPIATION OF TRANSGRESSIONS, THE REMISSION OF SINS, AND LIFE ETERNAL TO THEM THAT RECEIVE.

People. Amen.

Priest. Do this in remembrance of Me; for as often as ye shall eat this Bread and drink this Chalice, ye shall set forth My death, until I shall come.

People. (*As in* 18.)

R

73. Philoxenus of Mabug. I. (*Syro-Jacobite.*)

Priest. And when He willed of His own free will to taste death for us, and to accomplish the legal Passover, He took bread into His holy hands, and lifted up His eyes to Thee, God the Father; He gave thanks, He blessed, He sanctified, He brake, and gave to the order of His holy Apostles, and said : This is My Body, which for you and for many is broken and divided, for the remission of sins and life eternal.

People. Amen.

Priest. In like manner He also mingled the Chalice of wine and water, He gave thanks, He blessed, He sanctified, and gave to the company of His holy Apostles, and said : Take, drink ye all of it : This is My Blood, which for you and for many is poured forth for the remission of sins, and life eternal.

People. Amen.

Priest. Thus also He commanded and admonished them : As often as ye shall celebrate these Mysteries, ye shall do it to commemorate My Death and Resurrection, until I shall come.

People. (*As in* 18.)

74. Philoxenus of Mabug. II. (*Syro-Jacobite.*)

Priest. Who, when He had accomplished all His dispensation, salutary and full of life, and had exhibited virtues and miracles to all creatures, and had in all places destroyed the power of the Rebel and Seducer, and coming to His salutary Passion through love to us men, He had eaten that legal Lamb with the company of His disciples ; taking bread into His pure, holy, immaculate and unpolluted hands, raising His eyes to heaven, He looked up to Thee, God the Father, and gave thanks, blessed, sancti-

fied, brake, and gave to His holy disciples, saying:
Take, eat of it: THIS IS MY BODY, WHICH PREPARETH
YOU AND MANY FAITHFUL TO LIFE ETERNAL.

People. Amen.

Priest. In like manner also He took the Chalice,
tempered with wine and water, and gave thanks,
blessed, sanctified, and gave to the same disciples,
His Apostles, saying: Take, drink ye all of it:
THIS IS MY BLOOD OF THE NEW TESTAMENT, WHICH
PREPARETH YOU AND MANY FAITHFUL TO LIFE ETERNAL.

People. Amen.

Priest. And ever do this in remembrance of Me:
for as often as ye shall eat this Bread and shall
drink this Chalice, ye shall make memory of My
Death and announce My Resurrection, until I
come.

People. (*As in* 18.)

75. ROMAN.

Priest. Who, the day before He suffered, took
bread into His holy and venerable hands: and
having lifted up His eyes to heaven, to Thee His
Father GOD Almighty, He blessed, He brake, and
gave to His disciples, saying: Take and eat ye all
of this: FOR THIS IS MY BODY.

In like manner after they supped, taking also
this glorious Chalice into His holy and venerable
hands; also rendering thanks to Thee, He blessed
and gave to His disciples, saying: Take, and drink
ye all of it: FOR THIS IS THE CHALICE OF MY BLOOD,
OF THE NEW AND ETERNAL TESTAMENT, THE MYSTERY
OF FAITH: WHICH FOR YOU AND FOR MANY SHALL BE
POURED FORTH FOR THE REMISSION OF SINS. As often
as ye do these things, ye shall do them in memory
of Me.

* 76. ROMANO-CHALDEE. (47)

Glory to Thee, GOD the FATHER, who didst send Thy only SON for our deliverance; and He, on the day before His *Passion*, took bread in His holy hands, and lifted up His eyes unto Thee, GOD, His FATHER Omnipotent, and gave thanks to Thee, and blessed, and brake, and gave to His disciples, saying: Take, eat of it, all of you; THIS IS MY BODY.

In the same way, after they had supped, He took in His pure hands this pure Cup, and gave thanks to Thee, and blessed, and gave to His disciples, saying: Take, drink of it, all of you; THIS IS THE CUP OF MY BLOOD OF THE NEW TESTAMENT, WHICH IS FOR EVER THE MYSTERY OF FAITH, WHICH FOR YOU AND FOR MANY IS SHED FOR THE REMISSION OF SINS.

77.   SCOTTISH.

Priest. Who, (by His own oblation of Himself once offered,) made a full, perfect, and sufficient sacrifice, oblation, and satisfaction for the sins of the whole world; and did institute, and in His Holy Gospel command us to continue, a perpetual memorial of that His precious death and sacrifice, until His coming again. For in the night that He was betrayed, He took bread, and when He had given thanks, He brake it, and gave it to His disciples, saying: Take, eat: THIS IS MY BODY, WHICH IS GIVEN FOR YOU: do this in remembrance of Me.

Likewise, after supper, He took the cup; and when He had given thanks, He gave it to them, saying: *D*rink ye all of this: FOR THIS IS My

---

(47) Brit. Mus., Add. 25,874, fol. 21 *b*.

BLOOD OF THE NEW TESTAMENT, WHICH IS FOR YOU, AND FOR MANY, FOR THE REMISSION OF SINS : do this, as often as ye shall drink it, in remembrance of Me.

78. SEVERUS OF ANTIOCH (*Syro-Jacobite*).

Priest. Who, when He left His salutary Passion and Cross for a memorial to us, He, the Physician of our wickednesses, offering the oblation of Himself for us to Thee, GOD and FATHER, took bread into His hands, and stretching them to heaven, He blessed, He sanctified, He brake, and divided to His disciples the Apostles, saying : Take, eat of it : FOR THIS IS MY BODY, WHICH FOR YOU AND FOR MANY IS BROKEN AND GIVEN UNTO LIFE ETERNAL.

People. Amen.

Priest. In like manner also He took the Chalice, after they had supped, and mingling it with wine and water, He gave thanks, and sanctified, and divided to His disciples the Apostles, saying : Take, drink ye all of it : THIS IS MY BLOOD OF THE NEW TESTAMENT, WHICH FOR YOU AND FOR MANY IS POURED FORTH AND GIVEN FOR THE REMISSION OF SINS. Do this in remembrance of Me ; for as often as ye shall eat this Bread, and shall drink this Chalice, ye shall set forth My death.

People. (*As in* 18.)

79. THEODORE THE INTERPRETER (*Nestorian*).

Priest. Who, with His Apostles, in that night in which He was betrayed, celebrated this Mystery, great, tremendous, holy and divine : taking bread, He blessed and brake, and gave to His disciples,

and said : THIS IS MY BODY, WHICH FOR YOU IS
BROKEN FOR THE REMISSION OF SINS.

In like manner also the Chalice : He gave thanks,
and gave to them and said : THIS IS MY BLOOD OF
THE NEW TESTAMENT, WHICH FOR MANY IS POURED
FORTH FOR THE REMISSION OF SINS.   Take ye all,
therefore, and eat of this Bread and drink of this
Chalice, and do thus, as often as ye shall be gathered
together, in remembrance of Me.

80.   THOMAS OF HERACLEA (*Syro-Jacobite*). ([48])

Priest. Verily and certainly He took on Himself
the form of a servant, that in that form He might
accomplish the things that were to be for our salvation, and the life that was to be given us.   He took
bread and wine : He blessed, He sanctified, He
brake, and gave to His Apostles, saying : Take, use,
and thus do.   And when ye shall receive these
things, believe and be certain that ye eat My Body
and drink My Blood, doing it in remembrance of
My *Death*, until I shall come.

People. (*As in* 18.)

[This is one of the invalid formulæ : the words inserted in the
second clause, according to the judgment of the best
ritualists, scarcely avail to make good their omission in
the first.]

* 81.   THE THREE HUNDRED AND EIGHTEEN.
(Fathers of Nicæa).   (*Ethiopic*).   ([49])

He went along with them, and shewed them the
order of the mystery of the Sacrifice.   He took

([48]) Brit. Mus., Add. 14,692, fol. 36 *b*.

([49]) Brit. Mus., Orient. 545, fol. 97 *b*.

bread in their presence, blessed, and said : Take,
eat: THIS BREAD IS MY BODY, WHICH IS BROKEN
FOR YOU, FOR THE REMISSION OF SIN. And likewise
the Cup, He blessed, and said : Take, drink; THIS
CUP IS MY BLOOD, WHICH IS GIVEN FOR YOU, FOR THE
REMISSION OF SIN.

82. S. XYSTUS (*Syro-Jacobite*).([50])

Priest. Who, when He was prepared for His
salutary *P*assion, in the bread which by Him was
blessed, sanctified, broken, and distributed to His
holy Apostles, sanctifying His Body, He gave it to
us, saying : Eat ye of it : FOR THIS IS MY BODY,
WHICH FOR YOU AND FOR MANY IS BROKEN AND DIVIDED,
FOR THE EXPIATION OF TRANSGRESSIONS, AND THE RE-
MISSION OF SINS, TO ETERNAL LIFE.

People. Amen.

Priest. In like manner, in the Cup which was by
Him signed, sanctified, and given to the same holy
Apostles, giving to us, His propitiatory Blood, He
said : Take, drink ye all of it : FOR THIS IS THE
CHALICE OF MY BLOOD OF THE NEW TESTAMENT,
WHICH FOR YOU AND MANY IS GIVEN FOR THE EXPIATION
OF TRANSGRESSIONS, AND HATH GIVEN TO US THE RE-
MISSION OF ETERNAL LIFE.

People. Amen.

Priest. He also added this admonition, saying:
As often as ye shall communicate in this Bread,
ye shall set forth My *D*eath and Resurrection, until
I come.

People. (*As in* 18.)

([50]) Brit. Mus., Add. 14,691, fol. 100 *a*; 14,694, fol. 103 *a*.

APPENDIX II.

PRAYERS FOR THE FAITHFUL DEPARTED.

In the following Appendix I propose to give the more interesting among the intercessions for the faithful departed which occur in the whole body of Liturgies. The more they are examined, the more clearly two points will appear. 1. That prayers for the dead, and more especially the oblation of the blessed Eucharist for them, have been from the beginning the practice of the Universal Church. 2. And this without any idea of a purgatory of pain, or of any state from which the departed soul has to be delivered as from one of misery. The examples are arranged in alphabetical order ; and the many that are omitted, are omitted, not because they contravene the above statements, (a polemical deceit of which God forbid that I should be guilty,) but only, either because they say less strikingly what is better expressed in some example that I have given ; or as being conceived in precisely the same words.

1. ARMENIAN.

Remember, Lord, and have mercy, and be propitious to the souls of the departed, and give them repose and life, and set them with Thy Saints in

the kingdom of heaven, making them worthy of
Thy mercy.

2.   S. Basil (*Copto-Jacobite*).

In like manner, O Lord, remember also all those
who have already fallen asleep in the Priesthood,
and amidst the laity; vouchsafe to give rest to all
their souls, in the bosoms of our holy fathers,
Abraham, and Isaac, and Jacob.   Bring them in and
collect them in a place of greenness, by the water of
comfort in the paradise of pleasure, where grief and
misery and sighing are banished, in the brightness
of Thy Saints.

8.   S. Clement (*Syro-Jacobite*).

And at Thy spiritual and holy altar, O Lord,
grant rest, good memory, and felicity to all the
souls, bodies, and spirits of our fathers, brethren,
and sisters, corporal or spiritual, who have departed
in whatever regions, cities, or states; or have been
suffocated in the sea or in rivers, or who have died
in travel, and of whom there is no memory in the
Churches constituted on earth.   Thou, O Lord,
give them good memory, who have departed to Thee
in the orthodox faith, together with those whose
names are written in the book of life.

And to all of them who, having run the race of
this life, have appeared perfect and illustrious before
Thee, and having been set free from the ocean of
sins have reached Thee, our fathers and brethren
according to the flesh and the spirit,—give rest,
O Lord, in that spiritual and mighty bosom.   Give
them the spirit of joy in the habitations of light and
gladness, in the tabernacles of shade and rest, in
the treasures of happiness, whence every sorrow is

far banished, and the souls of the pious wait without labour for the first-fruits of life ; and the spirits of the righteous in like manner are waiting for the fulfilment of the promised reward : in that region, where the labourers and the weary look towards *Paradise*, and they that are invited to the wedding long for the celestial Bridegroom : when they that are called to that feast wait till they go up thither, and ardently desire to receive that new state of glory : where sorrows are banished and where joys are found ; for love only has appeared not entangled in the passions of sin of all who have been arrayed with the human body, namely, Thine Only-Begotten Son, Jesus Christ, our Lord, through Whom also we hope to obtain mercy for ourselves and for them.

4.   Gregory Abu'lfaraj (*Syro-Jacobite*).

Because Thou art the just remunerator of the living and the dead, and because in Thy hands are the spirits of all flesh, we pray Thee, Lord, for all men who have passed to Thee out of this temporal life, who have departed in the orthodox faith, that Thou wouldst remember them, of Thy mercy, and hear these our prayers, and neglect not these our supplications on their behalf; for they are created in Thy king-like image ; but spare them of Thy grace ; forgive them according to Thy clemency ; lead them into Thy dwellings ; direct them to Thee, adding them to the numbers of heavenly hosts, where Thy Only-Begotten Son is celebrated and glorified by hymns, and is honoured and extolled by hymns returning in a circle. According to the promises made by Him to us, we hope in Thy mercy and the remission of sins, as well for us as for them.

5. S. IGNATIUS (*Syro-Jacobite*).

*P*lacidly and tranquilly receive through Thy goodness, O LORD, the souls and spirits of Thy servants and worshippers, who have departed to Thee out of the present life; but chiefly them for whom, and on account of whom, this sacrifice is offered and perfected. Remember them, grant them rest, and place them in the habitations of light, in the abodes of blessed spirits, in the heavenly Jerusalem, in the Church of the First-born who are written in heaven: and bestowing on them good memory and a most happy rest, through Thy love to men, give them the life that knoweth not old age, the good things that pass not away, the delights that have no end. Mercy may they obtain through Thy clemency: rest may they be possessed of through Thy mercy: let them be hid under the wings of Thy grace and not condemned, because they have put their trust in Thee and Thine Only-Begotten SON, through Whom, &c.

6. JAMES BARADÆUS (*Syro-Jacobite*).

LORD GOD of spirits and of all flesh, grant that all they whom we have commemorated, and they also whom we have not commemorated, who have departed in the orthodox faith out of this mutable life, may become worthy of that indefectible existence in the bosom of Abraham, Isaac, and Jacob, where are all Saints: where griefs and straits are not found, but where beatitude and joy only reign: where Thine Only-Begotten SON is glorified with Thee by all; through whom also we hope to obtain mercy, and revelation of face, before Thee, and for His sake as well for them as for us.

7. JAMES OF SERUG (*Syro-Jacobite*).

Grant, O LORD, rest to their souls whom we

commemorate, and write their names in the book of life, and make them worthy of the pleasure which is received in Paradise. Set them in the region of the just, and join them to the ranks of the pious, and cause them to arrive in the harbour of life, where is the habitation of rest, where griefs, infirmities, groans and miseries fly; where all the Saints enjoy blessedness, where all the pious rest. Cast out none of them, or of us, in condemnation from Thy heavenly kingdom; for One only hath appeared upon earth without sin, &c.

8. John Bar-Maadan (*Syro-Jacobite*).

Them, who with true faith and confidence, and in the orthodox belief, have been set free from this temporal life, according to the sentence promulgated by Thy equity, and have returned to Thee, O God, as to their first omnipotent cause; spare them by Thy mercy: reckon them among the number of Thine elect: cover them with the bright cloud of Thy Saints: ([1]) set them with the lambs on Thy right hand, and bring them into Thy habitation: cause them to arrive in the blessed dwelling of Thy kingdom; grant that they may be invited to Thy banquet, and bring them into the region of exultation and joy, where place there is none for grief and misery, and passion and sighing is at an end. Examine them not severely, since they beseech Thee to deal mercifully with them, because of the errors to which this flesh, formed of clay and subject to sin, is liable; but in that terrible hour of judgments, let them be patterns, O Lord, for us and for themselves, for none is there without sin, &c.

([1]) A very beautiful allusion to the bright cloud which overshadowed the Apostles during the Transfiguration.

9. **S.** John Chrysostom (*Syro-Jacobite*).

And remember them who with purity of heart, and sanctity of soul and body, have departed from this world, and have come to Thee, O God. Them whom from the first Adam, the first made of our creation, in all generations have pleased Thee, and confessed Thee, and have hoped for and expected the manifestation of Thine Only-begotten Son, and have desired to see His great and glorious day. Them who in the spiritual bosom of Baptism have put Thee on splendidly and have believed in Thy Name. Give them rest in Thy celestial habitations, in the paradise of delights, in the tabernacles of light, in quiet dwelling-places. Enter not into judgment with them, O Lord, for in Thy sight shall no man living be justified; for there is only One Who hath appeared upon earth, pure and without blemish, &c.

10. John the Scribe (*Syro-Jacobite*).

Maker and Creator of all things, God and Father, grant that the bodies and spirits of Thy servants who have departed in Thy hope, may come to celestial good things and to those pleasures which have no end, to those joys which are without termination, to the indesinent banquet. Write their names in the book of life, gladden them with the aspect of Thy countenance; set them in the region of the righteous, count them among the bands of the pious. Grant that they may rejoice in the good things of the Saints; grant that they may lie down at Thy spiritual Table; forgive their sins through Thy mercy; save them from grief and sighing; deliver them from the burnings of Gehenna; cause them to pass beyond those terrible straits of the place of fear (²); set them in the tabernacle of light: grant them rest in the bosom of Abraham, Isaac, and Jacob, our fathers, in Thy celestial habitations, in places of quiet. Enter not into judgment with Thy servants, for in Thy sight shall no man living be justified.

11. S. MARUTHAS (*Syro-Jacobite.*

Remember, O LORD, through Thy grace, all those who by means of the sentence pronounced against our first father Adam, have departed out of this miserable life, and are gone where Thou only knowest ; and give them rest among those delights which Thou hast promised to them that love Thee, not calling to memory their sins and ours, for no man is without sin.

12. S. MARK (*Syro-Jacobite*).

And remember those who are worthy of pious commemoration through Thy mercy, O LORD, priests, deacons, and chaste sub-deacons, readers, singers, and all the departed faithful, especially our fathers, brethren, and masters, and all who have sought the prayers of our littleness, and all who have been made partakers of any ecclesiastical dignity, and all who have communicated to the necessities of all the poor of our society, and those whom we desire to remember. We beseech Thee, LORD GOD of the holy fathers, Abraham, Isaac, and Jacob, and of all the company of the just and pious, that Thou wouldst give rest to them,—to them all who

---

(²) It would almost seem as if constant association with Mahometan theology had somewhat influenced the writer's ideas of the passage from this world to the next.

have left us and departed to Thee, and to Thy blessed seats. Blot out, forgive, and remit all their sins, known and unknown, voluntary or involuntary; for none hath appeared upon earth without sin, excepting Thy Only-begotten SON, our LORD GOD and SAVIOUR, JESUS CHRIST, by Whom also we desire to obtain mercy and the remission of sins which is for His sake, both for them and for ourselves.

13. MICHAEL, PATRIARCH OF ANTIOCH.
(*Syro-Jacobite*).

O our GOD, Artificer of our nature, only to be adored and knowing all things, Who desirest the life and salvation of all, give by Thy mercy, good memory, and remission of transgressions and forgiveness of sins, to our fathers, masters, and doctors, and all the sons of Thy holy Church, who by the decree which Thy equity hath pronounced against us, drank of old time the sad cup of death, and of most bitter separation. Visit them, O LORD, and console them in the habitations in which they rest, by Thy divine and most wise decree, by Thy just dispensation, by the feeling of Thy SPIRIT, blessed, sweet, and full of clemency, by this mystical sacrifice, full of all blessed hope, LORD, receive our prayers for them, and blot out their sins and defects, and purify their faults; for there is none, &c.

14. PHILOXENUS OF MABUG. II. (*Syro-Jacobite*).

Grant, O LORD, that Thy servants who have departed with Thy hope in faith, may arrive at those celestial good things, and unfailing delights, and the pleasures which perish not: to the port in which the weary and tempest-tost rest together: to that feast in which martyrs and confessors exult, and to the supper prepared for all the blessed: preserving them from fire, darkness, and the worm that dieth not, because none is free from sin, &c.

15.   SEVERUS OF ANTIOCH (*Syro-Jacobite*).

And give rest in the bosom of Abraham, Isaac, and Jacob in the Paradise of pleasure, in the place of repose, in the tabernacles of the Saints, where is the multitude of them that keep the glorious holy-day, to the souls, bodies, and spirits of them who have come to Thee out of flesh and blood, to Thee, O LORD of all flesh : where is the perfection of life without molestation, and the first-fruits of ineffable promises; of the consummation whereof make them worthy, not reckoning to them their offences, not entering into judgment with Thy servants, for in Thy sight shall no man living be justified, for One only is without sin, &c.

16.   THEODORE THE INTERPRETER (*Nestorian*).

LORD, our GOD, receive from us, through Thy grace, this sacrifice of thanksgiving, namely, the reasonable fruits of our lips, that the memory may be good before Thee of the ancient righteous men, holy prophets, blessed Apostles, martyrs, and confessors, bishops, doctors, priests, deacons, and all the sons of the holy Catholic Church, who with true faith have departed out of this world, that by Thy grace, O LORD, Thou mayest give them pardon of all sins and transgressions, which, in this world, in a mortal body, and a soul, subject to temptation, they have sinned and offended, for there is no man that sinneth not.

CATALOGUE

OF

Theological Literature,

INCLUDING MANY

Standard Works by J. MASON NEALE, D.D. (the Celebrated Hymnologist), R. F. LITTLEDALE, D.D. (Historian of the Eastern Church), and others too numerous to detail.

A Large and Varied Selection of

CATHOLIC AND MISCELLANEOUS THEOLOGY;

Also a Select Assortment of

JUVENILE LITERATURE

Very suitable for

SUNDAY SCHOOL PRIZES, &c.

ON SALE BY

JOHN GRANT, Bookseller,

EDINBURGH,

AND ALL BOOKSELLERS.

CATALOGUE.

---*---

Works of John Mason Neale, D.D.,
1818-66 (*the Famous Hymnologist ; Founder of St Margaret's, East Grinstead ; author of "A Commentary on the Psalms from Primitive and Mediæval Writers," &c., &c.*), *and*

Rev. Dr R. F. Littledale, 1833-90
(*of St Mary Virgin, Soho, and author of " Short History of the Council of Trent," " Offices from the Service-Books of the Holy Eastern Church," &c., &c.*).

Primitive Liturgies — The Primitive Liturgies (in Greek) of S. Mark, S. Clement, S. James, S. Chrysostom, and S. Basil, edited by the late Rev. J. M. Neale, D.D., with new Preface by the Rev. Dr Littledale, fcap 8vo, cloth (pub 6s), 2s   J. T. Hayes.

"A new and most handsomely printed edition of Dr Neale's Primitive Liturgies has just been issued. . . . The study of these, next in importance to the Holy Scriptures, will do more to extend the Catholic revival and root Evangelical truths in the minds of those who do so than aught besides. The volume, which is remarkably cheap, should be found on the library shelves of every parish priest and every well-informed layman of our beloved and Apostolical Church."—*Church News.*

Primitive Liturgies—The Translations of the Primitive Liturgies, with Introduction and Appendices, by Rev. Dr Neale and the Rev. Dr Littledale, seventh edition, fcap 8vo, cloth (pub 4s), 2s   J. T. Hayes.

" We have here the concise results of a profound knowledge of the subject treated, and in the most unpretending form."—*Guardian.*

"This is more than a reprint. It is really a new edition, with improvements, notes, additions, and the Formulæ of Institution, from twenty-four Liturgies either unknown to Dr Neale or beyond his reach when the first edition (1859) was published. It is now for the first time that the Liturgy of S. Basil is given in an English form, and the thanks of all who wish to see the increase of sound liturgical knowledge facilitated are due to Dr Littledale for the pains he has taken over this unpretending but solidly useful volume. It is really a book for persons who wish to learn for themselves, and not only to imbibe some one else's ideas at second hand."—*Literary Churchman.*

4

Works of J. M. Neale and Dr Littledale—*continued.*

Holy Eastern Church (The), a Popular Outline of its History, Doctrines, Liturgies, and Vestments, by a Priest of the English Church, Preface by Dr Littledale, plates, crown 8vo, cloth (pub 3s 6d), 2s

J. T. Hayes

Principal Contents :—Vast Antiquity and Extent of the Greek Church, and its Three Great Divisions—Essential Doctrines of Eastern Christendom—Description of Eastern Churches—Vestments of Greek Church and their Origin—The Greek Liturgies, Services, and Service Books.

"A clear and handy account of Oriental Christendom. There are few to whom it will not be welcome and most serviceable."—*Literary Churchman.*

Armenian Church — Fortescue (*E. F. K.*) — The Armenian Church, a Sketch of the History, Liturgy, Doctrine, and Ceremonies of this Ancient National Church, including Dr Mason Neale's Translation of this Church's Liturgy, crown 8vo, cloth (pub 7s 6d), 2s 6d

J. T. Hayes

Catechetical Notes and Class Questions, Literal and Mystical, chiefly on the Earlier Books of Holy Scripture, by Rev. Dr J. M. Neale, crown 8vo, cloth (pub 5s), 2s 6d

J. T. Hayes

"Unless we are much mistaken, this will be one of the most practically useful of the various posthumous works of Dr Neale, for the publication of which we are indebted to the S. Margaret's Sisters and Dr Neale's literary executors. Besides 'class notes'—lecture notes as most people would call them—on the earlier books of Holy Scripture, there are some most excellent similar notes on the Sacraments, and then a collection of notes for catechising children. Throughout these notes are supplemented from other of Dr Neale's papers, and in particular we would specify an admirable appendix of extracts from Dr Neale's sermons (chiefly unpublished) bearing upon points touched on in the text."—*Literary Churchman.*

Grou (*Pere*)—The Spiritual Maxims of Pere Grou, translated from the French by Dr Neale and other Members of St Margaret's, East Grinstead, crown 8vo, cloth (pub 3s), 1s 6d

J. T. Hayes

"Primarily good for religious, but we strongly recommend it to all devout lay readers."—*Church Times.*

Hymns, suitable for Invalids, original or translated, with a Preface by the Rev. Dr Littledale, square fcap 8vo, cloth (pub 1s 6d), 6d

J. T. Hayes

Works of J. M. NEALE and Dr LITTLEDALE—*continued.*

Hymns of the Eastern Church (The), translated by the Rev. J. M. Neale, D.D., square 12mo, cloth (pub 2s 6d), 1s 6d   J. T. Hayes

—— The same, with Music from Greek and other sources, Verifications, Various Readings, and Prose Translations, by the Very Rev. S. G. Hatherley, Mus. B., Archpriest of the Patriarchal Œcumenical Throne, small 4to, cloth (pub 8s), 2s 6d

"Their great beauty in the original, the successful manner in which they have been translated, the demand which their publication so well supplies, have together tended to obtain for them the well-deserved *imprimatur* of Catholics in general."—*Union Review.*

Notes on the Divine Office, Historical and Mystical, from Ancient and Modern Sources, by Dr J. M. Neale, crown 8vo, cloth (pub 5s), 2s   J. T. Hayes

CONTENTS :—Sketch of the Origin and History of the Divine Office—The Offices Considered, Generally and Particularly—Of the Offices in General, Matins, Lauds, Prime, Chapter, Tierce, Sexts, and Nones, Vespers, Compline—Comparison of Eastern and Western Offices, some Minor Offices, &c.—Office of the Blessed Virgin, Office of the Faithful Departed, Psalm 119, Penitential Psalms, Gradual Psalms, Litany, Dignity of Festivals, Advent, Christmas, Epiphany, Septuagesima, Lent, Easter, Trinity—Of the Divine Office simply considered as Prayer, Extracts from an Essay on the Mystical Interpretation of the Psalms, by the Rev. J. M. Neale, D.D.—The Rule of S. Benedict, The Kalendar.

Occasional Sermons, preached in Various Churches, by Rev. Dr J. M. Neale, author of " Hymns of the Eastern Church," crown 8vo, cloth (pub 3s 6d), 2s
                J. T. Hayes

CONTENTS :—Festival of the Annunciation—The House of God and the Gate of Heaven—Easter Eve—The Rest of the Saints—Fourth Sunday after Easter, 1864—The Blessing of Isaac—The Key of the House of David—In the Octave of S. Barnabas, 1850—The Church's Extremity her Lord's Opportunity—S. Barnabas' Day—The City of David—The Potters and their Work—The Poor and Needy—Confirmation—Heavenly Music—Festival of All Saints—The Moulding of the Vessels—Our Debts—He said, Come—A Few Words of Hope on the Present Crisis in the English Church, 1850—The Bible, and the Bible only, the Religion of Protestants (a Lecture given at Brighton, 1852).

Works of J. M. NEALE and Dr LITTLEDALE—*continued.*

Original Sequences, Hymns, and other Ecclesiastical
Verses, with Prologue in "Dear Memory of John
Keble," square 18mo, cloth (pub 2s 6d), 1s 6d
J. T. Hayes

Sermons on the Blessed Sacrament, at the Oratory,
East Grinstead, by Dr J. M. Neale, fcap 8vo, cloth
(pub 2s 6d), 1s 6d
J. T. Hayes
"Abounding in originality of thought (sometimes, we think,
carried to excess), these sermons will be highly prized by all who
value mystical interpretation, of which Dr Neale was a constant
teacher."—*Church Herald.*

Sermons on Passages from the Prophets, by Dr J.
M. Neale, 2 vols, crown 8vo, cloth (pub 10s), 4s 6d
J. T. Hayes
SYNOPSIS OF CHAPTERS:—Pleasant Pictures—Then shall they
Fast—The Coal from the Altar—The Wells of Salvation—The
Sending of the Lamb—The Divine Sacrifice—In Safeguard—The
Mountain—Retreat—Strength in Battle — The Passage of the
Grounded Staff—Eyesight—Liberality, Consolation, and Exultation
—Our All in All—The Land of the Living—The Treasures of Our
King—Warfare Accomplished—Labour and Reward—The Trans-
figuration of Toil—Impossibility Impossible—Despondency—En-
couragement—True Glory—Sunbeams—The Flight of the Doves—
An Acceptable Year—Fellowship in Suffering—As the Days of a
Tree—Abide with Us—Your Own Land—To Approach unto Me—
The Time of Love—The Staff of Reed—Safe for Ever—To Receive
and to Give—Tekel—Jezreel—Gradually—The Leading of Love—
The Witness and Help of the Lord—High Places—The Tower of
the Flock—Perseverance to the End—Though He slay me, yet will
I trust Him—The Lord's House—Whose Builder and Maker is God
—Crowned with many Thorns—Bright Clouds—He Goeth before
Them—Strong in the Power of the Lord—Zechariah Fulfilled—The
Poor—Appendix.

Text Emblems : A Series of Twelve Beautiful Designs,
engraved by Dalziel, illustrative of the Mystical Interpretation of as many verses from the Old Testament,
by Dr J. M. Neale, square fcap 8vo, cloth (pub 2s), 1s
J. T. Hayes

The Rhythm of Bernard of Morlaix, on the Celestial
Country, edited and translated by the late Rev. J. M.
Neale, beautifully printed on handmade paper, within
red lines, 18mo, neatly bound in cloth, gilt bevelled
boards, gilt top, edges untrimmed (pub 3s 6d), 1s
J. T. Hayes
"A most elegant reprint of the world-famous translation by Dr
Neale. It may be regarded as a library edition of that charming
little work, or it is equally suitable as a present book."—*Church
Review.*

Catholic and Patristic Literature, also Lives of the Saints.

Biroat (*Jacques, Doctor in Theology of the Order in St Benedict, Councillor and Preacher to the King*)—The Eucharistic Life of Jesus Christ, Preached during the Octave of the Holy Sacrament, in Church of St André des Arcs, in 1657, translated from the 5th edition (Paris, 1676) by Edward G. Varnish, with an Introductory Preface by Rev. Arthur Tooth, M.A., 8vo, cloth (pub 6s). 1s 6d   London

Eucharist (The): Meditations on its Types, by Rev. W. E. Heygate, Brighstone, crown 8vo, cloth (pub 3s 6d), 1s 6d   J. T. Hayes

Fathers of the Church, by H. L. Sydney Lear, edited by the Rev. W. J. E. Bennett, containing Lives of St Clement of Rome, St Ignatius, St Polycarp, St Justin, St Irenæus, Tertullian, St Clement of Alexandria, Origen, St Cyprian, St Gregory Thaumaturgus, St Dionysius, St Athanasius, St Basil the Great, St Gregory Nazianzen, St Chrysostom, St Jerome, St Ambrose, St Augustine, St Cyril, St Ephrem, 3 vols, fcap 8vo, cloth (pub 15s), 4s 6d   J. T. Hayes

To be had separately, Vol 2, 1s ; Vol 3, 1s.

"Composed with care and skilful discrimination ; embraces nearly all the greatest lights of the first four centuries."—*Church Quarterly.*

Fenelon (*Archbishop of Cambrai*)—Counsels to Those who are Living in the World, translated by H. L. Sidney Lear, edited by the Rev. W. J. E. Bennett, fcap 8vo, cloth (pub 2s), 1s   J. T. Hayes

Morris (*Rev. John Brande, Professor at Prior Park*)—Jesus, the Son of Mary; or, The Doctrine of the Catholic Church upon the Incarnation of God the Son, considered in its Bearings upon the Reverence shown by Catholics to His Blessed Mother, 2 handsome volumes, 8vo, cloth (pub 24s), 3s 6d
London, James Toovey

St Charles Borromeo, 1538-84 (*Cardinal, Archbishop of Milan and Confessor*)—Life and Times, by C. A. Jones, fcap 8vo, cloth (pub 3s 6d), 1s 6d   J. T. Hayes

8

CATHOLIC AND PATRISTIC LITERATURE—*continued.*

St Elizabeth of Hungary—Life of, 1207-31, edited by C. A. Jones, author of "A History of the Church," with Preface by Rev. Dr Littledale, crown 8vo, cloth (pub 5s), 2s   J. T. Hayes

"Gives the details of a life, which, if half of what is here related be true, was certainly most wonderful and heavenly. The most astounding miracles are recorded, and there is a long extract from Dr J. M. Neale insisting that it is our duty to believe mediæval miracles—a duty which must sometimes be a very hard one. However, the author evidently does the utmost to follow the precept, and is justified in making the best of a very difficult case."—*Literary Churchman.*

St Jane de Chantal—Life of, 1573-1641, by C. A. Jones, crown 8vo, cloth (pub 5s), 1s 6d   J. T. Hayes

"It is well and feelingly written, and evidently done as a labour of love."—*Literary Churchman.*

St Thomas Aquinas: A Digest of the Doctrine of St Thomas Aquinas on the Mystery of the Incarnation, by Father Humphreys, author of "A Digest of the Doctrine of St Thomas on the Sacraments," crown 8vo, cloth (pub 6s), 2s   J. T. Hayes

"It is entirely to be commended."—*Church Review.*

St Vincent de Paul—Life of, by C. A. Jones, crown 8vo, cloth (pub 5s), 2s   J. T. Hayes

"Written with a sympathy for its subject which will make it pleasant reading."—*Literary Churchman.*

"Miss Jones always writes pleasantly and easily; and this will be perused with both pleasure and profit."—*Church Times.*

Virgin Mary (The) and the Traditions of Painters, by Rev. J. G. Clay, crown 8vo, cloth (pub 6s), 1s 6d
                                          J. T. Hayes

"A good deal of interesting matter, from the artistic point of view; showing how doctrinal changes in respect to the teaching concerning the Mother of God have been first chronicled, and then aided by alterations in the pictorial treatment of subjects in which she is represented."—*Union Review.*

9

Miscellaneous Theology.

Anecdotes for the Use of Preachers—The Missioner's Manual of Anecdotes, for the Use of Mission Preachers, Catechists, and Sunday-School Teachers, compiled by the Rev. Arthur G. Jackson, crown 8vo, cloth (pub 6s), 2s 6d   J. T. Hayes

Armfield (*Rev. H. T., author of " The Legend of Christian Art "*)—The Gradual Psalms, a Treatise on the Fifteen Songs of Degrees, with Commentary based on Ancient Hebrew, Chaldee, and Christian Authorities, crown 8vo, cloth (pub 8s), 1s   J. T. Hayes

Ashley (*Rev. John Marks, LL.B., of Fewston, Otley, author of " The Relations of Science," " The Pulpit Lectionary," &c.*)—A Festival Year with the Great Preachers; or, Twenty-Eight Sermons for the Festivals throughout the Year, crown 8vo, cloth (pub 6s), 2s   J. T. Hayes

List of Preachers :—William Alvernus, Joseph de Barzia, Gabriel Biel, Judoe Clichtove, Joseph Ignatius Claus, Escobar de Mendoza, Matthias Faber, S. Vincent Ferrer, Henry Harpius, Nicholas de Nys, Augustine Paoletti, Bernardin of Sienna, Laurentius de Villavincentio, Jacobus de Voragine.

Baird (*Rev. W.*)—The Mystery of Bethlehem : Lectures on the Incarnation, 12mo, cloth (pub 1s), 4d   J. T. Hayes

Christmas Carols—The Royal Cradle, and other Carols, for Christmas and all the Year round, by " S. D. N.," author of " The Chronicles of St Mary's," and " Holydays at St Mary's," &c., with 4 photographs depicting scenes and incidents in the life of Our Lord, 16mo, cloth extra (pub 2s 6d), 1   J. T. Hayes

Cobb (*Gerard F., M.A., Fellow of Trinity College, Cambridge*)—The Kiss of Peace; or, England and Rome at one on the Doctrine of the Holy Eucharist, also the sequel volume published at a later date, crown 8vo, cloth (pub 10s 6d), 2s 6d   J. T. Hayes

—— The Sequel, sold separately (pub 5s) 1s

Cox (*Samuel, D.D., editor of the " Expositor," &c. &c.*)—The House and its Builder, and other Discourses, a Book for the Doubtful, 12mo, cloth (pub 5s), 1s 6d   Fisher Unwin

MISCELLANEOUS THEOLOGY—*continued*.

Cresswell (*Rev. R. H., of Christ's Church, Clapham*)—
Aids to Meditation—1. Advent to Trinity; 2. Trinity
to Advent, with a few Hints on Mental Prayers, 2 vols,
fcap 8vo, cloth (pub 8s), 3s   J. T. Hayes

"A fuller guide to the divine art than its predecessors."
—*Church Review.*

"By far the most complete book we have seen."—*Church
Times.*

—— Preparation for Confirmation and First Communion,
18mo, cloth (pub 1s 6d), 9d   J. T. Hayes

"Is a complete clergyman's handbook for the instruction
and guidance of confirmation candidates, and is one of the
most thoroughly practical handbooks."—*Literary Churchman.*

Dunwell (*Rev. F. H.*)—A Commentary on the Author-
ised Version of the Gospel according to St John, compared with the Siniatic, Vatican, and Alexandrine
MSS., demy 8vo, cloth (pub 15s), 2s   J. T. Hayes

Eales (*Samuel John, D.C.L., author of "Via Crucis,"
"The Voice from the Cross," &c. &c.*)—The Mystic
Vine (Vitis Mystica), a Meditation on the Passion of
Our Lord and Saviour Jesus Christ, treated Mystically
and Devotionally, translated from the Latin of an
unknown Author, and edited by S. J. Eales, frontispiece, 12mo, cloth (pub 1s 6d), 9d   Sonnenschein

Epitaphs—Munby (*A. J., author of "Vestigia Retror-
sum"*)—Faithful Servants, being Epitaphs and Ohitu-
aries, recording their Names and Services, edited and
in part collected by A. J. Munby, M.A., F.S.A.,
contains many interesting and curious Epitaphs found
in the Graveyards of Great Britain, crown 8vo, cloth
(pub 6s), 1s 6d

A valuable addition to the collection of those who collect
books on epitaphs.

Grou (*Père*)—Meditations upon the Love of God, translated from the French by C. A. Jones, author of
"A History of the Church," fcap 8vo, cloth (pub 2s 6d),
1s 6d   J. T. Hayes

"Will be very welcome to very many."—*Church
Quarterly.*

11

MISCELLANEOUS THEOLOGY—*continued.*

Haddingtonshire—The Churches of Saint Baldred, Auldhame, Whitekirk, Tynninghame, Prestonkirk, with Copious Extracts from the Records of the Session of Tynninghame, by A. J. Ritchie, crown 8vo, cloth (pub 7s 6d), 1s 6d Edinburgh

Hatch (*Rev. W. M.*)—Early Counsels, being Sermons to the Schoolboys of St Paul, Stony Stratford, demy 8vo, cloth (pub 7s), 1s 6d J. T. Hayes

"We must say a word of p a se; they seem excellently adapted for a youthful audience, such as that to which they were addressed."—*Church Quarterly Review.*

Hunt (*Rev. John, D.D., author of " Religious Thought in England"*)—Pantheism and Christianity, 8vo, cloth (pub 12s 6d), 4s 6d London, 1884

Irons (*William Josiah, D.D., 1812-1882, the celebrated Hymnologist, and author of " Christianity as Taught by St Paul," being the Bampton Lecture for 1870*)— On Miracles and Prophecy, being a Sequel to the Argument of the "Bible and its Interpreters," with some Minor Notes, crown 8vo, cloth (pub 3s), 1s

J. T. Hayes

—— The Sacred Life and Words of Jesus Christ the Son of God, taken in Order from the Gospels, square fcap 8vo, cloth (pub 3s), 9d J. T. Hayes

"It is a novel undertaking—an attempt by Dr Irons to give the *events* of our Lord's life in his (the Editor's own words, merely just referring to the miracles and parables, which are afterwards tabulated according to their date."— *Ecclesiastic.*

Jones (*C. A., author of " Our English Church," " Life of St Vincent de Paul," and numerous works for the young*)—A History of the Church from the Day of Pentecost to the Present Time, with Preface by Rev. Dr Littledale, 2 vols, fcap 8vo, cloth (pub 11s), 3s J. T. Hayes

"A clever attempt to popularise Church History. The great historical facts, though of course very briefly told, are not related in the dry and repulsive fashion of the compendiums with which we used to be familiar years ago; but are relieved by personal sketches of the leading actors, and by notices of the lives and legends of the mediæval saints with whose names—if no more—every one is acquainted. The book is cleverly conceived, and we should think it would be popular."—*Literary Churchman.*

MISCELLANEOUS THEOLOGY—*continued.*

Knox (*John*) and the Reformation Times in Scotland, by Jean L. Watson, Preface by Rev. Robert Muir, Hawick, with frontispiece, crown 8vo, cloth (pub 3s 6d), 1s 6d

Lee (*Frederick George, D.D., D.C.L., of all Saints, Lambeth*)—Sancta Clara on the Thirty-Nine Articles—Paraphrastica Expositio Articulorum Confessionis Anglicanæ—The Articles of the Anglican Church paraphrastically considered and explained, by Franciscus A. Sancta Clara (Christopher Davenport), reprinted from the edition in Latin of 1646, with a Translation, together with Expositions and Comments in English from the Theological Problems and Propositions of the same writer, and with additional Notices and References, edited by the Rev. George Frederick Lee, D.C.L., small 4to, cloth (pub 7s), 2s
J. T. Hayes

Liturgies (Early) of the Scottish Church—Sprott (*Rev. George W.*)—The Booke of Common Prayer and Administration of the Sacraments, with other Rites and Ceremonies of the Church of Scotland, as it was sett down at first, before the change thereof made by Ye Archb. of Canterburie (from a MS. in the British Museum), also an Earlier Draft prepared before the troubles caused by the Articles of Perth, 1618 (from MS. in the Advocates' Library), edited with an Introduction and Notes by the Rev. George W. Sprott, B.A., crown 8vo, cloth, scarce, 3s 6d
Edmonston & Douglas, 1871

Liturgy of the Church of Sarum (The), Translated from the Latin, and with an Introduction and Explanatory Notes by Charles Walker, author of the "Ritual Reason Why," with Introduction by Rev. T. T. Carter, small 4to, cloth (pub 5s), 2s 6d J. T. Hayes

Longfellow's Complete Works, comprising Prose Works (2 vols), Poems (6 vols), and Translation of Dante's Commedia (3 vols), printed from the Author's latest revised Text, with new Notes relative to the history, various readings, subject-matter, &c., of these writings, &c., The Riverside Edition, 4 fine steel portraits, 11 vols. crown 8vo, cloth back, gilt tops (pub 38s 6d), 18s 6d

MISCELLANEOUS THEOLOGY—*continued.*

Luther—Luther's Hymns set to Original Melodies, with
an English Version, edited by Leonard Woolsey Bacon,
assisted by Nathan H. Allen, vignette portrait, handsome 4to volume (pub 6s), 1s 6d Hodder & Stoughton
"An exceedingly interesting volume."—*Athenæum.*

Macduff (*Dr J. R.*)—The Anchor and Haven of Hope;
or, Some of God's Words of Hope in the Old and New
Testaments, a Text-Book for every Morning and
Evening, beautifully illustrated with floral designs,
small 4to, padded cloth, gilt (pub 5s), 1s 6d
Marcus Ward

—— The same, Cheaper Edition, neatly printed within
borders, 16mo, cloth (pub 1s 6d), 6d

—— The Golden Gospel, beautifully printed in gold,
with borders, small 4to, padded cloth, gilt (pub 3s 6d),
1s 6d   Marcus Ward

Meditations on the Song of Songs, edited by Rev.
G. Crosby White, 12mo, cloth (pub 3s 6d), 1s
J. T. Hayes
"An intense spirit of devotion breathes in every page;
can hardly be read without mingled pleasure and
advantage."—*Scottish Guardian.*

A Marvellously Cheap Edition.
Nothing like it in the Book Market.

Pascal (*Blaise*)—Thoughts on Religion and Philosophy,
a New Translation, with an Original Memoir of the
Author, and an Introductory Essay by Isaac Taylor,
author of "Natural History of Enthusiasm," &c.,
printed in a fine large clear type, crown 8vo, cloth
(pub 6s), 1s 6d   Simpkin Marshall

Patrick (*Bishop S.*)—The Heart's Ease; or, A Remedy
against all Trouble, neatly printed on ribbed paper
with red border, 32mo, cloth, red edges, very neat
(pub 2s), a neat little devotional volume, 6d

Plutarch's Lives, the Translation called Dryden's,
corrected from the Greek and revised by A. H.
Clough, sometime Fellow and Tutor of Oriel College,
Oxford, and late Professor of the English Language
and Literature at University College, London, Best
Library Edition, 5 vols, large demy 8vo, cloth, uncut
edges (pub 42s net), 24s   Nimmo

MISCELLANEOUS THEOLOGY—*continued.*

Ponder and Pray: The Penitent's Pathway, translated by the Rev. Francis Humphrey, crown 8vo, cloth (pub 3s 6d), 1s   J. T. Hayes

"Most serviceably meets a special need. The first difficulty mission-priests have to overcome is to teach the very principle of repentance and to convince of sin. They will find a valuable help in this little book."—*Church Review.*

Rogers (*W. H. Hamilton, F.S.A., author of " Memorials of the West," &c.*)—The Strife of Roses, and Days of the Tudors in the West of England, with beautiful frontispiece on India paper, and numerous full-page plates of effigies, brasses, &c., from drawings by Roscoe Gibbs, 8vo, elegantly printed on fine paper, and splendidly bound in cloth extra gilt (pub 12s 6d), 6s   London

Ruined Abbeys of Britain (The), by Frederick Ross, F.R.H.S., illustrated with twelve beautifully coloured plates—each worthy of being framed—of the most celebrated Abbeys, and numerous fine wood engravings and plans from drawings by A. F. Lydon, and Descriptive Letterpress, folio, cloth, gilt edges (pub £3 3s), £1 7s 6d   London

Scottish Covenanters—Lives and Times of the Two Guthries; or, Sketches of the Covenanters, by Jean L. Watson, crown 8vo, cloth neat (pub 2s), 1s

—— Inscriptions on the Tombstones and Monuments Erected in Memory of the Covenanters, by James Gibson, editor of "Burns Calendar," "Burns Birthday Book," &c., illustrated, fcap 8vo, 292 pp, cloth, bevelled boards (pub 3s 6d), 1s 6d

"Every available source of information has been consulted which could throw light upon the names of the martyrs."—*Preface.*

—— Peden (*Rev. Alex., the Prophet*) and Rev. James Renwick, their Lives and Times, by Jean L. Watson, with Introductory Essay on Scottish Nationality by Rev. Dr John Kerr, crown 8vo, cloth (pub 2s), 1s

Shakespeare and Holy Writ, Parallel Passages, tabularly arranged by W. H. Malcolm, with Forewords by F. J. Furnivall, 18mo, cloth (pub 1s), 4d

MISCELLANEOUS THEOLOGY—*continued.*

Simpson (*M. E., author of " Ploughing and Sowing "*)— A Simple Commentary on the Psalms, as translated in the Prayer-Book, to which is prefixed a Commendation by Rev. Walsham How, crown 8vo, cloth (pub 5s), 1s   J. T. Hayes

Tracery from the Church Roof, a Book of Poems on the Various Services of the Church, by a Stone in the Pavement, square fcap 8vo, cl (pub 5s), 9d J.T. Hayes

Wilkinson (*Rev. J. B.*)—Repentance and Holy Living, being Meditations on the Lord's Prayer and the Seven Penitential Psalms, 12mo, cl (pub 2s 6d), 1s J.T. Hayes "Plain, sound, and devout."—*Guardian.*

Wilson (*Bishop*)—On the Lord's Supper, with Liturgical Notes, 12mo, cloth limp (pub 1s), 4d   J. T. Hayes

Wilson (*Rt. Rev. Thomas, D.D., Lord Bishop of Sodor and Man*)—Sacra Privata: Private Devotions and Prayers, with Notes and Appendix, printed in beautiful old-fashioned type, thick 24mo, cloth (pub 2s), 9d   J. T. Hayes

JUVENILE LITERATURE.

Published by J. T. Hayes, and of the Highest Religious and Moral Tendencies. A Popular Selection of Entertaining and Instructive Stories and Tales for Young People. All tastefully got up in neat cloth bindings, gilt:—

Aunt Atta, a Tale for Little Nephews and Nieces, by Author of "Tales of Kirkbeck," &c., 12mo, cloth (pub 2s 6d), 1s   J. T. Hayes

Aunt Atta Again; or, The Long Vacation, by the same Author, 12mo, cloth gilt (pub 2s 6d), 1s J. T. Hayes

A Commonplace Story, by H. L. Sidney Lear, author of "Cousin Eustace," "Tales of Kirkbeck," &c., 18mo, cloth (pub 2s 6d), 1s   J. T. Hayes

A Little Life in a Great City, by C. A. Jones, author of "Church Stories for Sundays and Holy Days," &c., 12mo, cloth extra (pub 2s), 1s   J. T. Hayes

Christine; or, The King's Daughter, by the Author of "Siegfried; or, The Lost Inheritance," 12mo, cloth extra (pub 2s), 1s   J. T. Hayes

Church Ballads (First Series), specially suitable for the Young, or for use in the Parish or Schools, 12mo, cloth (pub 3s 6d), 1s   J. T. Hayes

16

JUVENILE LITERATURE—*continued.*

Church Ballads (Second Series), for the Festivals
throughout the Year, 12mo, cloth (pub 3s 6d), 1s
J. T. Hayes

Church Stories for the Sundays, Holy-Days, and
Fast-Days of the Christian Year (90 in all), 8 vols,
12mo, cloth (pub 20s), 8s J. T. Hayes

—— The same, in 4 vols, 12mo, cloth (pub 20s), 8s

CONTENTS OF VOL. 1:—Roland—The Drummer Boy—
The Hope of Everlasting Life—The Hearts of the Dis-
obedient—The Peace which Passeth all Understanding—
Little Ben's Christmas—Signed with the Sign of Jesus—
The Good that Christmas brings us—The Light of the Star
—Heedless Willie's Prayer—Whatsoever He saith unto
you, do it—Coals of Fire—"A Great Calm"—Robin the
Reaper—The Heavenly Inheritance—The Race Won—All
Right—Thinketh No Evil—The Ghost of the Apple-Tree—
Mary Winslow—The Village where the Snowdrops Grow—
The Children of Light—Flowers of Paradise—Robert's
Forgiveness.

CONTENTS OF VOL. 2:—Leonard's Good Name—The
Still Week—The New Commandment—Dick, the Tele-
graph Boy—Mother's Rest—The Angel of the Resurrection
—Hugging's One's Wrongs—Gerald's Desire—The Gift of
Peace—The Good Shepherd—Hope Brandon—True Joys—
How the Prayer was Answered—The Excursion to Littleton
—The Track of Love—The Right Judgment—The Hope of
Whitsun-tide—Alfred Lawson—Stedfast in the Faith—
Stokesleigh Fair—The Lesson of Love—Angel's Joy—The
Mystery Solved.

CONTENTS OF VOL. 3:—Speaking One's Mind—The
Beautiful Country—Our Best—Piper Bobby—Mary's
Temptation—Angels' Faces—The Day of Small Things—
Bertha's Home—The Two Half-Crowns—Gideon's Last
Request—Casting all your Care upon Him—The Grave of
Sin—Fading Away—Always Ready—The Hetherington
Feud—Willing Service—The Soldier Boys—The Lesson of
St Martin—Ask Faithfully—The Bands of Sin—Works of
Mercy—Ruth's Prayer.

CONTENTS OF VOL. 4:—Everybody's Ralph—Harry
Wheeler—Faithful unto Death—Where the Cross Fell—
Poor Martin—The Two Homes—Self-Confidence—"Pure
in Heart"—Rest for the Heavy-Laden—The Angel's
Message—Ned's Will—The Queen of the May—Comfort's
True Son—Our Octave—The Loving Look—His Will—
Great Things—The Rainy Day—Tiny Harold—My Brother
Rupert—Joe Miller—Little May.

Climbing the Ladder, by Cecilia MacGregor, 12mo, cloth extra (pub 2s), 1s   J. T. Hayes

Days at Leighscombe, a New Tale, by Mrs John Francis Foster, 12mo, cloth gilt (pub 2s), 1s
          J. T. Hayes

Fables (Spanish), translated by M. R. Cresswell, from the "Fábulas Ascéticas" of Don Cayetano Fernandez, Canon of Seville, a book which has passed through several large editions, and is very highly esteemed in Spain, 16mo, cloth, gilt (pub 2s 6d), 1s   J. T. Hayes

From Darkness to Light, a Confirmation Tale, by Iota, with Preface by Rev. T. Fenton, of Ings, Westmoreland, 18mo, cloth, gilt (pub 2s 6d), 1s
          J. T. Hayes

Harold Austin, a Tale by the Author of "From Darkness to Light," 12mo, cloth, gilt extra (pub 2s), 1s
          J. T. Hayes

Harry Deane's Lifeboat, by Miss Florence Wilford, author of "No Man's Land," &c., 12mo, cloth extra (pub 2s), 1s   J. T. Hayes

Ingram (*Rev. Professor J. H., author of "The Throne of David," "Pillar of Fire," &c.*)—The Prince of the House of David; or, Three Years in the Holy City, frontispiece, crown 8vo, cloth neat, the cheapest edition in cloth in the market (pub 2s), 1s

In the Backwoods, a Tale, by Florence Wilford, author of "No Man's Land," "Vivia," "Harry Deane's Lifeboat," &c., 18mo, cloth extra (pub 2s), 1s   J. T. Hayes

Knight and the Dragon (The), a Legend of the Hougie Bie de Hambie in the Island of Jersey, by Harriet Gabourel, author of "Suzanne de L'Orme," "A Tale of France in Huguenot Times," crown 8vo, cloth (pub 5s), 1s 6d   J. T. Hayes

Laurie ; or, Willow Banks, a Story, by Helena Brett, 12mo, cloth extra (pub 3s 6d), 1s 6d   J. T. Hayes

Letty's Plan, a Book for the Children's Holidays, by Mrs J. Francis Foster, 12mo, cloth gilt (pub 2s 6d), 1s
J. T. Hayes

Love and Hate, a New Tale, by the author of "An Object in Life," "Our Christian Calling," &c., 12mo, cloth extra (pub 2s), 1s   J. T. Hayes

No Man's Land, and How the Church Came to it, by Miss Florence Wilford, author of "Vivia," &c., 12mo, cloth (pub 3s 6d), 1s 6d   J. T. Hayes

Norwegian Tales ; or, Evenings at Oakwood, translated from the work of Hannah Wisnes by Ellen White, Preface by Rev. S. Baring-Gould, 12mo, cloth extra (pub 3s 6d), 1s 6d   J. T. Hayes

Oswald, the Young Artist: Inculcating Reverence during Public Worship, by C. Walker, author of "The Ritual Reason Why," fcap 8vo, cloth (pub 1s 6d), 9d
J. T. Hayes

Our Childhood's Pattern : Nine Tales, based on Incidents in the Life of the Holy Child Jesus, by C. A. Jones, 18mo, cloth gilt extra (pub 2s 6d), 1s
J. T. Hayes

Pilgrim (The), Benedetto, The Shepherd's Little Lamb, A Legend of St Christopher, The Two Diadems, Allegories, 18mo, cloth gilt (pub 1s 6d), 9d   J. T. Hayes

Poor Milly, by Miss Jones, author of "Church Stories," &c., 12mo, cloth (pub 2s), 1s .   J. T. Hayes

Rhineland and its Legends, with other Tales, translated from the German by the Translator of "God Still Works Miracles," &c., with Preface by the Rev. W. J. E. Bennett, Froome-Selwood, fcap 8vo, cloth (pub 3s.6d), 2s   J. T. Hayes

JUVENILE LITERATURE—*continued.*

Self-Surrender; or, The Cruise of the Yacht "Aya-canora," by Miss E. Bussell, 18mo, cloth (pub 1s 6d), 4d   J. T. Hayes

Sir Henry Appleton, a Tale of the Great Rebellion, by Rev. W. E. Heygate, Brightstone, fcap 8vo, cloth (pub 5s), 2s   J. T. Hayes

. **Tales of Kirkbeck,** or the Parish in the Fells, by H. L. Sydney Lear, author of "The Life of Francis de Sales," "The Fathers of the Church," &c., Second Series, comprising Baldwin's Scar; Agnes, the Idiot Girl; The Flood; Kirkbeck Fair; Naomi; Bowsho Hall; The Pleasure Trip; Lilias's Trial; S. Bartholo-mew's Day; Abrie and Annie; The Twin Sisters; and Speak Gently, fcap 8vo, cloth gilt extra (pub 3s 6d), 1s
                                                      J. T. Hayes

By the same Author.

Our Doctor's Note-Book, being Twelve Further Tales of Kirkbeck, comprising The Outcast; Cottage Sor-rows; A Sea Story; A Chapter on Old Women; The Drunkard's Wife; Laith Butts; A Hospital Romance; Laneside; The "Strangers' Corner"; The Furnesses; Edy's Illness; The Doctor's Round, fcap 8vo, cloth gilt extra (pub 3s 6d), 1s   J. T. Hayes

Tales on the Parables, by C. A. Jones, author of "Church Stories," &c., fcap 8vo, cloth (pub 2s 6d), 1s
                                                      J. T. Hayes

The Bonny Kate, a Story of Adventure, Northward and Eastward, in the Sixteenth Century, by Rev. Henry Belcher, King's College School, London, fcap 8vo, cloth (pub 5s), 1s   J. T. Hayes

The Children's Guild, a Tale for the Young, to which are appended the Rules of a few Guilds and Kindred Societies in operation, by the author of the "Abbey Farm," &c., 12mo, cloth (pub 2s 6d), 1s   J. T. Hayes

20

JUVENILE LITERATURE—*continued.*

The City of the Plain, and other Tales, by the author of the "Moor Cottage," &c., edited by the Rev. E. H. Blyth, Hammersmith, 12mo, cloth extra (pub 2s), 1s
J. T. Hayes

The Life and Times of St Edward the Confessor, by Cecilia MacGregor, 12mo, cloth (pub 2s 6d), 1s
J. T. Hayes

The Old Home; or, The Rainbow Arch, a Simple Story of Family Life, by Helena Brett, author of "Emmanuel," with Preface by the late Robert Brett, Esq., 12mo, cloth extra (pub 3s 6d), 1s 6d   J. T. Hayes

The Use of a Flower, A Long Day, and While the Rain Lasted, Three Stories, by Mrs J. Francis Foster, 18mo, cloth gilt (pub 2s 6d), 1s
J. T. Hayes

CPSIA information can be obtained
at www.ICGtesting.com
Printed in the USA
LVHW04s0256240818
588006LV00024B/1419/P